T0289096

Lincoln-Lore

Lincoln-Lore:
Lincoln in the Popular Mind

2nd Edition

edited by
Ray B. Browne

with a foreword by
Russel B. Nye

Bowling Green State University Popular Press
Bowling Green, OH 43403

Shakespeare applied to our national bereavement

Abraham Lincoln

Born July 12, 1809—Died April 15, 1865

After life's fitful fever, he sleeps well:
Treason has done his worst; nor steel, nor poison
Malice, domestic, foreign levy, nothing
Can touch him further.

———————

Our Honored President, all agree,
Hath borne his faculties so meek, hath been
So clear in his great office that his virtues
Will plead like angels, trumpet-tongued, against
The deep damnation of his taking off.

———————

Duty of the Hour

Let's briefly put on manly readiness,
And question this most bloody piece of woe
And know it further—Ill deeds are seldom slow,
Nor single—Dread horrors still abound—
Our country—it weeps, it bleeds; and each new day
A gash is added to her wounds.

Broadside enclosed by black border, with woodcut. (Boston?) Mass., 1865.
(Library of Congress, Rare Book Room, Portfolio 333, No. 69.)

Copyright © 1996 Bowling Green State University Popular Press

Library of Congress Cataloging-in-Publication Data
Lincoln-lore : Lincoln in the popular mind / edited by Ray B. Browne : with
   a foreword by Russel B. Nye.
      p.   cm.
   ISBN 0-87972-719-5 (cloth). -- ISBN 0-87972-720-9 (pbk.)
   1. Lincoln, Abraham, 1809-1865--Anecdotes. I. Browne, Ray Broadus.
E457.15.L54   1996
973.7' 092--dc20   96-29461
                                                               CIP

Cover design by Dumm Art

Contents

To

PAT

GLENN

KEVIN

SHANNON

ALICIA

LARRY

Introduction to the Second Edition

Currently when the whole United States seems to be obsessed with learning all that can be known about the Civil War, the lore of Abraham Lincoln continues to grow in volume and to become more enriched in meaning and importance. This burning desire to understand our 16th President, the world around him, and the conditions in which he saved the Union prompted the reissuance of this earlier volume.

Much has been added to this collection because of the availability of hitherto hidden or generally inaccessible material. There are, for example, many more songs—both pro and con—about Lincoln. The picture of the singing world in favor of Lincoln has been enriched in this volume, and there are many songs from the anti-Lincoln forces which demonstrate just how much he was hated. There is, too, an added section from the folklore of Lincoln's period which centered on him. Such folklore is not easy to gather because of the evanescent nature of folklore. Among the slaves, as the items in this collection demonstrate, Lincoln was both god and devil.

The completely new section on how Lincoln was pictured by the cartoonists in *Frank Leslie's Illustrated Newspaper* gives an immediately accessible dimension of the visual newspaper illustrations over which the citizens laughed and cried. In Lincoln's day, as in our own, the media were at work illustrating and commenting on the President and his men. Seeing those comments is enlightening.

This revised edition of *Lincoln-Lore: Lincoln in the Popular Mind* should add a new chapter to our understanding and appreciation of Abraham Lincoln.

Bowling Green State University, 1996

Foreword

Abraham Lincoln, one hundred and nine years after his death, continues to influence profoundly the attitudes, values, and actions of modern Americans. What he said and did is embedded deep in our political philosophy, our cultural consciousness, our social inheritance. The fact that Lincoln was a wartime president and a martyred President (the only one in our history to be both) has obviously contributed much to the Lincoln legend—for such it is—but does not explain the whole story. We have had other legendary men, many of them, but the American people's fascination with Lincoln has never slackened; his reputation (unlike Jackson's or Washington's, for example) has never had any ups or downs.

William Herndon, Lincoln's law partner, friend and biographer, who knew him perhaps better than anyone else, said while books about him were pouring from the presses, "The man is not yet understood, his history is not known." Despite the fact that no other person in American history has ever been studied so constantly and intensively, Herndon's statement is still true. Though writing about Lincoln has become a profession—almost an art—in itself, yet the man and his meaning are still elusive. There have been the hagiographers and the filio-pietists, the chatty and the learned, dilettantists and encyclopaedists, psychoanalysts, iconoclasts, and revisionists, but Lincoln still remains. There are so many facets of his complex, shifting personality to evaluate that Lincoln presents, both to scholars and amateurs, a perennial challenge. He took many guises—upward bound backwoods boy, shrewd country lawyer, skilled politician, homespun philosopher, tall-tale-teller, compassionate parent and husband, commander-in-chief, peerless statesman, man of destiny and man of sorrows—personalities ranging from "Old Abe" to "Our Fallen Leader."

The facts of Lincoln's fifty-six years, two months, and four days of life have been fully recorded, no doubt, for over a half-century; it seems unlikely that anything more about him can be found out that would cause substantial changes in the biographical story. The meaning of his acts, and the significance of his impact on the events of American history, have likewise been thoroughly explored, argued, and agreed or disagreed upon. It is not with such facts or interpretations, however, that this book about Lincoln deals. It is concerned with the other Lincoln—not the "real" Lincoln—but the tall, lanky, legendary figure in the stovepipe hat (a silhouette instantly recognizable by any American) who was created by song, story, verse, anecdote, and reminiscence. This Lincoln arose from the vast accumulation of the apocryphal, fabulous, and spurious that began to gather about the man during his lifetime. This considerable folklore, which will never be exorcised, grows yet; "new" Lincoln stories appear yearly (traceable by scholars to stories about anybody from Alexander the Great to Winston Churchill) to augment the legend.

Collections of Lincoln stories began to appear within a few months of his death and multiplied by decades in almost geometrical progressions for the next fifty years. Whether they were true or not was irrelevant, for their purposes were clear—to hold for posterity evidences of the man's greatness, to keep alive the meaning of his life, to add a piece to the puzzle of his personality. J.B. McClure of Chicago, whose collection of Lincoln anecdotes was one of the better ones of the later nineteenth century, gathered them, he said, because in them "the great Lincoln still lives, with an influence for good among men." Such stories, which "lightened all pathways with radiance," he believed, would "reveal and perpetuate the soul life of him who spoke so often, so fully, and so truly of government of the people, for the people, and by the people." The present book, then, continues a long and honorable tradition of what might be called popular American history, that is, the legendary strain that runs beside and beneath formal history. Its aim is as valid and its accomplishments as timely as those of any of its predecessors. The lode of Lincoln lore is boundless, and some of the richest of it is in this collection.

Russel B. Nye
East Lansing, Michigan
1974

Introduction

Lincoln, probably more than any other President of the United States, saturated the consciousness and subconsciousness of the American popular mind, that is, of the people in general. The reason is obvious. In times of great national crisis people focus their minds on the President as the center of the storm. He becomes, in effect, the cause as well as the agent for the cure. The Civil War was an internal struggle and, therefore, doubly intense.

The degree to which our sixteenth President dominated people's thoughts on this popular level can well be gauged by the noisiness of their reaction and the forms this reaction assumed.

The Lincoln of this popular mind—or as our Madison Avenue hucksters would call it, the image he projected to the people—was a man of contradictory extremes, so widely antithetical that sometimes we today have difficulty in discovering the same man behind the two pictures. To those people who loved him, Lincoln the man was a gentle, melancholy storyteller and anecdotist who, without peer in the country, jested and drolled on every subject. He was the eternal raconteur. His latest saying or anecdote was broadcast throughout the country, by newspaper, magazine, letter, word of mouth, and by other media. It was eagerly caught up and repeated.

Although some persons who heard or read the President's witticisms thought they flirted with the risqué, generally the feeling was that they were harmless humor, demonstrating, as the editor of one book at a somewhat later period, *Wit and Humor of Abraham Lincoln*, remarked, "a moral, which every good story should have." The President's anecdotes, this editor added, contain "lessons that could be taught so well in no other way. Every one of them is a sermon. Lincoln, like the man of Galilee, spoke to the people in parables."

Without Lincolnisms to be passed around, popular conversation during the 1860s would not have been nearly as juicy and tart as it was. But because no one man could possibly talk enough or be sufficiently witty to satisfy the demands of a nation hungry for such things, numerous sayings, witticisms and pearls of repartee gravitated to Lincoln's name, as metal filings to a magnet. There was, however, a movement in the opposite direction. Often his sayings were caught up, separated from his name, and were thus taken into the great ocean of anonymous stories.

Take as examples of both kinds of movement the following three anecdotes, all of which were attributed to Lincoln but were also told without any association with his name.

"Boy," said an ill-tempered old fellow to a noisy lad, "what are you hollerin' for when I am going by ?" "Humph," returned the boy, "what are you going by for when I am hollerin'?"

Or this one.

A priest said to a peasant whom he thought rude, "You are better fed than taught." "Shud think I was," replied the clodhopper, "as I feeds myself and you teaches me."

Or, finally.

"Pray, Sir, what makes you walk so crookedly?" "Oh, my nose, you see, is crooked, and I have to follow it!"

Lincoln's name became so closely associated with the world of humor that the editor of a volume of such material—*Lincolniana; or the Humors of Uncle Abe*—pleaded with readers in general to send in jokes of all kinds and from all sources, "and duly [they] will appear in the 'complete' edition of Uncle Abe's jokes."

About such Lincolnisms and pseudo-Lincolnisms the present-day reader would agree, at least partially, with the assertion of the editor of *Wit and Humor*, cited above: "Nothing that can be written about Lincoln can show his character in such a true light as the yarns and stories he was so fond of telling, and at which he would laugh as heartily as anyone."

But the reader of today would insist that more is needed to give the full picture of Lincoln and his popular world—or Lincoln in his popular world. On the same level of society, often among the same people, there were numerous other kinds of comments on the President. There were many songs. Some painted him as an affable, kindly man, as a Father figure, or as a wise politician and statesman. Many political songs exploited his humble beginnings to demonstrate that he should be elected President of a threatened land, or re-elected as leader of a war-torn nation. Another kind of popular literature drew him as Father Abraham, and the Bible was rewritten around this figure. Further, Negro minstrels described him in song and skit, though the latter type all now seem lost or unavailable. Brief lives, generally sentimental though braced with humor, gave thumbnail sketches to people, thus making him more familiar and more a part of the general populace.

But even all these types do not give the full portrait of Lincoln in his popular world. For the other side of the coin of love is hate, and no President has been so bitterly hated and so unrestrainedly attacked as Lincoln was. The media for disseminating this hate were the same as those for sowing the love, with the obvious exception of the books of wit and humor.

Because of his constant humorizing, Lincoln's enemies pictured him as an inhuman monster who cracked jokes while sending boys to their death on the battlefield and while the nation was being shattered. Even members of his official family—as numerous comments attest—deplored his drollery. Gideon Welles, Secretary of the Navy, for example, thought it beneath contempt. Lincoln's physical appearance, his conduct of the war, his seeming vacillation, his assumption of extraordinary powers, his domestic and political life—in short, every aspect of him that could be seized upon was used as a club to beat him. Songs by Southerners and Copperheads burned at him. The Bible and other religious books and rites were rewritten, turning Father Abraham into Tyrant Abraham. Skits and playlets smeared him with pitch.

This book is a collection of these various comments on Lincoln in his world. Everything here reprinted comes from the popular level of society of Lincoln's time or almost surely, was known then or soon thereafter. It is all Lincoln-lore. Only such a full collection can reveal Lincoln from this point of view. This volume is designed to supplement other collections which center on Lincoln in contemporary newspapers, in anecdote, and in portrait and caricature. As such it pretty nearly rounds out these particular aspects of the world of Lincoln, though the subject will never be exhausted nor the workers fatigued.

Much of the material included here—roughly one half—has never been given in other collections of Lincolniana. Many more, and much more representative songs, for example, are included than can be found in other volumes on Lincoln or the Civil War. Most of the reworkings of the Bible and other religious material have never before been reprinted. And the amusing and revealing playlet *Abraham Africanus I* is reprinted here to make it readily available. Many of the jokes and humorous anecdotes—especially those about Lincoln—appear for the first time in a collection of this kind.

In arranging this volume I have mixed chronological and logical order. That is, I have generally followed chronology except where logic seemed to dictate a better placement. I have usually kept the long items together, as I have the songs, for clearest and most effective presentation.

In order to make the picture as complete as possible I have included material after the turn of the century, but to keep the volume somewhat within the bounds of bearable size I have made no attempt to cover the twentieth century. Occasionally I have given variants of the same item in order to demonstrate how stories were changed in the retelling. I have made no effort to authenticate or correct stories or statements of fact. Original spelling and punctuation have been followed throughout.

Undoubtedly it is not necessary at this time to state that this volume was made without regional or political bias. My desire was to include everything that would help us to see Lincoln as his popular society saw him. I have therefore included as much from friends as from enemies, and vice versa, where it was available. Lincoln belongs to the ages and to the whole nation. The present volume is intended to make him and his times easily accessible today.

Bowling Green University
Ray B. Browne
January 1974

Chapter 1

Wit

and

Humor

Introduction

The shadow of Lincoln hung over all aspects of the everyday life in America, permeating every one that the media—especially the oral medium—touched. Material about him in general was, of course, most widespread. Citizens of all walks of life delighted—or deplored—in stories about Lincoln's birth and youth, about his antics and wit as lawyer, about his homeliness and home life, his friends and his enemies, about how he was bested by the wits (and accepted the temporary put-downs) but about how he nearly always triumphed in the end, how he acted as President, and about his final evaluation after his assassination. He was the shadow and projection of nearly all people—what they needed for protection of their personalities and living evidence of what they too might become. He was the folk and popular hero and the incarnation of the people's very best.

It may be that it will never be possible to recapture all the wit and humor of and about Lincoln. But the following examples range wide and inclusively. They gauge the substance and the shadow of the man and of his society.

EARLY YEARS

A Teetotaler

When Lincoln was in the Black Hawk War as captain, the volunteer soldiers drank in with delight the jests and stories of the tall captain. Aesop's Fables were given a new dress, and the tales of the wild adventures that he had brought from Kentucky and Indiana were many, but his inspiration was never stimulated by recourse to the whiskey jug.

When his grateful and delighted auditors pressed this on him he had one reply: "Thank you, I never drink it." (*Wit and Humor*)

Uncle Abe's Good Bye

When Uncle Abe joined the Sangamon Militia and entered on the Black Hawk War campaign, his Colonel was a small snipe of a fellow about four feet three inches. Physically, of course, Uncle Abe looked down upon his Colonel. Abe had rather a slouching look and gait at that time, and attracted by his awkward appearance, the dapper little Colonel thus saluted the future Executive and manufacturer of both Colonels and Brigadiers. "Come, Uncle Abe, hold up your head; higher, fellow!" "Yes sir." "Higher, fellow—higher." Abe stretched his land neck to its greatest altitudinous tension and said, "What—so, Sir?" "Yes, fellow, a little higher." "And am I always to remain so?" "Yes, fellow, certainly!" "Then," said Uncle Abe, with a woeful countenance, "good bye, Colonel, for I shall never see you again!" (*Lincolniana*)

Incident in the Black Hawk War

An old Indian strayed, hungry and helpless, into the camp one day. The soldiers were conspiring to kill him as a spy.

A letter from General Cass, recommending him, for his past kind and faithful service to the whites, the trembling old savage drew from beneath the folds of his blankets; but failed in any degree to appease the wrath of the men who confronted him. "Make an example of him, they exclaimed; "the letter is a forgery, and he is a spy."

11

They might have put their threats into execution had not the tall form of their captain, his face swarthy with resolution and rage, interposed itself between them and their defenseless victim.

Lincoln's determined look and demand that it must not be done were enough. They sullenly desisted, and the Indian, unmolested, continued on his way. (*Wit and Humor*)

The Running Sickness

In the Black Hawk war, Uncle Abe belonged to a militia company in the service. On a scout, the company encountered the Indians, and in a brisk skirmish drove them some miles, when, night coming on, our forces encamped. Great was the consternation on discovering that Lincoln was missing. His absence, or rather his stories, from the bivouac, was a misfortune. Suddenly, however, he came into camp. "Maj. Abe, is that you? Thought you were killed. Where've you been?" were the startling speculations. "Yes," said Uncle Abe, "this is me-ain't killed either." "But where have you been all the time?" "Oh, just over there." "But what were you over there for? Didn't run away, did you? ...." "No," said he deliberately, "I don't think ! run away; but, after all, I reckon if anybody had seen me going, and had been told I was going for a doctor he would have thought somebody was almighty sick." (*Lincolniana*)

Colonel Baker Defended by Lincoln

On one occasion, Colonel Baker was speaking in a courthouse, which had been a storehouse, and, on making some remarks that were offensive to certain political rowdies in the crowd, they cried: "Take him off the stand!" Immediate confusion ensued, and there was an attempt to carry the demand into execution. Directly over the speaker's head was an old scuttle, at which it appeared Mr. Lincoln had been listening to the speech. In an instant, Mr. Lincoln's feet came through the scuttle, followed by his tall and sinewy frame, and he was standing by Colonel Baker's side. He raised his hand, and the assembly subsided into silence.

"Gentlemen," said Mr. Lincoln, "let us not disgrace the age and country in which we live. This is a land where freedom of speech is guaranteed. Mr. Baker has a right to speak, and ought to be permitted to do so. I am here to protect him, and no man shall take him from this stand if I can prevent it."

The suddenness of his appearance, his perfect calmness and fairness, and the knowledge that he would do what he had promised to do, quieted all disturbance, and the speaker concluded his remarks without difficulty. (*Wit and Humor*)

Admired the Strong Man

Governor Hoyt of Wisconsin tells a story of Mr. Lincoln's great admiration for physical strength. Mr. Lincoln, in 1859, made a speech at the Wisconsin State Agricultural Fair. After the speech, in company with the Governor, he strolled about the grounds, looking at the exhibits. They came to a place where a professional "strong man" was tossing cannon balls in the air and catching them on his arms and juggling with them as though they were as light as baseballs. Mr. Lincoln had never before seen such an exhibition, and he was greatly surprised and interested.

When the performance was over, Governor Hoyt, seeing Mr. Lincoln's interest, asked him to go up and be introduced to the athlete. He did so, and, as he stood looking down musingly on the man, who was very short, and evidently wondering that one so much smaller than he could be so much stronger, he suddenly broke out with one of his quaint speeches. "Why," he said, "why, I could lick salt off the top of your hat." (*"Abe" Lincoln's Anecdotes*)

A Mortifying Experience

A lady reader or elocutionist came to Springfield in 1857. A large crowd greeted her. Among other things she recited "Nothing to Wear," a piece in which is described the perplexities that beset "Miss Flora McFlimsey" in her efforts to appear fashionable.

In the midst of one stanza in which no effort is made to say anything particularly amusing, and during the reading of which the audience manifested the most respectful silence and attention, some one in the rear seats burst out with a loud, coarse laugh, a sudden and explosive guffaw.

It startled the speaker and audience, and kindled a storm of un-suppressed laughter and applause. Everybody looked back to ascertain the cause of the demonstration, and were greatly surprised to find that it was Mr. Lincoln.

He blushed and squirmed with the awkward diffidence of a school-boy. What caused him to laugh, no one was able to explain. He was doubtless wrapped up in a brown study, and recalling some amusing episode indulged in laughter without realizing his surroundings. The experience mortified him greatly. (*"Abe" Lincoln's Anecdotes*)

Uncle Abe as School Superintendent

When Uncle Abe kept grocery on the Sangamon he was elected as School Superintendent out of his district. It was his duty to examine the applicant teachers on mathematics; which he once did in this wise in his grocery story. "If two pigs weigh twenty pounds how much will a large hog weigh."

"Jump into the scales," said the wielder of the birch, "and I'll soon tell you."

Abe did not examine him further in mathematics. (*Lincolniana*)

A Handy Faculty

Whilst Uncle Abe was passing, in his flat-boat, a small town on the Wabash, an old chum accosted him from shore thus:—

"Uncle Abe, are you asleep?"

"Why?"

"Because, I want to borrow some whiskey."

"Then" said Abe, "*I am asleep.*"

And he rolled over drowsily on the flat-boat, and it passed on. (*Lincolniana*)

Symptoms of Civilization

Uncle Abe and his chums were wrecked and swamped once on a trip to New Orleans, and having waded ashore, were in search of shelter and refreshment, without much prospect of success, in a thickly timbered bottom. They had traveled through the forest a long distance, and were in despair of finding any human habitation, when they discovered a negro hanging on the projecting limb of a tree. "The joy," said Abe, when telling the adventure, "which this cheering view excited, cannot be described, for it convinced us that we were in a civilized country." (*Lincolniana*)

Could Stand It a Day or Two

About the time this occurred, there stood on one side of Capitol Square, in Springfield, a Hotel, now doubtless out of memory of most of the occupants of the out-lots and additions which speculators have hitched to the original village. In its day it was a "first-class hotel," but it waned before the "American" and is now among the "things that were." There were some who doubted the cleanliness of the *cuisine*, and "thereby hangs a tale."

Judge Brown arrived in town and put up at the aforesaid hotel, whereat, Uncle Abe, on meeting him, expressed his regret, begging him to become his guest. The Judge would fain not trouble his friend.

"But you know the reputation of the place—the kitchen?" said Uncle Abe.

"I've heard of it," said the Judge; "but as I want to keep my appetite, I always shun the kitchen, if not the cooks."

"But surely, can't you see by the table alone, Judge?"

"I know, Mr. Lincoln, but I'm going to stop only a day or two, and I guess I can stand for that time what the landlord's family stand all their lives." (*Lincolniana*)

'Twas "Moving Day"

Speed, who was a prosperous young merchant of Springfield, reports that Lincoln's personal effects consisted of a pair of saddlebags, containing two or three lawbooks, and a few pieces of clothing. Riding on a borrowed horse, he thus made his appearance in Springfield. When he discovered that a single bedstead would cost seventeen dollars he said, "It is probably cheap enough, but I have not enough money to pay for it." When Speed offered to trust him, he said: "If I fail here as a lawyer, I will probably never pay you at all." Then Speed offered to share a large double bed with him.

"Where is your room?" Lincoln asked.

"Upstairs," said Speed, pointing from the store leading to his room. Without saying a word, he took his saddle-bags on his arms, went upstairs, set them down on the floor, came down again, and with a face beaming with pleasure and smiles, exclaimed: "Well, Speed, I'm moved." (*Wit and Humor*)

Lincoln's First Speech

Lincoln made his first speech when he was a mere boy, going barefoot, his trousers held up by one suspender, and his shock of hair sticking through a hole in the crown of his cheap straw hat.

"Abe," in company with Dennis Hanks, attended a political meeting, which was addressed by a typical stump speaker—one of those loud-voiced fellows who shouted at the top of his voice, and waved his arms wildly.

At the conclusion of the speech, which did not meet the views either of "Abe" or Dennis, the latter declared that "Abe" could make a better speech than that. Whereupon he got a dry-goods box and called on "Abe" to reply to the campaign orator.

Lincoln threw his old straw hat on the ground, and, mounting the dry-goods box, delivered a speech which held the attention of the crowd and won him considerable applause. Even the campaign orator admitted that it was a fine speech and answered every point in his own "oration."

Dennis Hanks, who thought "Abe" was about the greatest man that ever lived, was delighted, and he often told how young "Abe" got the better of the trained campaign speaker. (*"Abe" Lincoln's Anecdotes*)

Root Hog or Die

...It reminds me of a man out in Illinois by the name of Case, who undertook, a few years ago, to raise a very large herd of hogs. It was a great trouble to feed them, and how to get around this was a puzzle to him. At length he hit on the plan of planting an immense field of potatoes, and when they were sufficiently grown, he turned the whole herd into the field, and let them have full swing, thus saving not only the labor of feeding the hogs, but also that of digging the potatoes!

Charmed with his sagacity, he stood one day leaning against the fence counting his hogs, when a neighbor came along.

"Well, well," said he, "Mr. Case, this is all very fine. Your hogs are doing very well just now, but you know out here in Illinois the frost comes early, and the ground freezes for a foot deep. Then what are you going to do?" This was a view of the matter Mr. Case had not taken into account. Butchering time for hogs was away on in December or January. He scratched his head, and at length stammered, "Well, it may come pretty hard on their snouts, but I don't see but that it will be 'root hog or die.'" (*Book of Anecdotes*)

LINCOLN AS LAWYER

Failure as a Business Man

One of Lincoln's business ventures was with William Berry in a general store, under the firm name of Lincoln & Berry, but it did not take long to show that he was not adapted for a business career. The firm failed, Berry died and the debts of the firm fell entirely upon Lincoln. Many of these debts he might have escaped legally, but he assumed them all and it was not until fifteen years later that the last indebtedness of Lincoln & Berry was discharged. During his membership in this firm he had applied himself to the study of law, beginning at the beginning, that is with Blackstone. Now that he had nothing to do he spent much of his time lying under the shade of a tree poring over law books, borrowed from a comrade in the Black Hawk War, who was then a practicing lawyer at Springfield. (*Wit and Humor*)

He "Broke" to Win

A lawyer, who was a stranger to Mr. Lincoln, once expressed to General Linder the opinion that Mr. Lincoln's practice of telling stories to the jury was a waste of time.

"Don't lay that flattering unction to your soul," Linder answered; "Lincoln is like Tansey's horse, he 'breaks to win.'" (*"Abe" Lincoln's Anecdotes*)

The Question of Legs

Whenever the people of Lincoln's neighborhood engaged in dispute; whenever a bet was to be decided; when they differed on points of religion or politics; when they wanted to get out of trouble, or desired advice regarding anything on the earth, below it, above it, or under the sea, they went to "Abe."

Two fellows, after a hot dispute lasting some hours, over the problem as to how long a man's legs should be in proportion to the size of his body, stamped into Lincoln's office one day and put the question to him.

Lincoln listened gravely to the arguments advanced by both contestants, spent some time in "reflecting" upon the matter, and then, turning around in his chair and facing the disputants, delivered his opinion with all the gravity of a judge sentencing a fellow-being to death.

"This question has been a source of controversy," he said, slowly and deliberately, "for untold ages, and it is about time it should be definitely decided. It has led to bloodshed in the past, and there is no reason to suppose it will not lead to the same in the future.

"After much thought and consideration, not to mention mental worry and anxiety, it is in my opinion, all side issues being swept aside, that a man's lower limbs, in order to preserve harmony of proportion, should be at least long enough to reach from his body to the ground." (*Wit and Humor*)

Find Out for Yourselves

"Several of us lawyers," remarked one of his colleagues, "in the eastern end of the circuit, annoyed Lincoln once while he was holding court for Davis by attempting to defend against a note to which there were many makers. We had no legal, but a good moral defense, but what we wanted most of all was to stave it off till the next term of court by one expedient or another.

"We bothered 'the court' about it till late on Saturday, the day of adjournment. He adjourned for supper with nothing left but this case to dispose of. After supper he heard our twaddle for nearly an hour, and then made this odd entry.

"'L.D. Chaddon vs. J.D. Beasley et al. April Term, 1856, Champaign County Court. Plea in abatement by B.Z. Green, a defendant not served, filed Saturday at 11 o'clock a.m., April 24, 1856, stricken from the files by order of court. Demurrer to declaration, if there ever was one, overruled. Defendants who are served now, at 8 o'clock p.m., of the last day of the term, ask to plead to the merits, which is denied by the court on the ground that the offer comes too late, and therefore, as by nil dicet, judgment is rendered for Pl'ff. Clerk assess damages. A. Lincoln, Judge pro tem.'

"The lawyer who reads his singular entry will appreciate its oddity if no one else does, After making it, one of the lawyers, on recovering from his astonishment, ventured to enquire: 'Well, Lincoln, how can we get this case up again?'

"Lincoln eyed him quizzically for a moment, and then answered, 'You have all been so mighty smart about this case, you find out how to take it up again yourselves.'" (*Wit and Humor*)

Discouraged Litigation

Lincoln believed in preventing unnecessary litigation, and carried out this in his practice, "Who was your guardian?" he asked a young man who came to him to complain that a part of the property left him had been withheld. "Enoch Kingsbury," replied the young man.

"I know Mr. Kingsbury," said Lincoln, "and he is not the man to have cheated you out of a cent, and I can't take the case, and advise you to drop the subject."

And it was dropped. (*Wit and Humor*)

His Financial Standing

A New York firm applied to Abraham Lincoln, some years before he became President, for information as to the financial standing of one of his neighbors. Mr. Lincoln replied:

"I am well acquainted with Mr. —, and know his circumstances. First of all, he has a wife and baby; together they ought to be worth $50,000 to any man. Secondly, he has an office in which there is a table worth $1.50 and three chairs worth, say $1. Last of all, there is in one corner a large rat hole, which will bear looking into. Respectfully, A. Lincoln." (*Wit and Humor*)

Rather Starve than Swindle

Ward Lamon, once Lincoln's law partner, relates a story which places Lincoln's high sense of honor in a prominent light. In a certain case, Lincoln and Lamon being retained by a gentleman named Scott, Lamon put the fee at $250, and Scott agreed to pay it. Says Lamon:

"Scott expected a contest, but, to his surprise, the case was tried inside of twenty minutes; our success was complete. Scott was satisfied, and cheerfully paid over the money to me inside the bar, Lincoln looking on. Scott then went out, and Lincoln asked, 'What did you charge that man?'

"I told him $250. Said he: 'Lamon, that is all wrong. The service was not worth that sum. Give him back at least half of it.'

"I protested that the fee was fixed in advance; that Scott was perfectly satisfied, and had so expressed himself. 'That may be,' retorted Lincoln, with a look of distress and of undisguised displeasure, 'but I am not satisfied. This is positively wrong. Go, call him back and return half the money at least, or I will not receive one cent of it for my share.'

"I did go, and Scott was astonished when I handed back half the fee.

"This conversation had attracted the attention of the lawyers and the court. Judge David Davis, then on our circuit bench (afterwards Associate Justice on the United States Supreme bench), called Lincoln to him. The judge never could whisper, but in this instance he probably did his best. At all events, in attempting to whisper to Lincoln he trumpeted his rebuke in about these words, and in rasping tones that could be heard all over the court-room: 'Lincoln, I have been watching you and Lamon. You are impoverishing this bar by your picayune charges of fees, and the lawyers have reason to complain of you. You are now almost as poor as Lazarus, and if you don't make people pay you more for your services you will die as poor as Job's turkey!'

"Judge O.L. Davis, the leading lawyer in that part of the State, promptly applauded this malediction from the bench; but Lincoln was immovable.

"'That money,' said he, 'comes out of the pocket of a poor, demented girl, and I would rather starve than swindle her in this manner.'" (*Wit and Humor*)

A Peculiar Lawyer

Lincoln was once associate counsel for a defendant in a murder case. He listened to the testimony given by witness after witness against his client, until his honest heart could stand it no longer; then, turning to his associate, he said: "The man is guilty; you defend him—I can't," and when his associate secured a verdict of acquittal, Lincoln refused to share the fee to the extent of one cent.

Lincoln would never advise clients to enter into unwise or unjust lawsuits, always preferring to refuse a retainer rather than be a party to a case which did not commend itself to his sense of justice. (*Wit and Humor*)

Creditor Paid Debtor's Debt

A certain rich man in Springfield, Illinois, sued a poor attorney for $2.50, and Lincoln was asked to prosecute the case. Lincoln urged the creditor to let the matter drop, adding, "You can make nothing out of him, and it will cost you a good deal more than the debt to bring suit." The creditor was still determined to have his way, and threatened to seek some other attorney. Lincoln then said, "Well, if you are determined that suit should be brought, I will bring it, but my charge will be $10."

The money was paid him, and peremptory orders were given that the suit be brought that day. After the client's departure Lincoln went out of the office, returning in about an hour with an amused look on his face. Asked what pleased him, he replied, "I brought suit against —, and then hunted him up, told him what I had done, handed him half of the $10, and we went over to the squire's office. He confessed judgment and paid the bill."

Lincoln added that he didn't see any other way to make things satisfactory for his client as well as the other. (*Wit and Humor*)

End for End

Judge H.W. Beckwith, of Danville, Ill., in his "Personal Recollections of Lincoln," tells a story which is a good example of Lincoln's way of condensing the law and the facts of an issue in a story: "A man, by vile words, first provoked and then made a bodily attack upon another. The latter, in defending himself, gave the other much the worst of the encounter. The aggressor, to get even, had the one who thrashed him tried in our Circuit Court on a charge of an assault and battery. Mr. Lincoln defended, and told the jury that his client was in the fix of a man who, in going along the highway with a pitchfork on his shoulder, was attacked by a fierce dog that ran out at him from a farmer's dooryard. In parrying off the brute with the fork, its prongs stuck into the brute and killed him.

"What made you kill my dog?" said the farmer.

"What made him try to bite me?"

"But why did you not go at him with the other end of the pitchfork?"

"Why did he not come after me with his other end?"

"At this Mr. Lincoln whirled about in his long arms an imaginary dog, and pushed its tail end toward the jury. This was the defensive plea of 'son assault demesne'—loosely, that 'the other fellow brought on the fight,'—quickly told, and in a way the dullest mind would grasp and retain." (*Wit and Humor*)

Lincoln Rescues a Pig from a Bad Predicament

An amusing incident occurred in connection with "riding the circuit," which gives a pleasant glimpse into the good lawyer's heart. He was riding by a deep slough, in which, to his exceeding pain, he saw a pig struggling, and with such faint efforts that it was evident that he could not extricate himself from the mud. Mr. Lincoln looked at the pig and the mud which enveloped him, and then looked at some new clothes with which he had but a short time before enveloped himself. Deciding against the claims of the pig, he rode on, but he could not get rid of the vision of the poor brute, and, at last, after riding two miles, he turned back, determined to rescue the animal at the expense of his new clothes. Arrived at the spot, he tied his horse, and coolly went to work to build of old rails a passage to the bottom of the hole. Descending on these rails, he seized the pig and dragged him out, but not without serious damage to the clothes he wore. Washing his hands in the nearest brook, and wiping them on the grass, he mounted his gig and rode along. He then fell to examining the motive that sent him back to the release of the pig. At the first thought it seemed to be pure benevolence, but, at length, he came to the conclusion that it was selfishness, for he certainly went to the pig's relief in order (as he said to the friend to whom he related the incident), "to take a pain out of his own mind." This is certainly a new view of the nature of sympathy; and one which it will be well for the casuist to examine. (*Wit and Humor*)

'Squire Bagly's Precedent

Mr. T.W.S. Kidd, of Springfield, says that he once heard a lawyer opposed to Lincoln trying to convince a jury that precedent was superior to law, and that custom made things legal in all cases. When Lincoln arose to answer him he told the jury he would argue his case in the same way.

"Old 'Squire Bagly, from Menard, came into my office and said, 'Lincoln, I want your advice as a lawyer. Has a man what's been elected justice of the peace a right to issue a marriage license?' I told him he had not; when the old 'squire threw himself back in his chair very indignantly, and said, 'Lincoln, I thought you was a lawyer. Now Bob Thomas and me had a bet on this thing, and we agreed to let you decide; but if this is your opinion I don't want it, for I know a thunderin' sight better, for I have been 'squire now for eight years and have done it all the time.'"
(*"Abe" Lincoln's Anecdotes*)

Catch 'Em and Cheat 'Em

The lawyers on the circuit traveled by Lincoln got together one night and tried him on the charge of accepting fees which tended to lower the established rates. It was the understood rule that a lawyer should accept all the client could be induced to pay. The tribunal was known as "The Ogmathorial Court."

Ward Lamon, his law partner at the time, tells about it:

"Lincoln was found guilty and fined for his awful crime against the pockets of his brethren of the bar. The fine he paid with great good humor, and then kept the crowd of lawyers in uproarious laughter until after midnight.

"He persisted in his revolt, however, declaring that with his consent his firm should never during its life, or after its dissolution, deserve the reputation enjoyed by those shining lights of the profession, 'Catch 'em and Cheat 'em.'" (*"Abe" Lincoln's Anecdotes*)

A Juryman's Scorn

Lincoln had assisted in the prosecution of a man who had robbed his neighbor's hen roosts. Jogging home along the highway with the foreman of the jury that had convicted the hen stealer, he was complimented by Lincoln on the zeal and ability of the prosecution and remarked: "Why, when the country was young, and I was stronger than I am now, I didn't mind packing off a sheep now and again, but stealing hens!" The good man's scorn could not find words to express his opinion of a man who would steal hens. (*"Abe" Lincoln's Anecdotes*)

Kept up the Argument

Judge T. Lyle Dickey of Illinois related that when the excitement over the Kansas-Nebraska bill first broke out, he was with Lincoln and several friends attending court. One evening several persons, including himself and Lincoln, were discussing the slavery question. Judge Dickey contended that slavery was an institution which the Constitution recognized, and which could not be disturbed. Lincoln argued that ultimately slavery must become extinct. "After a while," said Judge Dickey, "we went upstairs to bed. There were two beds in our room, and I remember that Lincoln sat up in his night shirt on the edge of the bed arguing the point with me. At last we went to sleep. Early in the morning I woke up and there was Lincoln half sitting up in bed. 'Dickey', said he, 'I tell you this nation cannot exist half slave and half free.' 'Oh, Lincoln,' said I, 'go to sleep.'" (*"Abe" Lincoln's Anecdotes*)

Settled out of Court

When Abe Lincoln used to be drifting around the country, practicing law in Fulton and Menard counties, Illinois, an old fellow met him going to Lewiston, riding a horse which, while it was a serviceable enough animal, was not of the kind to be truthfully called a fine saddler. It was a weatherbeaten nag, patient and plodding, and it toiled along with Abe—and Abe's books, tucked away in saddle-bags, lay heavy on the horse's flank.

"Hello, Uncle Tommy," said Abe,

"Hello, Abe," responded Uncle Tommy. "I'm powerful glad to see ye, Abe, fer I'm gwyne to have sumthin' fer ye at Lewiston co't, I reckon."

"How's that, Uncle Tommy?" said Abe.

"Well, Jim Adams, his land runs 'long o' mine, he's pesterin' me a heap, an' I got to get the law on Jim, I reckon."

"Uncle Tommy, you haven't had any fights with Jim, have you?"

"No."

"He's a fair to middling neighbor, isn't he?"

"Only tollable, Abe."

"He's been a neighbor of yours for a long time, hasn't he?"

"Nigh on to fifteen year."

"Part of the time you get along all right, don't you?"

"I reckon we do, Abe."

"Well, now, Uncle Tommy, you see this horse of mine? He isn't as good a horse as I could straddle, and I sometimes get out of patience with him, but I know his faults. He does fairly well as horses go, and it might take me a long time to get used to some other horse's faults. For all horses have faults. You and Uncle Jimmy must put up with each other, as I and my horse do with one another."

"I reckon, Abe," said Uncle Tommy, as he bit off about four ounces of Missouri plug, "I reckon you're about right."

And Abe Lincoln, with a smile on his gaunt face, rode on toward Lewiston. (*"Abe" Lincoln's Anecdotes*)

I'm an Inderlid

One day while Uncle Abe was attending to a case at Mount Pulaski,
(the county seat of Logan County, Illinois) he was beset by old B—s, a
worthy farmer, but a notorious malaprop, for an opinion as to his
amenability to the road tax. "You look here, Mr. Lincoln, these fellows
here want to make me work on the road."

"Well!" said Uncle Abe.

"Well, I tells them that they can't do it, cause I'm an *inderlid*, you
see."

(Of course Uncle Abe concurred in B—s opinion, and forgot to
charge a fee.)

"On another occasion, he wanted John G. Gillette, the great cattle
dealer, to *proximate* him because he'd got the best pair of cattle scales in
Logan County." (*Lincolniana*)

The Wrong Pig by the Ear

I never knew a flash phrase worse used up than was one by Uncle
Abe attending one of the neighboring Circuit Courts above Springfield.
He was employed to aid a young County Attorney to prosecute some
reputed hog thieves. The crime of hog stealing had become so common
that the people were considerably excited and an example was determined on. The first person tried was acquitted on a pretty clear *alibi* or
pretty hard swearing. As the fellow thus acquitted was lounging round
the Court House, Uncle Abe was passing, and he hailed him.

"Well, Mr. Lincoln, I reckon you got the wrong sow by the ear
when you undertook to pen me up."

"So it seems," replied Uncle Abe, blandly, "but really you must
excuse me, pigs are so very much alike! In fact, people up here don't all
seem to know their own." (*Lincolniana*)

"Abe" Got the Worst of It

When Lincoln was a young lawyer in Illinois, he and a certain
judge once got to bantering one another about trading horses; and it was
agreed that the next morning at nine o'clock they should make a trade,
the horses to be unseen up to that hour, and no backing out, under a for-
feiture of $25. At the hour appointed, the Judge came up, leading the sor-
riest-looking specimen of a horse ever seen in those parts. In a few min-

utes Mr. Lincoln was seen approaching with a wooden saw-horse upon his shoulders.

Great were the shouts and laughter of the crowd, and both were greatly increased when Lincoln, on surveying the Judge's animal, set down his saw-horse and exclaimed:

"Well, Judge, this is the first time I ever got the worst of it in a horse trade." (*"Abe" Lincoln's Anecdotes*)

Abe's Spelling

Being asked by a client in Springfield why he spelled so badly in his law papers, Uncle Abe replied, "Because, the Suckers are so cussed mean they won't pay for good spelling." (*Lincolniana*)

Cute

One night Uncle Abe came wet and cold to a cross road tavern in Indiana, and found the fire more thoroughly blockaded with Hoosiers than mother Welles has been able to blockade the Southern Confederacy. Abe ordered the landlord to carry his horse a peck of catfish. "He can't eat catfish," said Boniface. "Try him," said Abe, "there's nothing like trying." The crowd all rushed after the landlord to see Abe's horse eat the peck of catfish. "He won't eat them, as I told you," said the landlord, on returning. "Then," coolly responded Uncle Abe, who had squatted on the best seat, "bring them to me and I'll eat them myself." (*Lincolniana*)

Uncle Abe Puzzled

Uncle Abe was met one day near Springfield, by a conceited cox-comb, who had built him a house at some distance, and invited him to dinner. Uncle Abe did not much relish the Jackenape's acquaintance. In fact, as Justice Shallow has it, had "written him down as an Ass." However, Abe enquired very minutely where Snooks lived. "Thistle Grove," replied the verdant Snooks; "but there's no grove now, and not a single thistle!"

"Eh, what!" cries Uncle Abe, "not a single thistle! Then what on earth do you live on?" (*Lincolniana*)

Uncle Abe a Shakespearian

When Uncle Abe was making a plea in one of the county Circuit Courts, not far from Springfield, one of the lawyers becoming sensible that he was being out-generaled, remarked to Uncle Abe, as he sat down—

"I smell a mice,"

"Why don't you quote Shakespeare correctly?" said Uncle Abe.

"Why," said the other, "I was not aware that I was quoting Shakespeare at all."

"Certainly you were, and had you done it properly, it would have been more expressive and less vulgar. The correct expression is, "I smell a device." (*Lincolniana*)

LINCOLN'S PHYSICAL APPEARANCE

How Uncle Abe Got His Sobriquet

Someone ventured to ask Uncle Abe, soon after his arrival at the White House, how he got the sobriquet of "Honest Abe."

"Oh," said he, "I suppose my case was pretty much like that of a country merchant I once read of. Someone called him a 'little rascal.' 'Thank you for the compliment,' said he. 'Why so,' asked the stigmatizer. 'Because that title distinguishes me from my fellow trades-men, who are all great rascals.'"

"So honest lawyers were so scarce in Illinois that you were thus distinguished from them" persisted the questioner.

"Well," quoth Uncle Abe, glancing slyly at Douglas, Sweet and others from Illinois, "it's hard to say where the honest ones are." (*Lincolniana*)

Peter Cartwright's Description of Lincoln

Peter Cartwright, the famous and eccentric old Methodist preacher who used to ride a church circuit, as Mr. Lincoln and others did the court circuit, did not like Lincoln very well, probably because Mr. Lincoln was not a member of his flock and once defeated the preacher for Congress. This was Cartwright's description of Lincoln: "This Lincoln is a man six feet four inches tall, but so angular that if you should drop a plummet from the center of his head it would cut him three times before it touched his feet." (*"Abe" Lincoln's Anecdotes*)

Rough Sketch of President Lincoln

Senator Sherman of Ohio, in a speech at Sandusky in the fall of 1864 drew this rough but accurate outline of the lamented President's character:

"I know Old Abe; and I tell you there is not, at this hour, a more patriotic, or a truer man living than that man, Abraham Lincoln. Some say he is an imbecile; but he not only held his own in his debates with Douglas, whose power is admitted, and whom I considered the ablest intellect in the United States Senate, but got a little the better of him. He has been deliberate and slow, but when he puts his foot down, it is with the determination and certainty with which our generals take their steps; and, like them, when he takes a city he never gives it up. This firm old man is noble and kind-hearted. He is a child of the people. Go to him with a story of woe, and he will weep like a child. This man, so condemned, works more hours than any other President that ever occupied the chair. His solicitude for the public welfare is never-ceasing. I differed from him at first myself, but at last felt and believed that he was right, and shall vote for this brave, true, patriotic, kind-hearted man. All his faults and mistakes you have seen. All his virtues you never can know. His patience in labor is wonderful. He works far harder than any man in Erie County. At the head of this great nation—look at it! He has all the bills to sign passed by Congress. No one can be appointed to any office without his approval. No one can be punished without the judgment receives his signature, and no one pardoned without his hand. This man—always right, always just—we propose to re-elect now to the Presidency." (*Civil War in Song and Story*)

An American's Portrait of Father Abraham

In character and culture he is a fair representative of the average American. His awkward speech and yet more awkward silence, his uncouth manners, self-taught and partly forgotten, his style miscellaneous, concreted from the best authors, like a reading book, and yet oftentimes of Saxon force and classic purity; his argument, his logic a joke; both unseasonable at times and irresistable always; his questions answers, and his answers questions; his guesses prophecies and fulfillment ever beyond his promise; honest yet shrewd; simple yet reticent; heavy yet energetic; never despairing, never sanguine; careless in forms, conscientious in essentials; never sacrificing a good servant once trusted; never deserting a good principle once adopted; not afraid of new ideas, nor despising old ones; improving opportunities to confess mistakes, ready to learn, getting at facts, doing nothing when he knows not what to do; hesitating at nothing when he sees the right; lacking the recognized qualifications of a party leader, and leading his party as no other man can; sustaining his political enemies in Missouri in their defeat, sustaining his political friends in Maryland to their victory; conservative is his sympathies and radical in his acts, Socratic in his style and Baconian in his method; his religion consisting in truthfulness, temperance: asking good people to pray for him, and publicly acknowledging in events the hand of God, yet he stands before you as the type of 'Brother Jonathan,' a not perfect man and yet more precious than fine gold. (*Old Abe's Jokes*)

An Englishman's Portraits of Old Abe

To say that he is ugly, is nothing; to add that his figure is grotesque, is to convey no adequate impression.—Fancy a man six feet high, and then out of proportion; with long bony arms and legs, which somehow seem to be always in the way; with great rugged furrowed hands, which grasp you like a vice when shaking yours; with a long snaggy neck, and a chest too narrow for the great arms at its side. Add to this figure a head cocoa-nut shaped and somewhat too small for such a stature, covered with rough, uncombed and uncombable hair, that stands out in every direction at once; a face furrowed, wrinkled and indented, as though it had been scarred by vitrol; a high narrow forehead; and sunk deep beneath bushy eyebrows, two bright, dreamy eyes, that seem to gaze through you without looking at you; a few irregular blotches of black bristly hair, in the place where beard and whiskers ought to grow; a close-set, thin- lipped, stern mouth, with two rows of large white teeth, and a nose and ears which have been taken by mistake from a head of twice the size.—Clothe this figure, then, in a long, tight, badly-fitting suit of black, creased, soiled and puckered up at every salient point of the figure (and every point of this figure is salient) put on large, ill-fitting boots, gloves too long for the long bony fingers, and a fluffy hat, covered to the top with dusty, puffy crape; and then add to this an air of strength, physical as well as moral, and a strange look of dignity coupled with all this grotesqueness; and you will have the impression left upon me by Abraham Lincoln. (*Old Abe's Jokes*)

Six Foot Three Committee Man

Tall Judge Kelly, of Pennsylvania, who was one of the committee to inform Mr. Lincoln of his nomination at Chicago Convention, had been eyeing Mr. Lincoln's lofty form with a mixture of admiration, and very likely jealousy. This had not escaped Mr. Lincoln, and as he shook hands with the Judge he inquired: "What is your height?" "Six feet three; what is yours, Mr. Lincoln?" "Six feet four." "Then," said the Judge, "Pennsylvania bows to Illinois. My dear sir, for years my heart has been aching for a President that I could look up to, and I've found him at last in the land where we thought there were none but little giants." (*Wit and Humor*)

A Good One by Old Abe

The President is rather vain of his height, but one day a young man called on him who was certainly three inches taller than the former; he was like the mathematical definition of the straight line, length without breadth. "Really," said Mr. Lincoln, "I must look up to you; if you ever get into a deep place you ought to be able to wade out." (*Old Abe's Jokes*)

Long and Short of It

On the occasion of a serenade, the President was called for by the crowd assembled. He appeared at a window with his wife (who was somewhat below the medium height), and made the following "brief remarks":

"Here I am, and here is Mrs. Lincoln. That's the long and the short of it." (*"Abe" Lincoln's Anecdotes*)

A General Bustification

Many amusing stories are told of President Lincoln and his gloves. At about the time of his third reception he had on a tight-fitting pair of white kids, which he had with difficulty got on. He saw approaching in the distance an old Illinois friend named Simpson, whom he welcomed with a genuine Sangamon county (Illeenoy) shake, which resulted in bursting his white kid glove, with an audible sound. Then, raising his brawny hand up before him, looking at it with an indescribable expression, he said, while the whole procession was checked, witnessing this scene:

"Well, my old friend, this is a general bustification. You and I were never intended to wear these things. If they were stronger they might do well enough to keep out the cold, but they are a failure to shake hands with between old friends like us. Stand aside, Captain, and I'll see you shortly."

Simpson stood aside, and after the unwelcome ceremony was terminated he rejoined his old Illinois friend in familiar intercourse. (*Wit and Humor*)

Make Something Out of It, Anyway

From the day of his nomination by the Chicago convention, gifts poured in upon Lincoln. Many of these came in the form of wearing apparel. Mr. George Lincoln, of Brooklyn, who brought to Springfield, in January, 1861, a handsome silk hat to the President-elect, the gift of a New York hatter, told some friends that in receiving the hat Lincoln laughed heartily over the gifts of clothing, and remarked to Mrs. Lincoln: "Well, wife, if nothing else comes out of this scrape, we are going to have some new clothes, are we not?" (*"Abe" Lincoln's Anecdotes*)

Abe's Long Legs

When the President landed at Aquia Creek, going to see Burnside, there were boards in the way on the wharf, which the men hastened to remove, but the President remarked, in his usual style, "Never mind, boys; my legs are pretty long, have brought me thus far through life and I think they will take me over this difficulty." (*Old Abe's Jokes*)

"Long Abe's" Feet "Protruded Over"

George M. Pullman, the great sleeping car builder, once told a joke in which Lincoln was the prominent figure. In fact, there wouldn't have been any joke had it not been for "Long Abe." At the time of the occurrence, which was the foundation for the joke—and Pullman admitted that the latter was on him—Pullman was the conductor of his only sleeping-car. The latter was an experiment, and Pullman was doing everything possible to get the railroads to take hold of it.

"One night," said Pullman in telling the story, "as we were about going out of Chicago—this was long before Lincoln was what you might call a renowned man—a long, lean, ugly man, with a wart on his cheek, came into the depot. He paid me fifty cents, and half a berth was assigned him. Then he took off his coat and vest and hung them up, and they fitted the peg about as well as they fitted him. Then he kicked off his boots, which were of surprising length, turned into the berth, and undoubtedly having an easy conscience, was sleeping like a healthy baby before the car left the depot.

"Pretty soon along came another passenger and paid his fifty cents. In two minutes he was back at me, angry as a wet hen.

"'There's a man in that berth of mine,' said he hotly, 'and he's about ten feet high. How am I going to sleep there, I'd like to know? Go and look at him.'

"In I went—mad, too. The tall, lank man's knees were under his chin, his arms were stretched across the bed and his feet were stored comfortably—for him. I shook him until he awoke, and then told him if he wanted the whole berth he would have to pay $1.

"'My dear sir,' said the tall man, 'a contract is a contract. I have paid you fifty cents for half this berth, and, as you see, I'm occupying it. There's the other half,' pointing to a strip about six inches wide. 'Sell that and don't disturb me again.'

"And so saying, the man with a wart on his face went to sleep again. He was Abraham Lincoln, and he never grew any shorter afterward. We became great friends, and often laughed over the incident." (*"Abe" Lincoln's Anecdotes*)

He's Just Beautiful

Lincoln's great love for children easily won their confidence. A little girl, who had been told that the President was very homely, was taken by her father to see the President at the White House.

Lincoln took her upon his knee and chatted with her for a moment in his merry way, when she turned to her father and exclaimed:

"Oh, Pa! he isn't ugly at all; he's just beautiful!" (*Lincolniana*)

The Ugliest Man

Mr. Lincoln enjoyed a joke at his own expense. Said he: "In the days when I used to be in the circuit, I was accosted in the cars by a stranger, who said, 'Excuse me, sir, but I have an article in my possession which belongs to you.' 'How is that?' I asked, considerably astonished.

"The stranger took a jacknife from his pocket. 'This knife,' said he, 'was placed in my hands some years ago, with the injunction that I was to keep it until I had found a man uglier than myself. I have carried it from that time to this. Allow me to say, sir, that I think you are fairly entitled to the property.'" (*Lincolniana*)

Lincoln Asked to be Shot

Lincoln was, naturally enough, much surprised one day, when a man of rather forbidding countenance drew a revolver and thrust the weapon into his face. In such circumstances "Abe" at once concluded that any attempt at debate or argument was a waste of time and words.

"What seems to be the matter?" inquired Lincoln with all the calmness and self-possession he could muster.

"Well," replied the stranger, who did not appear at all excited, "some years ago I swore an oath that if I ever came across an uglier man than myself I'd shoot him on the spot."

A feeling of relief evidently took possession of Lincoln at this rejoinder, as the expression upon his countenance lost all suggestion of anxiety.

"Shoot me," he said to the stranger; "for if I am an uglier man than you I don't want to live." (*"Abe" Lincoln's Anecdotes*)

Uncle Abe Swapped When a Baby

Abe, when asked whether he could account for his excessive homeliness said, "when I was two months old I was the handsomest child in Kentuck, but my nigger nurse swapped me off for another boy just to please a friend who was going down the river whose child was rather plain looking." (*Lincolniana*)

Uncle Abe's Nose

Uncle Abe being asked once why he walked so crookedly? said, "Oh my nose, you see, is crooked, and I have to follow it!"

"Fixed Up" a Bit for the "City Folks"

Mrs. Lincoln knew her husband was not "pretty," but she liked to have him presentable when he appeared before the public. Stephen Fiske, in "When Lincoln Was First Inaugurated," tells of Mrs. Lincoln's anxiety to have the President-elect "smoothed down" a little when receiving a delegation that was to greet them upon reaching New York City.

"The train stopped," writes Mr. Fiske, "and through the windows immense crowds could be seen; the cheering drowning the blowing off of steam of the locomotive. Then Mrs. Lincoln opened her handbag and said:

"'Abraham, I must fix you up a bit for these city folks.'

"Mr. Lincoln gently lifted her upon the seat before him; she parted, combed and brushed his hair and arranged his black necktie.

"'Do I look nice now, mother?' he affectionately asked.

"'Well, you'll do, Abraham,' replied Mrs. Lincoln critically. So he kissed her and lifted her down from the seat, and turned to meet Mayor Wood, courtly and suave, and to have his hand shaken by the other New York officials." (*"Abe" Lincoln's Anecdotes*)

"Abe's" Hair Needed Combing

"By the way," remarked President Lincoln one day to Colonel Cannon, a close personal friend, "I can tell you a good story about my hair. When I was nominated at Chicago, an enterprising fellow thought that a great many people would like to see how 'Abe' Lincoln looked, and, as I had not long before sat for a photograph, the fellow, having seen it, rushed over and bought the negative.

"He at once got no end of wood-cuts, and so active was their circulation that they were soon selling in all parts of the country.

"Soon after they reached Springfield, I heard a boy crying them for sale on the streets. 'Here's your likeness of "Abe" Lincoln!' he shouted. 'Buy one; price only two shillings! Will look a great deal better when he gets his hair combed!'" (*"Abe" Lincoln's Anecdotes*)

The President's Repartee

A distinguished foreigner, dining at the White House, wished to congratulate President Lincoln on the self-possession of the hostess, and her apparent indifference to the peculiar vexations of her new position. Having an imperfect knowledge of our language, he expressed his idea by saying: 'Your Excellency's lady makes it very indifferent!' Observing the twinkle of the President's eye, he endeavored to correct his language, and immediately said with emphasis: 'Your Excellency's lady has a very indifferent face!' (*Old Abe's Jokes*)

He Wanted a Steady Hand

When the Emancipation Proclamation was taken to Mr. Lincoln by Secretary Seward for the President's signature, Mr. Lincoln took a pen, dipped it in the ink, moved his hand to the place for the signature, held it a moment, then removed his hand and dropped the pen. After a little hesitation, he again took up the pen and went through the same movement as before. Mr. Lincoln then turned to Mr. Seward and said:

"I have been shaking hands since nine o'clock this morning, and my right arm is almost paralyzed. If my name ever goes into history, it will be for this act, and my whole soul is in it. If my hand trembles when I sign the Proclamation, all who examine the document hereafter will say, 'He hesitated.'"

He then turned to the table, took up the pen again, and slowly, firmly wrote "Abraham Lincoln," with which the whole world is now familiar.

He then looked up, smiled, and said, "That will do." (*Wit and Humor*)

"Fooling" the People

Lincoln was a strong believer in the virtue of dealing honestly with the people.

"If you once forfeit the confidence of your fellow-citizens," he said to a caller at the White House, "you can never regain their respect and esteem.

"It is true that you may fool all the people some of the time; you can even fool some of the people all the time; but you can't fool all of the people all the time." (*"Abe" Lincoln's Anecdotes*)

Lincoln's Religion

He once remarked to a friend that his religion was like that of an old man named Glenn, in Indiana, whom he heard speak at a church meeting, and who said, "When I do good, I feel good; when I do bad, I feel bad; and that's my religion."

Mrs. Lincoln herself has said that Mr. Lincoln had no faith—no faith, in the usual acceptance of those words. "He never joined a church: but still, as I believe, he was a religious man by nature. He first settled to think about the subject when our boy Willie died, and then more than ever about the time he went to Gettysburg; but it was a kind of poetry in his nature, and he never was a technical Christian." (*Wit and Humor*)

LINCOLN AS POLITICIAN

A Slow Horse

On one occasion when Mr. Lincoln was going to attend a political convention, one of his rivals, a liveryman, provided him with a slow horse, hoping that he would not reach his destination in time. Mr. Lincoln got there, however, and when he returned with the horse he said: "You keep this horse for funerals, don't you?" "Oh, no," replied the liveryman. "Well, I'm glad of that, for if you did you'd never get a corpse to the grave in time for the resurrection." (*"Abe" Lincoln's Anecdotes*)

A "Free for All"

Lincoln made a political speech at Pappysville, Illinois, when a candidate for the Legislature the first time. A free-for-all fight began soon after the opening of the meeting, and Lincoln, noticing one of his friends about to succumb to the energetic attack of an infuriated ruffian, edged his way through the crowd, and, seizing the bully by the neck and the seat of his trousers, threw him, by means of his strength and long arms, as one witness stoutly insists, "twelve feet away." Returning to the stand, and throwing aside his hat, he inaugurated his campaign with the following brief but pertinent declaration:

"Fellow-citizens, I presume you all know who I am. I am humble Abraham Lincoln. I have been solicited by many friends to become a candidate for the Legislature. My politics are short and sweet, like the old woman's dance. I am in favor of the national bank; I am in favor of the internal improvement system and a high protective tariff. These are my sentiments; if elected, I shall be thankful: if not, it will be all the same." (*"Abe" Lincoln's Anecdotes*)

His Teeth Chattered

During the Lincoln-Douglas debates of 1858, the latter accused Lincoln of having, when in Congress, voted against the appropriation for supplies to be sent the United States soldiers in Mexico. In reply, Lincoln said: "This is a perversion of the facts. I was opposed to the policy of the administration in declaring war against Mexico; but when war was declared I never failed to vote for the support of any proposition looking to the comfort of our poor fellows who were maintaining the dignity of our flag in a war that I thought unnecessary and unjust."

He gradually became more and more excited; his voice thrilled and his whole frame shook. Sitting on the stand was O.B. Ficklin, who had served in Congress with Lincoln in 1857. Lincoln reached back, took Ficklin by the coat-collar, back of his neck, and in no gentle manner lifted him from his seat as if he had been a kitten, and roared: "Fellow-citizens, here is Ficklin, who was at that time in Congress with me, and he knows it is a lie."

He shook Ficklin until his teeth chattered. Fearing he would shake Ficklin's head off, Ward Lamon grasped Lincoln's hand and broke his grip.

After the speaking was over, Ficklin, who had warm personal friendship with him, said: "Lincoln, you nearly shook all the Democracy out of me today." (*"Abe" Lincoln's Anecdotes*)

A Lincoln Man Ducked

During the canvass between Uncle Abe and Peter Cartright, the celebrated Pioneer Preacher, it chanced that Cartright was returning to his home from the Williamsville and Wiggins Lane settlement. The nearest crossing of the Sangamon was at Carpenter's Mills, where there was the convenience of a ferry instead of a bridge, as is now the case. Upon the hill on the western side of the river, Cartright saw a man elevated upon a barrel in front of a little grocery—and on nearing him, he discovered that he was giving the Democrats in general, and Uncle Peter Cartright in particular, a perfect fusilade of small shots of slang and abuse.

"I tell you, boys, I'm a Whig—a real Harrison Tippecanoe and Tyler too, Whig," said he, "I'm for putting down all these cuss'd locofocos, and if we can't vote 'em down, why I go for lickin' 'em down. There's long Abe Lincoln that's runnin' for the Legislature—he's the chap to vote for. He's one of the people—split rails and got his edycation by moonlight. He don't go round the country prayin' and preachin' like that mean Methodist cuss, Peter Cartright, that's runnin' agin him. I'd like to know what we wants of a parson to make laws for us? Just elect him, and fust you know he'll have a bill into the Legislature to fine us for not goin' to meetin' or for drinkin' a glass of whisky. I'll tell you what, if he ever comes round here, I'll pass him inter the Sangamon— certain—sure."

Just here Uncle Peter Cartright enquired for the ferryman.

"I'm the ferry-*man*, old boss," sung out the rustic orator, "and ken put ye cross the river in no time."

Uncle Peter signified his desire to cross, and the twain started towards the ferry boat. The Preacher stepping into the boat, hitched his horse to the side, while the ferryman shoved out into the stream.

"So you are a Lincoln man?" queried Uncle Peter.

"I'm that, boss."

"And so I presume you would douse a Cartright man if you had a chance?"

"I mought do it stranger."

"Certainly you would douse Mr. Cartright?"

"Sure's winkin', old fellow."

"Well Sir, I am Peter Cartright at your service," and before the ferryman recovered from his surprise Uncle Peter pitched him into the river, took the pole and put himself across the river.

The ferryman didn't vote for Uncle Peter but he altered his opinion of Methodist preachers in general and Uncle Peter in particular. (*Lincolniana*)

Smoke That

During the session of the Legislature of Illinois, in 1836-7, the Sangamon County delegation of nine members became known as the "Long Nine," from the fact of their remarkable average height. In this delegation were Uncle Abe, Gen. Baker, (killed at Bull's Bluff), N.W. Edwards, (brother-in-law of Uncle Abe, and now Captain commissary), and some others of note in their day. A law had passed the previous session to remove the capital from Vandalia to Springfield, to be carried out as soon as a new capitol could be built. In the meantime, Gen. W.L.D. Ewing, an influential Egyptian member, made periodical efforts to repeal the law and keep the capital at Vandalia. During the session of 1837, we had a regular tilt with the "long nine," during which, whenever Uncle Abe or Gen. Baker made a point, Ewing would be saluted with the cry "smoke that!" in allusion to "long nines," a popular kind of cigars used at that day. This probably gave rise to saying, "put that in your pipe and smoke it." (*Lincolniana*)

Smelt No Royalty in Our Carriage

On one occasion, in going to meet an appointment in the southern part of the Sucker State—that section of Illinois called Egypt—Lincoln, with other friends, was traveling in the "caboose" of a freight train, when the freight was switched off the main track to allow a special train to pass.

Lincoln's more aristocratic rival (Stephen A. Douglas) was being conveyed to the same town in this special. The passing train was decorated with banners and flags, and carried a band of music, which was playing "Hail to the Chief."

As the train whistled past, Lincoln broke out in a fit of laughter, and said: "Boys, the gentleman in that car evidently smelt no royalty in our carriage." (*"Abe" Lincoln Anecdotes*)

Damn Your Manners

Old Abe was once canvassing for himself for a local office, when he came to a blacksmith's shop.

"Sir," said he to the blacksmith, "will you vote for me?"

"Mr. Lincoln," said the son of Vulcan, "I admire your head, but damn your heart!"

"Mr. Blacksmith," returned Abe, "I admire your candor, but damn your manners!" (*Old Abe's Jokes*)

How Uncle Abe Felt

Soon after Uncle Abe's defeat by Judge Douglas in 1848, (whereby Douglas unwittingly made a President) someone asked Uncle Abe how he felt over the result.

"Well," said he, "I feel a good deal like a big boy I knew in Kentuck. After he'd got a terrible pounding by the school master, some one asked him how he felt? 'Oh!' said he, 'it hurt so awful bad I couldn't laugh, and I was too big to cry over it,' That's just my case."

It is presumed the questioner got an idea how a defeated politician feels. (*Lincolniana*)

Uncle Abe's Honor

At one time Uncle Abe aspired to a position on the bench, and Mrs. Lincoln, so as to be prepared for the event, practiced the habit of calling her husband "his Honor," or "your Honor," as the case might be. Uncle Abe never, however, succeeded to the dignity of the ermine; but attending Circuit at Chicago, and stopping at the — Hotel, Mrs. L. accompanied her husband, as was her custom. Uncle Abe had donned a brand new pair of boots, which were anything but comfortable, and almost as uncertain as a pair of skates to a learner on the keenest of ice. Mrs. Lincoln was enjoying herself in the parlor in a chit-chat with a number of other ladies, and putting on as many airs as her provincial position in Springfield would admit, when a strange, rumbling sound disturbed the pleasant company, who rushed out to learn what was the matter. Lo and behold! there was Uncle Abe in the undignified predicament of tumbling down stairs and bumping the end of his spine upon every step. The new boots, or the swig of forty-rod which he had taken in his bed-room, had proved traitor to him. Mrs. Lincoln was nearly non-plussed, but exclaimed in a consoling voice, "Is your Honor hurt?"

"No," said Uncle Abe, sitting gracefully on the carpet, with legs spread out amidst the bevy of tittering damsels, and rubbing the seat of his trowsers, "No, my honor is not hurt but my-my-my head is!" (*Lincolniana*)

Boat Had to Stop

Lincoln never failed to take part in all political campaigns in Illinois, as his reputation as a speaker caused his services to be in great demand. As was natural, he was often the target at which many of the "Smart Alecks" of that period shot their feeble bolts, but Lincoln was so ready with his answers that few of them cared to engage him a second time.

In one campaign Lincoln was frequently annoyed by a young man who entertained the idea that he was a born orator. He had a loud vice, was full of language, and so conceited that he could not understand why the people did not recognize and appreciate his abilities.

This callow politician delighted in interrupting public speakers. At last Lincoln determined to squelch him. One night while addressing a large meeting at Springfield, the fellow became so offensive that "Abe" dropped the threads of his speech and turned his attention to the tormentor.

"I don't object," said Lincoln, "to being interrupted with sensible questions, but I must say that my boisterous friend does not always make inquiries which properly come under that head. He says he is afflicted with headaches, at which I don't wonder, as it is a well-known fact that nature abhors a vacuum, and takes her own way of demonstrating it.

"This noisy friend reminds me of a certain steamboat that used to run on the Illinois river. It was an energetic boat, was always busy. When they built it, however, they made one serious mistake, this error being in the relative sizes of the boiler and the whistle. The latter was usually busy, too, and people were aware that it was in existence.

"This particular boiler to which I have reference was a six-foot one, and did all that was required of it in the way of pushing the boat along; but as the builders of the vessel had made the whistle a six-foot one, the consequence was that every time the whistle blew the boat had to stop." (*Wit and Humor*)

The Dead Man Spoke

Mr. Lincoln once said in a speech: "Fellow-citizens, my friend, Mr. Douglas, made the startling announcement today that the Whigs are all dead.

"If that be so, fellow-citizens, you will now experience the novelty of hearing a speech from a dead man; and I suppose you might properly say, in the language of the old hymn:

"'Hark! from the tombs a doleful sound.'" (*"Abe" Lincoln's Anecdotes*)

Good Memory of Names

The following story illustrates the power of Mr. Lincoln's memory of names and faces. When he was a comparatively young man, and a candidate for the Illinois Legislature, he made a personal canvass of the district. While "swinging around the circle" he stopped one day and took dinner with a farmer in Sangamon county.

Years afterward, when Mr. Lincoln had become President, a soldier came to call on him at the White House. At the first glance the Chief

Executive said: "Yes, I remember; you used to live on the Danville road. I took dinner with you when I was running for the Legislature. I recollect that we stood talking out at the barnyard gate while I sharpened my jack-knife."

"Y-a-a-s," drawled the soldier, "you did. But say, wherever did you put that whetstone? I looked for it a dozen times, but I never could find it after the day you used it. We allowed as how mabby you took it 'long with you."

"No," said Lincoln, looking serious and pushing away a lot of documents of state from the desk in front of him. "No, I put it on top of that gatepost—that high one."

"Well!" exclaimed the visitor, "mabby you did. Couldn't anybody else have put it there, and none of us ever thought of looking there for it."

The soldier was on his way home, and when he got there the first thing he did was to look for the whetstone. And sure enough, there it was, just where Lincoln had laid it fifteen years before. The honest fellow wrote a letter to the Chief Magistrate, telling him that the whetstone had been found, and would never be lost again. (*Wit and Humor*)

Thank God for the Sassengers

Almost as good an anecdote is told by Uncle Abe of one of his old friends, a Mr. Sawyer, who merchandized either in Macon or Champaign County. Sawyer was a Yankee and distinguished for little besides an immoderate liking for "sassengers," as he called that "linked sweetness" which polite people call sausages. When Uncle Abe was stumping the Sangamon District for Congress, it befell that he and Sawyer met at the same country hotel, which was kept by a hardshell Baptist, whose foible was long prayers and blessings at table. They—Lincoln and Sawyer— happened to be going to the same town by the same coaches. So they were up betimes and ready, but breakfast was delayed. They at last got to the table, and the Deacon was just closing his eyes preliminary to the blessing, when the stage horn blew.

"Bless me, Deacon, there's the stage ready," cried Sawyer; "thank God for the sassengers, and let us fall to," I hardly need say the Deacon's blessing—and perhaps his breakfast were spoiled. But Sawyer had his "sassengers." (*Lincolniana*)

Trusted Till the "Britchen" Broke

In the campaign of 1852, Lincoln in reply to Douglas' speech, wherein he speaks of confidence in Providence, replied: "Let us stand by our candidate (General Scott) as faithfully as he has always stood by our country, and I much doubt if we do not perceive a slight abatement of Judge Douglas's confidence in Providence as well as the people. I suspect that confidence is not more firmly fixed with the Judge than it was with the old woman whose horse ran away with her in a buggy. She said she 'trusted in Providence till the britchen broke,' and then she 'didn't know what in airth to do.'

"The chance is, the Judge will see the britchen broke,' and then he can, at his leisure, bewail the fate of Locofocism as the victim of misplaced confidence." (*Wit and Humor*)

Lincoln's Deep Musings

Mr. Herndon took me into the law office where Mr. Lincoln used to sit and toil. It is plain and unpretending. Indeed, everything about the man was indicative of the simplicity of his character. And yet, though so transparent and unassuming, he was sagacious. His friend told me that he was a man of profound policy. His neighbor, to whom I have referred, said he was a great thinker—that he was accustomed to think much on the affairs of the nation. Sometimes he would pass his friends on the street without a sign of recognition—lost in his deep musings. Again, as a neighbor approached him, he would cast up his eye, smile, and remark, "I've been thinking," and then proceed to unfold the subject of his thoughts.

"Assassination cast its shadow on the hearts of his friends as early as the Presidential election of 1860. Mr. Herndon told me that himself and two other friends guarded Mr. Lincoln to the polls in Springfield on that day to prevent a stiletto from being aimed at his heart. At length he fell, but not until his great work was done, and he was enthroned among the chiefest of the illustrious benefactors of humanity." (*Civil War in Song and Story*)

"Linkums" Sold Cheap

During the Presidential contest of 1860, there was an Italian artist of plaster figures in Springfield, who supplied "leetel Linkums," as he called his figures, faster than ever Uncle Abe did. He succeeded in putting one of these Republican penates into every Republican house in town, but they finally became a "drug" in the market. However, he kept his "asking price" up; but his selling price was as various as his buyers, and hard to deal with.

One day, with a load of these upon his head, he entered a jeweller's shop, and accosted the man behind the counter with—

"You buys 'em leetel Linkums?"

"No-don't want 'em."

"Sells 'em cheap," persisted the Italian.

"Well, how do you sell to-day ?"

"Fifty cent piece."

"I'll give you a dollar for the lot," said A—, expecting to pose the Italian.

"You takes 'em," greedily exclaimed the artist, and he left Mr. L.A. A—n with a lot of plaster on hand which he had hard work to give away. (*Lincolniana*)

I Am Not Fit for the Presidency

The opening of the year 1860 found Mr. Lincoln's name freely mentioned in connection with the Republican nomination for the Presidency. To be classed with Seward, Chase, McLean, and other celebrities was enough to stimulate any Illinois lawyer's pride; but in Mr. Lincoln's case, if it had any such effect, he was most artful in concealing it. Now and then, some ardent friend, an editor, for example, would run his name up to the masthead, but in all cases he discouraged the attempt.

"In regard to the matter you spoke of," he answered one man who proposed his name, "I beg you will not give it a further mention. Seriously, I do not think I am fit for the Presidency." (*Wit and Humor*)

A Little Shy on Grammar

When Mr. Lincoln had prepared his brief letter accepting the Presidential nomination he took it to Dr. Newton Bateman, the State Superintendent of Education. "Mr. Schoolmaster," he said,, "here is my letter of acceptance. I am not very strong on grammar and I wish you to see if it is all right. I wouldn't like to have any mistakes in it."

The doctor took the letter and after reading it, said:

"There is only one change I should suggest, Mr. Lincoln, you have written 'It shall be my care to not violate or disregard it in any part,' you should have written 'not to violate.' Never split an infinitive, is the rule,"

Mr. Lincoln took the manuscript, regarding it a moment with a puzzled air, "So you think I better put those two little fellows end to end, do you?" he said as he made the change. (*Wit and Humor*)

The Unpardonable Sin

Probably next to Mr. Lincoln, the best story-teller in Washington was Senator Nye of Nevada, commonly known as "Jim Nye." Unfortunately, however, like some of Mr. Lincoln's, many of his stories will not bear repetition. (*Scissors*)

Old Abe and the Blasted Powder

A western correspondent writes: "A visitor, congratulating Mr. Lincoln on the prospects of his re-election, was answered by that indefatigable story-teller with an anecdote of an Illinois farmer, who undertook to blast his own rocks. His first effort at producing an explosion proved a failure. He explained the cause by exclaiming, 'Pshaw, this powder has been shot before!' " (*Old Abe's Jokes*)

OLD ABE'S STORIES

Abraham Tells a Story

Dr. Hovey, of Dansville, N.Y., thought he would call and see the President, and on arriving at the White House found him on horseback, ready for a start. Approaching him, he said:

"President Lincoln, I thought I would call and see you before leaving the city, and hear you tell a story."

The President greeted him pleasantly, and asked where he was from.

The reply was: "From Western New York."

"Well, that's a good enough country without stories," replied the President, and off he rode. That was the story. (*Old Abe's Jokes*)

46 Lincoln-Lore

Gains Fame as a Story-Teller

It was about this time, too, that Lincoln's fame as a story-teller began to spread far and wide. His sayings and his jokes were repeated throughout that section of the country, and he was famous as a story-teller before anyone ever heard of him as a lawyer or a politician. (*Wit and Humor*)

One Thing "Abe" Didn't Love

Lincoln admitted that he was not particularly energetic when it came to real hard work.

"My father," said he one day, "taught me how to work, but not to love it. I never did like to work, and I don't deny it. I'd rather read, tell stories, crack jokes, talk, laugh—anything but work." (*"Abe" Lincoln's Anecdotes*)

A Sufficient Reason

Some one recently asked Uncle Abe why he didn't promote merit? "Because merit never helped promote me," said our Uncle Abe. (*Lincolniana*)

More Pegs than Holes

Some gentlemen were once finding fault with the President because certain generals were not given commands.

"The fact is," replied President Lincoln "I have got more pegs than I have holes to put them in." (*"Abe" Lincoln's Anecdotes*)

Hit at Antietam

Another story of Uncle Abe, too good to be lost, has leaked out. It seems he had accompanied a young lady to one of the hospitals in the capitol where the sympathizing creature, as in duty bound became interested in a wounded soldier. To all her inquiries as to the location of the wound, however, she could only get one reply, thus: "My good fellow where were you hit!" "At Antietam." "Yes, but where did the bullet strike you?" "At Antietam." "But where did it hit you ?" "At Antietam." Becoming discouraged, she deputized Uncle Abe to prosecute the inquiry, which he did successfully. Upon his rejoining her, she was more curious than ever when the President, taking both her hands in his said in his most impressive style. "My dear girl, the ball that hit him would not have injured you." (*Lincolniana*)

Every Little Helped

As the time drew near at which Mr. Lincoln said he would issue the Emancipation Proclamation, some clergymen, who feared the President might change his mind, called on him to urge him to keep his promise.

"We were ushered into the Cabinet room," says Dr. Sunderland. "It was very dim, but one gas jet burning. As we entered, Mr. Lincoln was standing at the farther end of the long table, which filled the center of the room. As I stood by the door, I am so very short that I was obliged to look up to see the President. Mr. Robbins introduced me, and I began at once by saying: 'I have come, Mr. President, to anticipate the new year with my respects, and if I may, to say to you a word about the serious condition of this country.'

"'Go ahead, Doctor,' replied the President; 'every little helps.' But I was too much in earnest to laugh at his sally at my smallness." (*"Abe" Lincoln's Anecdotes*)

Good on the Chop

During one of the last visits that the martyred President made to James River, a short time before the capture of Richmond, he spent some time in walking around among the hospitals, and in visiting various fatigue parties at work in putting up cabins and other buildings.

He came upon one squad who were cutting logs for a house; and, chatting a moment with the hardy woodsmen, asked one of them to let him see his axe. Mr. Lincoln grasped the helve with the easy air of one perfectly familiar with the tool, and remarked that he "used to be good on the chop."

The President then let in on a big log, making the chips fly, and making as smooth a cut as the best lumberman in Maine could do.

Meantime the men crowded around to see the work; and, as he handed back the axe, and walked away with a pleasant joke, the chop-pers gave him three as hearty cheers as he ever heard in the whole of his political career. (*Civil War in Song and Story*)

And—Here I Am

An old acquaintance of the President visited him in Washington. Lincoln desired to give him a place. Thus encouraged, the visitor, who was an honest man, but wholly inexperienced in public affairs or business, asked for a high office, Superintendent of the Mint.

The President was aghast, and said: "Good gracious! Why didn't he ask to be the Secretary of the Treasury, and have done with it?"

Afterward, he said: "Well, now, I never thought Mr. — had anything more than average ability, when we were young men together. But, then, I suppose he thought the same thing about me, and—here I am!" (*"Abe" Lincoln's Anecdotes*)

A Grateful Postmaster

Said a long legged hoosier, on receiving the appointment of Postmaster, in Sangamon County, "I tell you Uncle Abe, you're a hoss." "Yes," replied Uncle Abe, "a draft horse." (*Lincolniana*)

A White House Anecdote

An old farmer, from the West, who knew President Lincoln in days be-gone, called to pay his respects at the Presidential mansion. Slapping the Chief Magistrate upon the back, he exclaimed: "Well, old hoss, how are you?" Old Abe, being thoroughly democratic in his ideas, and withal relishing a joke, responded: "So I'm an old hoss—am I? What kind of a hoss, pray?" "Why all old draft hoss, to be sure," was the rejoinder. (*Civil War in Song and Story*)

A Bullet Through His Hat

A soldier tells the following story of an attempt upon the life of Mr. Lincoln:

"One night I was doing sentinel duty at the entrance of the Soldiers' Home. This was about the middle of August, 1864. About eleven o'clock I heard a rifle shot, in the direction of the city, and shortly afterwards I heard approaching hoof-beats. In two or three minutes a horse came dashing up. I recognized the belated President. The President was bareheaded. The President simply thought his horse had taken fright at the discharge of the firearms.

"On going back to the place where the shot had been heard, we found the President's hat. It was a plain silk hat, and upon examination we discovered a bullet hole through the crown.

"The next day, upon receiving the hat, the President remarked that it was made by some foolish marksman, and was not intended for him; but added that he wished nothing said about the matter.

"The President said, philosophically: 'I long ago made up my mind that if anybody wants to kill me, he will do it. Besides, in this case, it seems to me, the man who would succeed me would be just as objectionable to my enemies—if I have any.'

"One dark night, as he was going out with a friend, he took along a heavy cane, remarking, good-naturedly: 'Mother (Mrs. Lincoln) has got a notion into her head that I shall be assassinated, and to please her I take a cane when I go over to the War Department at night—when I don't forget it.'" (*"Abe" Lincoln's Anecdotes*)

God with a Little "g"

Abraham Lincoln
   his hand and pen
he will be good
   but god Knows When

These lines were found written in young Lincoln's own hand at the bottom of a page whereon he had been ciphering. Lincoln always wrote a clear, regular "fist." In this instance he evidently did not appreciate the sacredness of the name of the Deity, when he used a little "g."

Lincoln once said he did not remember the time when he could not write. (*"Abe" Lincoln's Anecdotes*)

Giving Away the Case

Between the first election and inauguration of Mr. Lincoln the disunion sentiment grew rapidly in the South, and President Buchanan's failure to stop the open acts of secession grieved Mr. Lincoln sorely. Mr. Lincoln had a long talk with his friend, Judge Gillespie, over the state of affairs. One incident of the conversation is thus narrated by the Judge:

"When I retired, it was the master of the house and chosen ruler of the country who saw me to my room. 'Joe,' he said, as he was about to leave me, 'I am reminded and I suppose you will never forget that trial down in Montgomery county, where the lawyer associated with you gave away the whole case in his opening speech. I saw you signaling to him, but you couldn't stop him.

"'Now, that's just the way with me and Buchanan. He is giving away the case, and I have nothing to say, and can't stop him. Good-night.'" (*Wit and Humor*)

President Nominated First

The day of Lincoln's second nomination for the Presidency he forgot all about the Republican National Convention, sitting at Baltimore, and wandered over to the War Department. While there, a telegram came, announcing the nomination of Johnson as Vice-President.

"What," said Lincoln to the operator, "do they nominate a Vice-President before they do a President?"

"Why," replied the astonished official, "have you not heard of your own nomination? It was sent to the White House two hours ago."

"It is all right," replied the President; "I shall probably find it on my return." (*Wit and Humor*)

Reduced to a Portable Shape

Mr. Lincoln said many funny things. One of them was that he knew a fellow once who had saved up fifteen hundred dollars, and had placed it in a private banking establishment. The bank soon failed, and he afterward received ten per cent of his investment. He then took his one hundred and fifty dollars and deposited it in a savings bank, where he was sure it would be safe. In a short time this bank also failed, and he received at the final settlement ten per cent on the amount deposited. When the fifteen dollars was paid over to him, he held it in his hand and looked at it thoughtfully; then he said, "Now, darn you, I have got you reduced to a portable shape, so I'll put you in my pocket." Suiting the action to the word, Mr. Lincoln took his address from the bag and carefully placed it in the inside pocket of his vest, but held on to the satchel with as much interest as if it still contained his "certificate of moral character." (*"Abe" Lincoln's Anecdotes*)

The Enemy are "Ourn"

Early in the Presidential campaign of 1864, President Lincoln said one night to a late caller at the White House:

"We have met the enemy and they are 'ourn'! I think the cabal of obstructionists 'am busted.' I feel certain that, if I live, I am going to be reelected. Whether I deserve to be or not, it is not for me to say; but on the score even of remunerative chances for speculative service, I now am inspired with the hope that our disturbed country further requires the valuable services of your humble servant. 'Jordan has been a hard road to travel,' but I feel now that, notwithstanding the enemies I have made and the faults I have committed, I'll be dumped on the right side of that stream.

"I hope, however, that I may never have another four years of such anxiety, tribulation and abuse. My only ambition is and has been to put down the rebellion and restore peace, after which I want to resign my office, go abroad, take some rest, study foreign governments, see something of foreign life, and in my old age die in peace with all of the good of God's creatures." (*Wit and Humor*)

Lincoln's Estimate of the "Honors"

As a further elucidation of Mr. Lincoln's estimate of Presidential honors, a story is told of how a supplicant for office, of more than ordinary pretensions, called upon him, and, presuming on the activity he had shown in behalf of the Republican ticket, asserted as a reason why the office should be given to him, that he had made Mr. Lincoln President.

"You made me President, did you ?" said Mr. Lincoln, with a twinkle of his eye. "I think I did," said the applicant. "Then a pretty mess you've got me into, that's all," replied the President, and closed the discussion. (*Old Abe's Jokes*)

Making a President

Uncle Abe, in elucidating his estimate of Presidential honors, tells a clever story, as he always does, when he sets about it. It seems that Windy Billy, who is a politician of no ordinary pretensions, was a candidate for the Consulship of Bayonne, and he urged his appointment with the eloquence of a Clay or a Seward. He boasted vociferously of his activity in promoting the success of the Republican ticket, and averred with his impassioned earnestness that he and he alone had made Uncle Abe President.

"Ah!" exclaimed Uncle Abe, "and it was you who made me President, was it?" a twinkle in his eye all the time.

"Yes," said Billy, rubbing his hands and throwing out his chest, as a baggage-master would a small valise, "yes, I think I may say I am the man who made you President."

"Well, Billy, my boy, if that's the case, it's a h-ll of a muss you got me into, that's all." (*Lincolniana*)

Lincoln's Love of Humor

It was once said of Shakespeare that the great mind that conceived the tragedies of "Hamlet," "Macbeth," etc., would have lost its reason if it had not found vent in the sparkling humor of such comedies as "The Merry Wives of Windsor" and "The Comedy of Errors."

The great strain on the mind of Abraham Lincoln produced by four years of civil war might likewise have overcome his reason had it not found vent in the yarns and stories he constantly told. No more fun-loving or humor-loving man than Abraham Lincoln ever lived. He enjoyed a joke even when it was on himself, and probably, while he got his greatest enjoyment from telling stories, he had a keen appreciation of the humor in those that were told him.

His favorite humorous writer was David R. Locke, better known as "Petroleum V. Nasby," whose political satires were quite famous in their day. Nearly every prominent man who has written his recollections of Lincoln has told how the President, in the middle of a conversation on some serious subject, would suddenly stop and ask his hearer if he ever read the Nasby letters.

Then he would take from his desk a pamphlet containing the letters and proceed to read them, laughing heartily at all the good points they contained. There is probably no better evidence of Mr. Lincoln's love of humor and appreciation of it than his letter to Nasby, in which he said: "For the ability to write these things I would gladly trade places with you." (*Wit and Humor*)

Massa Linkum Like de Lord!

By the Act of Emancipation President Lincoln built for himself forever the first place in the affections of the African race in this country. The love and reverence manifested for him by many of these people has, on some occasions, almost reached adoration. One day, Colonel McKaye, of New York, who had been one of a committee to investigate the condition of the freedmen, upon his return from Hilton Head and

Beaufort called upon the President, and in the course of the interview said that up to the time of the arrival among them in the South of the Union forces they had no knowledge of any other power. Their masters fled upon the approach of our soldiers, and this gave the slaves the conception of a power greater than their masters exercised. This power they, called "Massa Linkum."

Colonel McKaye said their place of worship was a large building they called "the praise house," and the leader of the "meeting," a venerable black man, was known as "the praise man."

On a certain day, when there was quite a large gathering of the people, considerable confusion was created by different persons attempting to tell who and what "Massa Linkum" was. In the midst of the excitement the white-headed leader commanded silence. "Brederen," said he, "you don't know nosen' what you'se talkin' 'bout. Now, you just listen to me. Massa Linkum, he ebery whar. He know ebery ting."

Then, solemnly looking up, he added: "He walk de earf like de Lord!" (*"Abe" Lincoln's Anecdotes*)

"Abe" Resented the Insult

A cashiered officer, seeking to be restored through the power of the executive, became insolent, because the President, who believed the man guilty, would not accede to his repeated requests, at last said, "Well, Mr. President, I see you are fully determined not to do me justice!"

This was too aggravating even for Mr. Lincoln; rising, he suddenly seized the disgraced officer by the coat collar, and marched him forcibly to the door, saying as he ejected him into the passage:

"Sir, I give you fair warning never to show your face in this room again. I can bear censure, but not insult. I never wish to see your face again." (*"Abe" Lincoln's Anecdotes*)

Lincoln on Vice and Virtue

Someone was smoking in the presence of the President, and complimented him on having no vices, neither drinking or smoking. "That is a doubtful compliment," answered the President; "I recollect once being outside a stage in Illinois, and a man sitting by me offered me a segar. I told him I had no vices. He said nothing, smoked for some time, and then grunted out, 'It's my experience that folks who have no vices have plagued few virtues.'" (*Old Abe's Jokes*)

The President on "Mud"

By special permission of the "Censor of the Press," we are allowed to mention that the President, on alighting from his carriage, after his late Aquia Creek excursion, remarked, "that it was all nonsense to say Virginia was disaffected, as he had found it a Clay State up to the hub." (*Old Abe's Jokes*)

Abe Passing Counterfeit Money

One day a poor woman ran into Uncle Abe's law office in great fright exclaiming:—

"Oh, Mr. Lincoln, my boy has swallowed a penny!"

"Was it a counterfeit," coolly asked Mr. Lincoln.

"No, certainly not," replied the woman, somewhat indignantly.

"Oh! well, then it will pass, of course," said Uncle Abe.

It is hardly necessary to add that the anxious mother went home comforted and that the boy who "swallowed the penny," at the last Presidential election voted for "Honest Old Abe." (*Lincolniana*)

The Man Down South

An amusing instance of the President's preoccupation of mind occurred at one of his levees, when he was shaking hands with a host of visitors passing him in a continuous stream.

An intimate acquaintance received the usual conventional handshake and salutation, but perceiving that he was not recognized, kept his ground instead of moving on, and spoke again, when the President, roused to a dim consciousness that something unusual had happened, perceived who stood before him, and, seizing his friend's hand, shook it again heartily, saying:

"How do you do? How do you do? Excuse me for not noticing you. I was thinking of a man down South."

"The man down South" was General W.T. Sherman, then on his march to the sea. (*Wit and Humor*)

No "Second Coming" for Springfield

Soon after the opening of Congress in 1861, Mr. Shannon, from California, made the customary call at the White House. In the conversation that ensued, Mr. Shannon said: "Mr. President, I met an old friend of yours in California last summer, a Mr. Campbell, who had a good deal to say of your Springfield life."

"Ah," returned Mr. Lincoln, "I am glad to hear of him. Campbell used to be a dry fellow in those days," he continued. "For a time he was Secretary of State. One day during the legislative vacation, a meek, cadaverous-looking man, with a white neckcloth, introduced himself to him at his office, and, stating that he had been informed that Mr. C. had the letting of the hall of representatives, he wished to secure it, if possible, for a course of lectures he desired to deliver in Springfield.

" 'May I ask,' said the Secretary, 'what is to be the subject of your lectures?'

" 'Certainly,' was the reply, with a very solemn expression of countenance. 'The course I wish to deliver is on the Second Coming of our Lord.'

" 'It is of no use,' said C.; 'if you will take my advice, you will not waste your time in this city. It is my private opinion that, if the Lord has been in Springfield once, He will never come the second time!' " (*Wit and Humor*)

Where Did It Come From?

"What made the deepest impression upon you?" inquired a friend one day, "when you stood in the presence of the Falls of Niagara, the greatest of natural wonders?"

"The thing that struck me most forcibly when I saw the Falls," Lincoln responded, with characteristic deliberation, "was, where in the world did all that water come from?" (*Wit and Humor*)

Quick Repartee

During the famous Lincoln and Douglas campaign the two men met in joint debate. The latter twitted the former on having once sold liquor.

Lincoln quickly replied: "It is perfectly true, fellow-citizens, that I once sold liquor in a country store, as was customary in those days, in connection with the grocery business. I merely wish to remark that Judge Douglas was very attentive on the other side of the counter!" (*Scissors*)

Onkle Abe Ish Tare

A gentleman, about whose Teutonic origin there could be but one opinion, was passing along the street, when he came to a halt before one of the huge posters announcing the coming of the Panorama of Paradise Lost. He read this line, "A Rebellion in Heaven," when he broke forth as follows: "A Rebellion in Heaven: mine Got! that lasts not long now— Onkle Abe ish tare." (*Civil War in Song and Story*)

The President's Choice

During a conversation on the approaching election, in 1864, a gentleman remarked to President Lincoln that nothing could defeat him but Grant's capture of Richmond, to be followed by his nomination at Chicago and acceptance. "Well," said the President, "I feel very much like the man who said he didn't want to die particularly, but if he had got to die, that was precisely the disease he would like to die of." (*Civil War in Song and Story*)

Why Didn't They?

While a person in Newport, N.H., was reading the account of the murder of the president, and escape of the assassins on the "stage," one of the listeners jumped up much excited, and eagerly inquired, "Why in the world didn't they stop the stage? Why didn't they shoot the driver?" (*Book of Anecdotes*)

We Think Not

If President Lincoln had kicked his secretary of state, William H. Seward, as a reward for his service, would that have been a proper way of *footing the Bill*?" (*Book of Anecdotes*)

At It with a Will

The President and Secretary of State were closeted together, overwhelmed by the affairs of the nation.

"Seward, you look puzzled," said Sec'y Chase as he entered and found that able functionary half buried among papers, scratching his head and biting his pen.

"Never fear," quoth Old Abe, laughing gaily and slapping the Secretary of State approvingly on the back. "Where there's a Will, there's a way!" (*Old Abe's Jokes*)

Every Man to His Own Choice

"Hurrah for Abe Lincoln!" shouted a little patriot on Cedar Street, the other day.

"Hurrah for the devil." rejoined an indignant Southern sympathizer.

"All right," said the juvenile; "you hurrah for your man, and I'll hurrah for mine." (*Old Abe's Jokes*)

Done with the Bible

Lincoln never told a better story than this:

A country meeting-house, that was used once a month, was quite a distance from any other house.

The preacher, art old-line Baptist, was dressed in coarse linen pantaloons, and shirt of the same material. The pants, manufactured after the old fashion, with baggy legs, and a flap in the front were made to attach to his frame without the aid of suspenders.

A single button held his shirt in position, and that was at the collar. He rose up in the pulpit, and with a loud voice announced his text thus: "I am the Christ whom I shall represent today."

About this time a little blue lizard ran up his roomy pantaloons. The old preacher, not wishing to interrupt the steady flow of his sermon, slapped away on his leg, expecting to arrest the intruder, but his efforts were unavailing, and the little fellow kept on ascending higher and higher.

Continuing the sermon, the preacher loosened the central button which graced the waistband of his pantaloons and with a kick off came that easy-fitting garment.

But, meanwhile, Mr. Lizard had passed the equatorial line of the waistband, and was calmly exploring that part of the preacher's anatomy which lay underneath the back of his shirt.

Things were now growing interesting, but the sermon was still grinding on. The next movement on the preacher's part was for the collar button, and with one sweep of his arm off came the tow linen shirt.

The congregation sat for an instant as if dazed; at length one old lady in the rear part of the room rose up, and, glancing at the exited object in the pulpit, shouted at the top of her voice: "If you represent Christ, then I'm done with the Bible." (*"Abe" Lincoln's Anecdotes*)

Metalic Ring

The new practical postal currency have upon the face, a faint oval ring of bronze, encircling the vignette. Uncle Abe, being asked its use, replied that it was a faint attempt on the part of Mr. Chase to give the new currency a metalic ring. (*Lincolniana*)

Lincoln's Name for "Weeping Water"

"I was speaking one time to Mr. Lincoln," said Governor Saunders, of Nebraska, "of a little Nebraskan settlement on the Weeping Water, a stream in our State."

"'Weeping Water!' said he.

"Then with a twinkle in his eye, he continued:

"'I suppose the Indians out there call it Minneboohoo, don't they? They ought to, if Laughing Water is Minnehaha (in their language.)'" (*"Abe" Lincoln's Anecdotes*)

No Deaths in His House

A gentleman was relating to the President how a friend of his had been driven away from New Orleans as a Unionist, and how, on his expulsion, when asked to see the writ by which he was expelled, the deputation which called on him told him the Government would do nothing illegal, and so they had issued to illegal writs, and simply meant to make him go of his own free will.

"Well," said Mr. Lincoln, "that reminds me of a hotel-keeper down at St. Louis, who boasted that he never had a death in his hotel, for whenever a guest was dying in his house, he carried him out to die in the gutter." (*"Abe" Lincoln's Anecdotes*)

Couldn't Let Go the Hog

When Governor Custer of Pennsylvania described the terrible butchery at the battle of Fredericksburg, Mr. Lincoln was almost brokenhearted.

The governor regretted that his description had so sadly affected the President. He remarked: "I would give all I possess to know how to rescue you from this terrible war." Then Mr. Lincoln's wonderful recuperative powers asserted themselves and this marvelous man was himself.

Lincoln's whole aspect suddenly changed, and he relieved his mind by telling a story.

"This reminds me, Governor" he said, "of an old farmer out in Illinois that I used to know.

"He took it into his head to go into hog-raising. He sent out to Europe and imported the finest breed of hogs he could buy.

"The prize hog was put in a pen, and the farmer's two mischievous boys, James and John, were told to be sure not to let it out. But James, the worst of the two, let the brute out the next day. The hog went straight for the boys, and drove John up a tree; then the hog went for the seat of James' trousers, and the only way the boy could save himself was by holding on to the hog's tail.

"The hog would not give up his hunt, nor the boy his hold! After they had made a good many circles around the tree, the boy's courage began to give out, and he shouted to his brother, 'I say, John, come down quick, and help me let go this hog!'

"Now, Governor, that is exactly my case. I wish someone would come and help me to let the hog go." (*"Abe" Lincoln's Anecdotes*)

No Vanderbilt

In February, 1860, not long before his nomination for the Presidency, Lincoln made several speeches in Eastern cities. To an Illinois acquaintance, whom he met at the Astor House, in New York, he said:

"I have the cottage at Springfield, and about three thousand dollars in money. If they make me Vice-President with Seward, as some say they will, I hope I shall be able to increase it to twenty thousand, and that is as much as any man ought to want." (*"Abe" Lincoln's Anecdotes*)

Stories Better than Doctors

A gentleman, visiting a hospital at Washington, heard an occupant of one of the beds laughing and talking about the President, who had been there a short time before and gladdened the wounded with some of his stories. The soldier seemed in such good spirits that the gentleman inquired:

"You must be very slightly wounded?"

"Yes," replied the brave fellow," very slightly—I have only lost one leg, and I'd be glad enough to lose the other, if I could hear some more of 'Old Abe's stories.'" (*"Abe" Lincoln's Anecdotes*)

Took Nothing but Money

During the War, Congress appropriated $10,000 to be expended by the President in defending United States Marshals in case of arrests and seizures where the legality of their actions was tested in the courts. Previously the Marshals sought the assistance of the Attorney-General in defending them, but when they found that the President had a fund for that purpose they sought to control the money.

In speaking of these Marshals one day, Mr. Lincoln said:

"They are like a man in Illinois, whose cabin was burned down, and, according to the kindly custom of early days in the West, his neighbors all contributed something to start him again. In his case they had been so liberal that he soon found himself better off than before the fire, and he got proud. One day a neighbor brought him a bag of oats, but the fellow refused it with scorn.

"'No,' said he, 'I'm not taking oats now. I take nothing but money.'" (*"Abe" Lincoln's Anecdotes*)

Old Abe and the Woodcock

The President one day dined at Richmond. When the landlord produced his bill, he thought it very exorbitant, and asked his name, 'Partridge! an't please you,' replied the host. 'Partridge!' said he; 'it should be woodcock, by the length of your bill.' (*Old Abe's Jokes*)

Old Abe and the Bull-Frogs

"A few days ago, Paine, a lawyer of some note in Cincinnati, paid a visit to the Presidential mansion, that he might return with his garments scented with loyal perfume to the Porkopolis Courts.

"During the interview the President asked him what was the feeling of the people of Ohio in reference to the Presidential election. Mr. Paine informed him that the great talk about Chase all amounted to nothing. At this announcement the President seemed well pleased and rubbing his hands, he exclaimed, 'That reminds me of a story. Some years ago two Irishmen landed in this country, and taking the way out into the interior after labor, came suddenly near a pond of water, and to their great horror they heard some bull-frogs singing their usual song, —B-a-u-m!—B-a-u-m!—B-a-u-m! They listened and trembled, and feeling the necessity of bravery they clutched their shellalies and crept cautiously forward, straining their eyes in every direction to catch a glimpse of the enemy, but he was not to be found. At last a happy idea came to the most forward one and he sprang to his mate, and exclaimed, 'and sure, Jamie, it is my opinion it's nothing but a *noise.*'" (*Old Abe's Jokes*)

A Tight Squeeze

President Lincoln says the prospect of his election for a second term reminds him of old Jake Tullwater who lived in Ill. Old Jake got fever once, and he became delirious, and while in this state he fancied that the last day had come and he was called to judge the world. With all the vagaries of insanity he gave both questions and answers himself, and only called up his acquaintances, the millers, when something like this followed:

'Shon Schmidt, come up here! Vat bees you in dis lower worlds?'

'Well, Lort, I bees a miller.'

'Well, Shon, did you ever take too much toll?'

'Oh, yes, Lord, when the water was low, and the stones were dull, I did take too much toll.'

'Well, Shon,' old Jake would say, 'You must go to the left among the goats.'

So he called up all he knew and put them through the same course, till finally he came to himself.

'Shake Tullwater, come up here! Well, Shake, what bees you in this lower world?'

'Well, Lord, I bees a miller.'

'And, Shake, didn't you ever take too much toll?'

'Ah, yes, Lort, when the water was low, and the stones was dull, I did take too much toll.'

'Well, Shake—well Shake (scratching his head)—well Shake, what did you do mit dat toll?'

'Well, Lort, I gives him to the poor.'

'Ah! Shake—gave it to the poor, did you? Well Shake, you can go to the right among the sheep—but it's a tam'd tight squeeze!' (*Old Abe's Jokes*)

Where Abe Said It Had Gone

When the Sherman expedition which captured Port Royal was fitting, there was great curiosity to learn where it had gone. A person visiting the Chief Magistrate at the White House importuned him to disclose the destination to him. 'Will you keep it entirely secret?' asked the President. 'Oh, yes, upon my honor.' 'Well,' said the President, 'I'll tell you.' Assuming an air of great mystery, and drawing the man close to him, he kept him a moment awaiting the revelation with an open mouth and great anxiety. 'Well,' said he in a loud whisper which was heard over the room, 'the expedition has gone to—sea!' (*Old Abe's Jokes*)

The President's Interview with a New Yorker

A man from New York tells of an interview he had with the President. 'How are you,' said he. 'I saw your card, but did not see you. I was glad, however, that you carded me, and I was reminded of an anecdote of Mr. Whittlesey. When Mr. Cox, then a young man, first came here, Mr. Whittlesey said to him: 'Sir, have you carded the senators?' 'No, sir; I thought I would curry favor first, and then comb them,' 'It is no joking matter, sir,' said Mr. Whittlesey, seriously. 'It is your duty to card the senators sir; and it is customary I believe, to card the cabinet also, and you ought to do it, sir. But,' he added after a moment's thought, 'I think I am wrong, the cabinet may card you.' (*Old Abe's Jokes*)

Old Abe's Mistakes

Old Abe being questioned one day in regard to some of his reputed 'mistakes' replied, 'That reminds me of a minister and a lawyer who were riding together; says the minister to the lawyer—

'Sir, do you ever make mistakes in pleading?'

'I do,' says the lawyer.

'And what do you do with mistakes?' inquired the minister.

'Why, sir, if large ones, I mend them; if small ones, I let them go,' said the lawyer. 'And pray, sir,' continued he, 'do you ever make mistakes in preaching?'

'Yes, sir, I have.'

'And what do you do with mistakes?' said the lawyer.

'Why, sir, I dispose of them in the same manner that you do. Not long since,' continued he, 'as I was preaching, I meant to observe that the devil was the father of *liars*, but made a mistake and said the father of *lawyers*. The mistake was so small that I let it go.' (*Old Abe's Jokes*)

President Lincoln on Grant's New Sword

Just before Grant's arrival, Representative Washburne took to the White House a handsome sword, presented to General Grant by some admirers in Illinois, to show the President and Mrs. Lincoln. 'Yes,' said the President, 'it is very pretty. It will do for a Commander-in-Chief.' Old Abe then turned to a general officer then present and asked him if he had any sword presentation lately. The reply was 'I have not.' 'Humph,' said Abe, 'that's a joke then that *you* have seen the *point* of yet.' (*Old Abe's Jokes*)

"Salmon the Solemn," vs. "Abraham the Jocular"

The solemn versus the jocular are brought into curious juxtaposition by the present state of affairs. The committee of 'the friends of Mr. Chase,' in their Ohio circular, called Mr. Lincoln 'our jocular President.' Against him they set up Mr. Chase, of whom a prominent Boston lawyer said some years ago, 'I don't like the Governor. He is too solemn—altogether too solemn.' More than a year ago, Mr. Lincoln said that he had just discovered that the initials of Salmon P. Chase mean shinplaster currency. Perhaps he will now say that they mean shinplaster candidate. An old Greek rhetorician advises to answer your adversary's sober arguments with ridicule, and his ridicule with sober argument. (*Old Abe's Jokes*)

Potomac! Bottomic!! Buttermilk

An amusing story is told by Old Abe of the 'Iowa First,' about the changes which a certain password underwent about the time of the battle of Springfield. One of the Dubuque officers, whose duty it was to furnish the guards with a password for the night, gave the word 'Potomac.' A German on guard, not understanding distinctly the difference between Bs and Ps, understood it to be 'Bottomic,' and this, on being transferred to another, was corrupted to 'Buttermilk.' Soon afterward, the officer who had given the word wished to return through the lines, and on approaching a sentinel was ordered to halt and the word demanded. He gave 'Potomac,' 'Nicht right—you don't pass mit me dis way.' 'But this is the word, and I will pass.' 'No, you stan'; at the same time placing a bayonet at his breast in a manner that told the officer that 'Potomac' didn't pass in Missouri. 'What is the word, then?' 'Buttermilk.' 'Well, then, Buttermilk.' 'Dat is right; now you pass mit yourself all about your piziness.' There was then a general overhauling of the password; and the difference between Potomac and Buttermilk being understood, the joke became one of the laughable incidents of the campaign. (*Old Abe's Jokes*)

The President Says that Jeff Is on His Last Legs

Because we gave him the grant (Grant) of Vicksburg and he couldn't hold it; we gave him the banks (Banks) of Port Hudson and they destroyed his best gardner (Gardner) and all he raised during the last two years; we gave him mead (Meade) at Gettysburg and he couldn't swallow it; we have his best wagoner (Wagner) fast at Charleston; compelled him to haul in his brag (Bragg) and get in the lee (Lee) of his rebel army. (*Old Abe's Jokes*)

Father Abraham's Good Clothes

At the beginning of the war, John Perry, then a resident of Georgia, was compelled to take the oath of allegiance to the Southern confederacy and agreed not to bear arms against it. He removed to West Troy soon afterwards and in September was drafted. Before the time of his appearance at Albany he wrote to the Provost Marshal General, Colonel Fry, stating the dilemma, and asking whether he could not be released from his obligation to serve Uncle Sam. The reply of Col. Fry has just been received. He states that he fully appreciates Mr. Perry's position, and has no idea of making him violate his oath. He kindly consents, therefore, that the conscript Perry shall be sent to the Northwest to fight Indians; but he can't for a moment think of absolving him from wearing "Father Abraham's good clothes." (*Old Abe's Jokes*)

Putting Salt on the Monitor's Tail

War is a pretty serious business; but they are not always gloomy at the War Department. When the foolish rumor was current in Washington that the Monitor had been captured, the President walked over to the War Department and asked whether the report was true.

"Certainly," replied an officer with due gravity.

"How did the rebels succeed in capturing her?" asked the President.

"By putting salt on her tail," was the reply.

The President's only answer was, "I owe you one." (*Old Abe's Jokes*)

Abe Thinks T.R. Strong, but Coffee are Stronger

It is told by an intelligent contraband, who is probably reliable, that Mr. Lincoln was walking up Pennsylvania Avenue the other day, relating 'a little story' to Secretary Seward, when the latter called his attention to a new sign bearing the name of 'T.R. Strong,' "Ha!" says old Abe his countenance lighting up with a peculiar smile, "T.R. Strong, but coffee are stronger." Seward smiled, but made no reply. (*Old Abe's Jokes*)

Old Abe "C's" It

I consoled the President this morning by relating to him what an unfortunate letter 'C' was in the Presidential Chase. A joke—do you take? I related the fate of Crawford, Calhoun, Clay and Cass. The Presidential eye brightened up. I saw hope displayed in every lineament of his countenance. He replied, "I see it." How quick he is at *repartee*. How pointed too. I think the Presidential heart has beat easier since the administry of my last solace. (*Old Abe's Jokes*)

I Mean 'Honest Old Abe'

A good story is told of an old Cleveland deacon, who just after Lincoln started on his journey for Washington, went to an evening prayer meeting, and being somewhat in a hurry, went down immediately on his knees, and made an earnest prayer in behalf of the President of the United States, asking that God would strengthen him and bless him in all his undertakings. Rising from his knees he left the church, apparently having an earnest call elsewhere. Presently he returned in a great hurry, and plumping again on his knees, thus addressed himself; "Oh, Lord, it may be as well for me to add as an explanation to my prayer just uttered, that by the President of the United States I mean honest old Abe Lincoln, and not that other chap who is yet sitting in the national nest, and for whom I don't care shucks. Amen." (*Old Abe's Jokes*)

Mr. Lincoln and the Millerite

A gentleman, it is said, sometime ago hinted to the President that it was deemed quiet settled that he would accept a re-nomination for his present office, whereupon Mr. Lincoln was reminded of a story of Jesse Dubois, out in Illinois. Jesse, as State Auditor, had charge of the State House at Springfield. An itinerant preacher came along and asked the use of it for a lecture. "On what subject?" asked Jesse. "On the second coming of our Saviour," answered the long-faced Millerite. "Oh, bosh," retorted Uncle Jesse, testily, "I guess if our Saviour had ever been to Springfield, and had got away with his life, he'd be too much smart to think of coming back again." This, Mr. Lincoln said, was very much his case about the succession. (*Old Abe's Jokes*)

What Old Abe Says of Tennessee

It is a fertile country, and the people are putting in crops after a fashion, and under difficulties. He asked a lady from there not long ago,
"Will you make a crop of cotton this year?"
"I am going to try."
"How many hands have you got?"
"One woman."
It struck me, says Abe, that a crop of cotton "made" by one female citizen of African descent would not be what is generally nominated a *Big Thing*. (*Old Abe's Jokes*)

The Presidential Hymn of Thanks

Miles O'Rielly, the soldier who was arrested on Morris Island, S.C., for making poetry, and pardoned by the President, in response to a witty poetical petition, has sent a hymn of thanks to the President, beginning:

"Long life to you, Misther Lincoln;
May you die both late and aisy;
An' whin you lie wid the top of aich toe
Turned up to the roots of a daisy,
May this be your epitaph, nately writ:
'Though traitors abused him vilely,
He was honest an' kindly, he loved a joke,
An' he pardoned Myles O'Reilly.'" (*Old Abe's Jokes*)

Honest Abe's Replies

Old Abe being asked what he had done for his country, made the following reply:

1st. I confiscated their cotton, but in return gave them Wool.

2d. I have exercised a Foster-ing care over North Carolina.

3d. I gave them a 'Pope' to control their misguided zeal.

4th. Notwithstanding the financial condition of their country, I established 'Banks' in New Orleans.

5th. I furnished them with a 'Butler' and 'Porter.'

6th. When the slaves in South Carolina fled from their masters, I sent them a Hunter, who found them by hundreds.

7th. When they invaded Pennsylvania to reap a harvest, I furnished the 'Sickles' and gave them 'Meade' to cool their heated blood. (*Old Abe's Jokes*)

Old Abe's Story of New Jersey

One terribly stormy night in bleak December, a United States vessel was wrecked off the coast of Jersey, and every soul save one, went down with the doomed craft. This one survivor seized a floating spar and was washed toward the shore, while innumerable kind-hearted tools of the Camden and Amboy railroad clustered on the beach with boats and ropes. Slowly the unhappy mariner drifted to land and as he exhaustedly caught at the rope thrown to him, the kindly natives uttered an encouraging cheer. 'You are saved!' they shouted. 'You are saved, and must show the conductor your ticket!' With the sea still boiling about him, the drowning stranger resisted the efforts to haul him ashore, 'Stop!' said he, in faint tones 'tell me where I am! What country is this?' They answered 'New Jersey.' Scarcely had the name been uttered when the wretched stranger let go the rope, ejaculating, as he did so, 'I guess I'll float a little farther!' (*Old Abe's Jokes*)

One of Abe's Last

'I can't say for certain who will be the people's choice for President, but to the best of my belief it will be the successful candidate.' (*Old Abe's Jokes*)

Father Abe on the Wood-Legged Amateur

Old Abe, once reminded of the enormous cost of the war, remarked, 'ah yes! that reminds me of a wooden legged amateur who happened to be with a Virginia skirmishing party when a shell burst near him, smashing his artificial limb to bits, and sending a piece of iron through the calf of a soldier near him. The soldier 'grinned and bore it' like a man, while the amateur was loud and emphatic in his lamentation. Being rebuked by the wounded soldier, he replied: 'Oh, yes; it's all well enough for you to bear it. Your leg didn't cost you anything, and will heal up; but I paid two hundred dollars for mine!' (*Old Abe's Jokes*)

Abe's Curiosity

Father Abraham says he lately discovered in an old drawer which had not been opened for years, a remarkable silver coin, which had on one side a head with the word 'Liberty' surrounded by thirteen stars, and the date 1860. On the opposite was an eagle with the motto 'E Pluribus Unum,' the words 'United States of America,' and the figures '10¢!' (*Old Abe's Jokes*)

Old Abe as a Mathematician

Mr. Lincoln has a very effective way sometimes of dealing with men who trouble him with questions. Somebody asked him how many men the rebels had in the field. He replied very seriously, 'Twelve hundred thousand, according to the best authority.' The interrogater blanched in the face, and ejaculated 'My God!' 'Yes, sir, twelve hundred thousand—no doubt of it. You see, all of our Generals, when they get whipped, say the enemy outnumbers them from three or five to one, and I must believe them. We have four hundred thousand men in the field, and three times four make twelve. Don't you see it?' The inquisitive man looked for his hat soon after 'seeing it.' (*Old Abe's Jokes*)

Never-Failing Patience

It would be hardly necessary to inform the nation that our President, in the midst of the anxieties of a state of war that continually torture his mind, is wont to find occasional relief in an appropriate anecdote or well-turned jest.

No man, says Mrs. Stowe, has suffered more and deeper, albeit with a dry, weary, patient pain, that seemed to some like insensibility, than President Lincoln. 'Whichever way it ends,' he said to the writer, 'I have the impression that I shan't last much longer after it is over.'

After the dreadful repulse of Fredericksburg, he is reported to have said: 'If there is a man out of Hell that suffers more than I do, I pity him.' In those dark days his heavy eyes and worn and weary air told how our reverses wore upon him, and yet there was a never-failing fund of patience at the bottom, that sometimes rose to the surface in some droll, quaint saying or story, that forced a laugh even from himself. (*Old Abe's Jokes*)

Call Again

When Uncle Abe was taken sick recently, and Mrs. Lincoln had sent for the doctor, Uncle Abe, having an aversion to physic, said he had better call another time, as he was too sick then to joke with him. (*Lincolniana*)

Handy in Case of Emergencies

During the fall of 1863, Uncle Abe was riding on the Virginia side of the Potomac, between Arlington Heights and Alexandria, accompanied by Dr. N— of New Jersey. Passing the huge earth-work fortifications, the Doctor observed: "Mr. President, I have never yet been enabled to discover the utility of constructing and maintaining those forts. What is your opinion about them?"

"Well doctor," replied Uncle Abe, "you are a medical man! and I will ask you a question in the line of your profession. Can you tell me the use of a man's nipples?" "No I can't" said the doctor. "Well I can tell you," said Uncle Abe,—"They would be mighty handy if he happened to have a child." (*Lincolniana*)

Abe on Rome

"Some conclusions," said Uncle Abe on one occasion, "are nonsequential. To say that Rome was not built in a day, does not prove that it was built in a night." (*Lincolniana*)

Old Abe's Uncle

'My deceased uncle,' says Old Abe, 'was the most polite gentleman in the world. He was making a trip on the Mississippi when the boat sank. He got his head above the water for once, took off his hat, and said, "Ladies and gentlemen, will you please excuse me?" and down he went.' (*Old Abe's Jokes*)

Matrimonial Advice

For a while during the Civil War, General Fremont was without a command. One day in discussing Fremont's case with George W. Julian, President Lincoln said he did not know where to place him, and that it reminded him of the old man who advised his son to take a wife, to which the young man responded: "All right; whose wife shall I take?" (*"Abe" Lincoln's Anecdotes*)

Abe on Taking Something

Old Abe tells the following anecdote of a prisoner, a Union soldier, a droll-looking fellow. I accosted him with, 'Well, my fine fellow, what are you in here for?' 'For taking something,' he replied. 'What do you mean?' 'Why,' said he, 'one morning I did not feel very well, and went to see the surgeon. He was busy writing at the time, and when I went in he looked at me saying, 'Well, you do look bad; you had better take something.' He then went on with his writing, and left me standing behind him. I looked around, and saw nothing I could take except his watch, and I took that. That's what I am in here for.' (*Old Abe's Jokes*)

Lincoln Mistaken for Once

President Lincoln was compelled to acknowledge that he made at least one mistake in "sizing up" men. One day a very dignified man called at the White House, and Lincoln's heart fell when his visitor approached. The latter was portly, his face was full of apparent anxiety, and Lincoln was willing to wager a year's salary that he represented some Society for the Easy and Speedy Repression of Rebellions.

The caller talked fluently, but at no time did he give advice or suggest a way to put down the Confederacy. He was full of humor, told a clever story or two, and was entirely self-possessed.

At length the President inquired, "You are a clergyman, are you not, sir?"

"Not by a jug full," returned the stranger heartily.

Grasping him by the hand Lincoln shook it until the visitor squirmed. "You must lunch with us. I am glad to see you. I was afraid you were a preacher."

"I went to the Chicago Convention," the caller said, "as a friend of Mr. Seward. I have watched you narrowly ever since your inauguration, and I called merely to pay my respects. What I want to say is this: I think you are doing everything for the good of the country that is in the power of man to do. You are on the right track. As one of your constituents I now say to you, do in future as you d— please, and I will support you!"

This was spoken with tremendous effect.

"Why," said Mr. Lincoln, in great astonishment, "I took you to be a preacher. I thought you had come here to tell me how to take Richmond," and he again grasped the hand of his strange visitor.

Accurate and penetrating as Mr. Lincoln's judgment was concerning men, for once he had been wholly mistaken. The scene was comical in the extreme. The two men stood gazing at each other. A smile broke from the lips of the solemn wag and rippled over the wide expanse of his homely face like sunlight overspreading a continent, and Mr. Lincoln was convulsed with laughter.

He stayed to lunch. (*"Abe" Lincoln's Anecdotes*)

Old Abe a Coward

If Lincoln should be renominated for the Presidency, why would he be a cowardly antagonist? Because he would be sure to run. (*Old Abe's Jokes*)

GETTING ON WITH PEOPLE

Too Many Hogs

There used to be a clerk in the Register's office in Washington who belonged to one of those Washington families which, ever since the foundation of the government, have considered themselves, by prescriptive right, entitled to be provided for by it. At the same time, his father was chief of one of the bureaus in the War Department, and he had a brother who was employed in the Interior Department. He had also another brother who had been in the army, but, becoming disabled by illness, had been honorably discharged. For this brother, too, he was determined to secure a place in the civil service. With this object he went from department to department, but always without success. Finally he determined to go directly to the President himself, to appeal to him to intervene in behalf of the discharged soldier. Mr. Lincoln, it would seem, had heard of the case before the Treasury clerk secured the audience with him which he sought. When the interview had terminated, the disappointed clerk commenced, in the most indiscreet and intemperate manner, to express his disgust with the President. "It is a disgrace to the country," he said, "that such a boor should be President of the United States!" The story of what had occurred between the President and himself was something like this: Mr. Lincoln received him kindly, and listened to his request. "Why don't you go directly to the Secretaries?" he asked. "I have been to them all, and failed with all," was the answer. "Hasn't your brother sufficiently recovered his health to enable him to return to the army?" inquired the President. "No, sir, he has not," was the reply. "Let me see," continued Mr. Lincoln "I believe that you yourself are a clerk in one of the departments—which one is it ?"—"The Treasury Department, sir."—"I thought so. Has your brother as good clerical capacity as you possess?"—"Yes, sir."—"I think that I have somewhere met your father. Doesn't he hold an office in Washington?"—"Yes, sir; he is the chief of the — bureau in the War Department."—"Oh, yes! I now recollect him perfectly well. Has your

brother good references as to character?"—"Yes, sir; the very best."—
"Is there *any other* of your family holding office under the government?"—"Yes, sir; I have a younger brother in the Interior Department."—"Well, then, all I have to say to you, Mr. —, is *that there are
too many hogs and too little fodder!*" (*Scissors*)

What Ailed the Boys

Mr. Roland Diller, who was one of Mr. Lincoln's neighbors in
Springfield, tells the following:
I was called to the door one day by the cries of children in the
street, and there was Mr. Lincoln, striding by with two of his boys, both
of whom were wailing aloud. 'Why, Mr. Lincoln, what's the matter with
the boys?' I asked.
"'Just what's the matter with the whole world,' Lincoln replied.
'I've got three walnuts, and each wants two.'" (*"Abe" Lincoln's Anecdotes*)

A Major

At one of Uncle Abe's levees recently, among the Company was a
Pennsylvania Avenue tailor whom Abe recognized but could not name.
"My dear Sir, I remember your face, but I forget your name," said Uncle
Abe. The knight of the needle whispered confidentially into Uncle Abe's
ear. "I made your breeches." Uncle Abe took him most affectionately by
the hand and exclaimed enthusiastically "Major Breeches, I am happy to
meet you at the White House!" (*Lincolniana*)

Fix the Date

Uncle Abe was conversing with some friends and remarked,
"There's a good Time coming." A countryman stepped up to Uncle Abe,
and said: "Mister, you couldn't fix to date, could yous?" (*Lincolniana*)

Reminded Him of "A Little Story"

When Lincoln's attention was called to the fact that, at one time in
his boyhood, he had spelled the name of the Deity with a small "g," he
replied:

"That reminds me of a little story. It came about that a lot of Confederate mail was captured by the Union forces, and, while it was not exactly the proper thing to do, some of our soldiers opened several letters written by the Southerners at the front to their people at home.

"In one of these missives the writer, in a postscript, jotted down this assertion:

"'We'll lick the Yanks termorrer, if goddlemity (God Almighty) spares our lives.'

"That fellow was in earnest, too, as the letter was written the day before the second battle of Manassas." (*"Abe" Lincoln's Anecdotes*)

A Poor Crop

An old acquaintance of Uncle Abe's called upon him a short time since with the view to getting hold of a contract. Uncle Abe told him that contracts were not what they were in Cameron's time. "In fact, said he, "they remind me now of a piece of meadow land on the Sangamon bottoms during a drouth." "How was that?" said the Sucker—"Why," said Abe, looking rather quizical, "the grass was so short that they had to lather before they could mow it." (*Lincolniana*)

"Thought He Must Be Good for Something"

An Illinois man who had known the "boy Mayor," John Hay, from boyhood, was expressing to Uncle Abe, after the massacre at Olustee, some regret that he should have supposed him capable of any military position.

"About Hay," said Uncle Abe, "the fact was, I was pretty much like Jim Hawks, out in Illinois, who sold a dog to a hunting neighbor, as a first-rate coon dog. A few days after, the fellow brought him back, saying he 'wasn't worth a cuss for coons.' 'Well,' said Jim, 'I tried him for everything else, and he wasn't worth a d—n, and so I thought he must be good for coons.'" (*Lincolniana*)

The Dandy and the Boys

President Lincoln appointed as consul to a South American country a young man from Ohio who was a dandy. A wag met the new appointee on his way to the White House to thank the President. He was dressed in the most extravagant style. The wag horrified him by telling him that the country to which he was assigned was noted chiefly for the bugs that abounded there and made life unbearable.

"They'll bore a hole clean through you before a week has passed," was the comforting assurance of the wag as they parted at the White House steps. The new consul approached Lincoln with disappointment clearly written all over his face. Instead of joyously thanking the President, he told him the wag's story of the bugs. "I am informed, Mr. President," he said, "that the place is full of vermin and that they could eat me up in a week's time." "Well, young man," replied Lincoln, "if that's true, all I've got to say is that if such a thing happened they would leave a mighty good suit of clothes behind." (*Wit and Humor*)

Douglas Held Lincoln's Hat

When Mr. Lincoln delivered his first inaugural he was introduced by his friend, United States Senator E.D. Baker, of Oregon. He carried a cane and a little roll—the manuscript of his inaugural address. There was a moment's pause after the introduction, as he vainly looked for a spot where he might place his high silk hat.

Stephen A. Douglas, the political antagonist of his whole public life, the man who had pressed him hardest in the campaign of 1860, was seated just behind him. Douglas stepped forward quickly, and took the hat which Mr. Lincoln held helplessly in his hand.

"If I can't be President," Douglas whispered smilingly to Mrs. Brown, a cousin of Mrs. Lincoln and a member of the President's party, "I at least can hold his hat." (*"Abe" Lincoln's Anecdotes*)

Justice vs. Numbers

Lincoln was constantly bothered by members of delegations of "goody-goodies," who knew all about running the War, but had no inside information as to what was going on. Yet they poured out their advice in streams, until the President was heartily sick of the whole business, and wished the War would find some way to kill off these nuisances.

"How many men have the Confederates now in the field?" asked one of these bores one day.

"About one million two hundred thousand," replied the President.

"Oh, my! Not so many as that, surely, Mr. Lincoln."

"They have fully twelve hundred thousand, no doubt of it. You see, all of our generals when they get whipped say the enemy outnumbers them from three or five to one, and I must believe them. We have four hundred thousand men in the field, and three times four make twelve,— don't you see it? It is as plain to be seen as the nose on a man's face; and at the rate things are now going, with the great amount of speculation and the small crop of fighting, it will take a long time to overcome twelve hundred thousand rebels in arms.

"If they can get subsistence they have everything else, except a just cause. Yet it is said that 'thrice is he armed that hath his quarrel just.' I am willing, however, to risk our advantage of thrice injustice against their thrice in numbers." (*"Abe" Lincoln's Anecdotes*)

Abraham Advises the "Springs"

It is stated that Old Abe being much disgusted at the crowd of officers who some time ago used to loiter about the Washington hotels, and he is reported to have remarked to a member of Congress: "These fellows, *and the Congressmen* do vex me sorely, they should certainly visit the 'Springs.'" (*Old Abe's Jokes*)

He Loved a Good Story

Judge Breese, of the Supreme bench, one of the most distinguished of American jurists, and a man of great personal dignity, was about to open court at Springfield, when Lincoln called out in his hearty way: "Hold on, Breese! Don't open court yet! Here's Bob Blackwell just going to tell a story!" The Judge passed on without replying, evidently regarding it as beneath the dignity of the Supreme Court to delay proceedings for the sake of a story. (*"Abe" Lincoln's Anecdotes*)

Graphic and True

When Hon. Emerson Etheridge escaped from Tennessee during the summer of 1862, his opinions on Tennessee affairs were eagerly listened to in Washington. Among other questions, Uncle Abe asked:

"Do the Methodist clergy in your State take to secession?"

"Take? Why, sir, they take to it like a duck to water, or a sailor to a duff kid." (*Lincolniana*)

Couldn't Make a Presidential Chair

"Mr. Lincoln," said an ardent sovereignty man just at the beginning of the last Presidential contest, "Mr. Douglas is a cabinet maker."

"He *was* when I first knew him," said Uncle Abe, "But he gave up the business so long ago, that I don't think he can make a Presidential chair now."

Uncle Abe proved himself a prophet, although at a tremendous cost to the country. (*Lincolniana*)

The Same Old Rum

One of President Lincoln's friends, visiting at the White House, was finding considerable fault with the constant agitation in Congress of the slavery question. He remarked that, after the adoption of the Emancipation policy, he had hoped for something new.

"There was a man down in Maine," said the President, in reply, "who kept a grocery store, and a lot of fellows used to loaf around for their toddy. He only gave 'em New England rum, and they drank pretty considerable of it. But after a while they began to get tired of that, and kept asking for something new—something new—all the time. Well, one night, when the whole crowd were around, the grocer brought out his glasses, and says he, 'I've got something New for you to drink, boys, now.'

"'Honor bright?' says they.

"'Honor bright,' says he, and with that he sets out a jug. 'That,' says he, 'that's something New; it's New England rum!' says he.

"Now," remarked the President, in conclusion, "I guess we're a good deal like that crowd, and Congress is a good deal like that store-keeper!" (*"Abe" Lincoln's Anecdotes*)

Lincoln Agreeable Disappointed

Mr. Lincoln, as the highest public officer of the nation is necessarily very much bored by all sorts of people calling upon him.

An officer of the Government called one day at the White House, and introduced a clerical friend. 'Mr. President,' said he, 'allow me to present to you my friend the Rev. Mr. F. of —. Mr. F. has expressed a desire to see you and have some conversation with you, and I am happy to be the means of introducing him.' The President shook hands with

Mr. F., and desiring him to be seated took a seat himself. Then—his countenance having assumed an air of patient waiting—he said: 'I am now ready to hear what you have to say.' 'O, bless you, sir,' said Mr. F., 'I have nothing especially to say, I merely called to pay my respects to you, and, as one of the million, to assure you of my hearty sympathy and support.' 'My dear sir,' said the President, rising promptly—his face showing instant relief, and with both hands grasping that of his visitor, 'I am very glad to see you, indeed. I thought you had come to preach to me!' (*Old Abe's Jokes*)

Abraham's Going to Pot

'A deputation of gentlemen from New York waited upon Old Abe with the determination to impress his mind with the great injustice done their department of trade by the Committee on Taxation.

'Gentlemen,' said the President, 'why do you come to me? The committee will hear you and do you justice. I cannot interfere.'

'But,' urged the spokesman, 'if they are going to tax all the commodities of life,—'

'My friends,' responded the rail-splitter, 'if they tax all the necessaries, I'm afraid we must all go to pot.' (*Old Abe's Jokes*)

Uncle Abe's Estimate of the Senate

Uncle Abe says that in the Senate, he "owns nine of the Senators and one-half of another," "Who owns the other half?" asked a gentleman to whom Uncle Abe was speaking. "Henry Wilson of Massachusetts," replied the Chief Magistrate. "Wilson is for me," says the President, "before breakfast; rather against me while his digestion is going on after it; loves me like pie during the hours which he spends visiting the various departments and asking for places and patronage; and bitterly my enemy from seven every evening until he goes to bed, drops asleep and commences snoring. Wilson is carrying water on both shoulders but I guess he'll get a wetting and soil his clothes before he gets through." (*Lincolniana*)

How Old Abe Had Never Read It

'The Loyal League Convention, which was in secret session in Washington, brought a strong pressure to bear on the President for the removal of some obnoxious members of the cabinet on account of their supposed conservative views, and also for the appointment of a radical commander in Missouri, in place of Gen. Scofield. At an interview, a committee of the Leaguers indignantly asked the President whether he endorsed Mr. Blair's Rockville speech; to which he replied, that he 'had never read it.' The feelings of the excited radicals may be more easily imagined than described at this Lincolnian stroke, and they retired from the White House with no dim perception of the meaning of 'Abe's latest and best joke.' (*Old Abe's Jokes*)

How Old Abe Settled the Point

The town is laughing at an amusing story of a recent interview between Mr. Lincoln and the president of the Baltimore and Ohio railroad. 'The draft has fallen with great severity upon the employes of our company,' said the R.R. President. 'Indeed!' responded the President of the U.S. 'If something is not done to relieve us, it is hard to foresee the consequences.' 'Let them pay the commutation.' 'Impossible! the men can't stand such a tax.' 'They have a rich company at their back and that's more than other people have.' 'They ought to be exempted, because they are necessary to the working of the road for the government.' 'That can't be.' 'Then I will stop the road.' 'If you do, I will take it up and carry it on.' The discussion is said to have dropped at this point, and the very worthy president is still working the road as successfully as ever. (*Old Abe's Jokes*)

More Pegs than Holes

President Lincoln, in replying to the St. Louis delegation, which recently waited on him to urge the prosecution of the war on ultra Abolition principles, replied that 'he had more *pegs* than he had *holes* to put them in.' This answer is peculiarly appropriate, as the Abolitionists, since the commencement of hostilities, have been so much engaged in stealing as to render the war nothing but a game of cribbage. (*Old Abe's Jokes*)

"Plough All 'Round Him"

Governor Blank went to the War Department one day in a towering rage:

"I suppose you found it necessary to make large concessions to him, as he returned from you perfectly satisfied," suggested a friend.

"Oh, no," the President replied, "I did not concede anything. You have heard how that Illinois farmer got rid of a big log that was too big to haul out, too knotty to split, and too wet and soggy to burn.

"'Well, now,' said he, in response to the inquiries of his neighbors one Sunday, as to how he got rid of it, 'well, now, boys, if you won't divulge the secret, I'll tell you how I got rid of it—I ploughed around it.'

"Now," remarked Lincoln, in conclusion, "don't tell anybody, but that's the way I got rid of Governor Blank. I ploughed all round him, but it took me three mortal hours to do it, and I was afraid every minute he'd see what I was at." (*"Abe" Lincoln's Anecdotes*)

"All Sicker'n Your Man"

A Commissioner to the Hawaiian Islands was to be appointed, and eight applicants had filed their papers, when a delegation from the South appeared at the White House on behalf of a ninth. Not only was their man fit—so the delegation urged—but was also in bad health, and a residence in that balmy climate would be of a great benefit to him.

The President was rather impatient that day, and before the members of the delegation had fairly started in, suddenly closed the interview with this remark:

"Gentlemen, I am sorry to say that there are eight other applicants for that place, and they are all 'sicker'n' your man." (*"Abe" Lincoln's Anecdotes*)

Old Abe on the Congressmen

As the President and a friend were sitting on the House of Representatives steps, the session closed, and the members filed out in a body. Abraham looked after them with a sardonic smile.

'That reminds me,' said he, 'of a little incident. When I was quite a boy, my flat-boat lay up at Alton, on the Mississippi, for a day, and I strolled about the town. I saw a large stone building, with massive walls, not so handsome, though, as this; and while I was looking at it, the iron gateway opened, and a great body of men came out. 'What do you call that;' I asked a by-stander. 'That,' said he, 'is the State Prison, and those are all thieves going home. Their time is up.' (*Old Abe's Jokes*)

Old Abe's Generosity

While President Lincoln was confined to his house with the varioloid, some friends called to sympathize with him, especially on the character of his disease. 'Yes,' he said, 'it is a bad disease, but it has its advantages. For the first time since I have been in office, I have something now to give to every person that calls.' (*Old Abe's Jokes*)

A Petitioner's Sudden Change of Mind

The President was feeling indisposed, and had sent for his physician, who upon his arrival informed the President that his trouble was either varioloid, or mild smallpox. "They're all over me. Is it contagious?" said Mr. Lincoln. "Yes," answered the Doctor, "very contagious, indeed."

"Well," said a visitor, "I can't stop. I just called to see you."

"Oh, don't be in a hurry sir," placidly said the President.

"Thank you, sir; I'll call again," retreating abruptly.

"Some people," said the Executive, looking after him, "said they could not take very well to my proclamation, but now, I am happy to say, I have something that everybody can take." (*Wit and Humor*)

Uncle Abe and the Pass to Richmond

A gentleman called upon the President, and solicited a pass for Richmond. 'Well,' said the President, 'I would be very happy to oblige, if my passes were respected; but the fact is, sir, I have, within the past two years, given passes to two hundred and fifty thousand men to go to Richmond, and not one has got there yet.' The applicant quietly and respectfully withdrew on his tip-toes. (*Old Abe's Jokes*)

The President and the Paymaster

One of the numerous paymasters at Washington sought an introduction to Mr. Lincoln. He arrived at the White House quite opportunely, and was introduced to the President by the United States Marshal, with his blandest smile. While shaking hands with the President the paymaster remarked, "I have no official business with you, Mr. President, I only called to pay my compliments." "I understand," replied "honest Abe," "that from the complaints of the soldiers, I think that is all you do pay." (*Civil War in Song and Story*)

Lincoln's Advice to the Commodore

In Mr. P.T. Barnum's "Struggles and Triumphs; or, Forty Years' Recollections" he mentions having been in Washington in the year 1862, with Commodore Nutt. President Lincoln sent Mr. Barnum an invitation to visit the White House, and bring his short friend. The Cabinet happened to be there, and the President introduced the little mariner to them. When Mr. Chase was introduced as Secretary of the Treasury, the Commodore remarked,—

"I suppose you are the gentleman who is spending so much of Uncle Sam's money?"

"No, indeed," said Secretary Stanton: "I am spending it."

"Well," said the Commodore, "it is in a good cause, and I guess it will come out all right."

Mr. Lincoln then bent down his long, lank body, and, taking Nutt by the hand, said,—

"Commodore, permit me to give you a parting word of advice. When you are in command of your fleet, if you find yourself in danger of being taken prisoner, *I advise you to wade ashore.*"

The Commodore, placing himself at the side of the President, and gradually raising his eyes up the whole length of Mr. Lincoln's very long legs replied, "I guess Mr. President, you could do that better than I could." (*Scissors*)

His Ideas Old, After All

One day, while listening to one of the wise men who had called at the White House to unload a large cargo of advice, the President interjected a remark to the effect that he had a great reverence for learning.

"This is not," President Lincoln explained, "because I am not an educated man. I feel the need of reading. It is a loss to a man not to have grown up among books."

"Men of force," the visitor answered, "can get on pretty well without books. They do their own thinking instead of adopting what other men think."

"Yes," said Mr. Lincoln, "but books serve to show a man that those original thoughts of his aren't very new, after all."

This was a point the caller was not willing to debate, and so he cut his call short. (*Wit and Humor*)

Outran the Rabbit

Mr. Lincoln enjoyed the description of how this Congressman led the race from Bull's Run, and laughed at it heartily.

"I never knew but one fellow who could run like that," he said, "and he was a young man out in Illinois. He had been sparking a girl, much against the wishes of her father. In fact, the old man took such a dislike to him that he threatened to shoot him if he ever caught him around his premises again.

"One evening the young man learned that the girl's father had gone to the city, and he ventured out to the house. He was sitting in the parlor, with his arm around Betsy's waist, when he suddenly spied the old man coming around the corner of the house with a shotgun. Leaping through a window into the garden, he started down a path at the top of his speed. He was a long-legged fellow, and could run like greased lightning. Just then a jack-rabbit jumped up in the path in front of him. In about two leaps he overtook the rabbit. Giving it a kick that sent it high in the air, he exclaimed: 'Git out of the road, gosh dern you, and let somebody run that knows how.'

"I reckon," said Mr. Lincoln, "that the long-legged Congressman, when he saw the rebel muskets, must have felt a good deal like that young fellow did when he saw the old man's shot-gun." (*Wit and Humor*)

Menace to the Government

The persistence of office-seekers nearly drove. President Lincoln wild. They slipped in through the half-opened doors of the Executive Mansion; they dogged his steps if he walked; they edged their way through the crowds and thrust their papers in his hands when he rode; and, taking it all in all, they well-nigh worried him to death.

He once said that if the Government passed through the Rebellion without dismemberment there was the strongest danger of its falling a prey to the rapacity of the office-seeking class.

"This human struggle and scramble for office, for a way to live without work, will finally test the strength of our institutions," were the words he used. (*Wit and Humor*)

Office Seekers Worse than War

When the Republican party came into power, Washington swarmed with office-seekers. They overran the White House and gave the President great annoyance. The incongruity of a man in his position, and with the very life of the country at stake, pausing to appoint postmasters, struck Mr. Lincoln forcibly. "What is the matter, Mr. Lincoln," said a friend one day, when he saw him looking particularly grave and dispirited. "Has anything gone wrong at the front?"

"No," said the President, with a tired smile. "It isn't the war; it's the postoffice at Brownsville, Missouri." (*Wit and Humor*)

LINCOLN AND THE ARMY

Old Abe on Banks' Expedition

When Gen. Banks was fitting out his expedition to New Orleans, it will be remembered that the President used to answer all questions as to its destination with great frankness, by saying that it was going South. (*Old Abe's Jokes*)

Father Abraham a Disciple of "Father Matthew"

When Gen. Hooker was ordered to join Gen. Grant at Chattanooga, the president advised him to avoid '*Bourbon*' county, when passing through Kentucky. (*Old Abe's Jokes*)

Five O'Clock to Gissober In

Abe tells the following story about a drunken captain who met a private of his company in the same condition. The captain ordered him to 'halt,' and endeavoring in vain to assume a firm position on his feet, and to talk with dignified severity, exclaimed: 'Private Smith, I'll give you t'l (hic) four o'clock to gissober in.' 'Cap'n' replied the soldier, 'as you'r (hic)—sight drunkerniam, I'll give you t'l five o'clock to gissober in.' (*Old Abe's Jokes*)

My Mary Ann

Many months ago the post commander at Cairo was a certain West Point colonel of a Northwestern regiment, noted for his soldierly qualities and rigid discipline. One day he passed by the barracks and heard a group of soldiers singing the well-known street piece, "My Mary Ann." An angry shade crossed his brow, and he forthwith ordered the men to be placed in the guard-house, where they remained all night. The next morning he visited them, when one ventured to ask the cause of their confinement.

"Cause enough," said the rigid colonel; "you were singing a song in derision of Mrs. Colonel B—."

The men replied by roars of laughter, and it was some time before the choler of the Colonel could be sufficiently subdued to understand that the song was an old one, and sung by half the school-boys in the land, or the risibles of the men be calmed down to learn that the Colonel's wife rejoiced in the name of "Mary Ann."

Uncle Abe made the Colonel a Brigadier the moment he heard this story. (*Lincolniana*)

Advises an Angry Officer

An officer, having had some trouble with General Sherman, being very angry, presented himself before Mr. Lincoln, who was visiting the camp, and said, "Mr. President, I have a cause of grievance. This morning I went to Colonel Sherman and he threatened to shoot me." "Threatened to shoot you?" said Mr. Lincoln. "Well [in a stage whisper], if I were you and he threatens to shoot, I would not trust him, for I believe he would do it." (*Wit and Humor*)

Grant "Tumbled" Right Away

General Grant told this story about Lincoln some years after the War:

"Just after receiving my commission as lieutenant-general the President called me aside to speak to me privately. After a brief reference to the military situation, he said he thought he could illustrate what he wanted to say by a story. Said he:

"'At one time there was a great war among the animals, and one side had great difficulty in getting a commander who had sufficient confidence in himself. Finally they found a monkey by the name of Jocko, who said he thought he could command their army if his tail could be made a little longer. So they got more tail and spliced it on to his caudal appendage.

"'He looked at it admiringly, and then said he thought he ought to have still more tail. This was added, and again he called for more, The splicing process was repeated many times until they had coiled Jocko's tail around the room, filling all the space.

"'Still he called for more tail, and, there being no other place to put it, they began wrapping it around his shoulders. He continued his call for more, and they kept on winding the additional tail around him until its weight broke him down.'

"I saw the point, and, rising from my chair, replied, 'Mr. President, I will not call for any more assistance unless I find it impossible to do with what I already have.'" (*Wit and Humor*)

A Vain General

In an interview between President Lincoln and Petroleum V. Nasby, the name came up of a recently deceased politician of Illinois whose merit was blemished by great vanity. His funeral was very largely attended.

"If General— had known how big a funeral he would have had," said Mr. Lincoln, "he would have died years ago." (*"Abe" Lincoln's Anecdotes*)

Cold Molasses Was Swifter

"Old Pap," as the soldiers called General George H. Thomas, was aggravatingly slow at a time when the President wanted him to "get a move on"; in fact, the gallant "Rock of Chickamauga" was evidently entered in a snail-race.

"Some of my generals are so slow," regretfully remarked Lincoln one day, "that molasses in the coldest days of winter is a race horse compared to them.

"They're brave enough, but somehow or other they get fastened in a fence corner, and can't figure their way out." (*"Abe" Lincoln's Anecdotes*)

Grant Held on All the Time

(Dispatch to General Grant, August 17th, 1864)
"I have seen your dispatch expressing your unwillingness to break your hold where you are. Neither am I willing.

"Hold on with a bulldog grip." (*"Abe" Lincoln's Anecdotes*)

Profanity as a Safety-Valve

Lincoln never indulged in profanity, but confessed that when Lee was beaten at Malvern Hill, after seven days of fighting, and Richmond, but twelve miles away, was at McClellan's mercy, he felt very much like swearing when he learned that the Union general had retired to Harrison's Landing.

Lee was so confident his opponent would not go to Richmond that he took his army into Maryland—a move he would not have made had an energetic fighting man been in McClellan's place.

It is true McClellan followed and defeated Lee in the bloodiest battle of the War—Antietam—afterwards following him into Virginia; but Lincoln could not bring himself to forgive the general's inaction before Richmond. (*"Abe" Lincoln's Anecdotes*)

Couldn't See It in That Light

A delegation of temperance men recently sought to influence Uncle Abe to take some stringent steps to suppress intemperance in our armies. Among other reasons urged, they said our armies were often beaten because of intemperance.

"Is that so?" said Uncle Abe. "I've heard on all sides that the rebels drink more than our boys do, and I can't see why our boys, who drink less, are more liable to get whipped."

"But you know the corrupting influence of the army in regard to drinking habits," pursued the Committee.

"I've heard that, too," said Uncle Abe, "but I think they will do pretty well if I can keep them out of Washington!"

The Committee didn't carry their measure by a jug full. (*Lincolniana*)

Aptly Said

To a man who was condoling Uncle Abe on the disaster at Olustee, and suggesting how it might have been prevented, he said:

"Your remarks are well intended, doubtless; but they do little less than aggravate a thing which I can't help thinking might have been helped. It reminds me of a story that I read when I was a boy. An old fellow who had clambered rather high into an apple tree, fell and broke his arm. A sympathizing and philosophic neighbor, seeing his mishap, went to his aid. 'Ah,' said he, 'if you had followed my plan you would have escaped this.' 'Indeed, what is your plan?" enquired the groaning man. 'Why, never to let go both hands, till you get one hold somewhere else.'"

The would-be Brigadier saw the point, and left. (*Lincolniana*)

A Soldier's Theory of the War

The soldiers at Helena, in Arkansas, used to amuse the inhabitants of that place, on their first arrival, by telling them yarns, of which the following is a sample:

"Some time ago Jeff Davis got tired of the war and invited President Lincoln to meet him on neutral ground to discuss terms of peace. They met accordingly, and after a talk, concluded to settle the war by dividing the territory and stopping the fighting. The North took the Northern States, and the South the Gulf and seaboard Southern States. Lincoln took Texas and Missouri, and Davis Kentucky and Tennessee; so that all were parcelled off excepting Arkansas. Lincoln didn't want it—Jeff wouldn't have it. Neither would consent to take it, and on that they split; and the war has been going on ever since." (*Lincolniana*)

Sorry for the Horses

When President Lincoln heard of the Confederate raid at Fairfax, in which a brigadier-general and a number of valuable horses were captured, he gravely observed:

"Well, I am sorry for the horses."

"Sorry for the horses, Mr. President!" exclaimed the Secretary of War, raising his spectacles and throwing himself back in his chair in astonishment.

"Yes," replied Mr. Lincoln, "I can make a brigadier-general in five minutes, but it is not easy to replace a hundred and ten horses." (*"Abe" Lincoln's Anecdotes*)

Old Abe and the "Brigadiers"

The President has been perpetrating one of his pungent sayings about that luckless wight, Brigadier-General Stoughton, who was so unceremoniously picked up by guerillas. 'Pretty serious business, this, Mr. President,' said a visitor, 'to have a Brigadier-General captured at Fairfax Court House!' 'Oh, that doesn't trouble me,' was the response, 'I can make a better Brigadier any time in five minutes; but it did worry me to have all those horses taken. Why, sir, these horses cost us a hundred and twenty-five dollars a head!' (*Old Abe's Jokes*)

Uncle Abe's Last

Yesterday a Western correspondent, in search for something definite in relation to the fighting now going on, stepped into the White House and asked the President if he had anything authentic from Gen. Grant. The President stated that he had not, as Grant was like the man that climbed the pole and then pulled the pole up after him.—*Washington Union*, May 16. (*Lincolniana*)

Feeling Patriotic

'I feel patriotic," said an old rowdy. 'What do you mean by feeling 'patriotic?' inquired the President, who was standing by. 'Why, I feel as if I wanted to kill somebody or steal something.' The Tennessee authorities felt the same kind of patriotism on the Fourth of July; and as they didn't like to venture upon killing anybody, they stole the trains of the Louisville and Nashville Railroad. (*Old Abe's Jokes*)

Wanted to "Borrow" the Army

During one of the periods when things were at a standstill, the Washington authorities, being unable to force General McClellan to assume an aggressive attitude, President Lincoln went to the general's headquarters to have a talk with him, but for some reason he was unable to get an audience.

Mr. Lincoln returned to the White House much disturbed at his failure to see the commander of the Union forces, and immediately sent for two general officers, to have a consultation. On their arrival, he told them he must have some one to talk to about the situation, and as he had failed to see General McClellan, he wished their views as to the possibility or probability of commencing active operations with the Army of the Potomac.

"Something's got to be done," said the President, emphatically, "and done right away, or the bottom will fall out of the whole thing. Now, if McClellan doesn't want to use the army for a while, I'd like to borrow it from him and see if I can't do something or other with it.

"If McClellan can't fish, he ought at least to be cutting bait at a time like this." (*"Abe" Lincoln's Anecdotes*)

Lincoln and Nobility

A lieutenant, whom debts compelled to leave his fatherland, and service, succeeded in being admitted to the late President Lincoln, and, by reason of his commendable and winning deportment and intelligent appearance, was promised a lieutenant's commission in a cavalry regiment. He was so enraptured with his success, that he deemed it a duty to inform the President that he belonged to one of the oldest noble houses in Germany. "Oh, never mind that," said Mr. Lincoln; "you will not find that to be an obstacle to your advancement." (*Civil War in Song and Story*)

LINCOLN AND THE CABINET

Lincoln and Chase's Bills

"There's an odor of nationality about those bills," said Secretary Chase, showing a lot of the firstlings of his greenbacks to Uncle Abe.

"A very good figure of speech," replied Uncle Abe, "but you must not get too many under the public nostril, or your figure of speech will be an odor of fact."
April 1, 1862, greenbacks, 100. April 1, 1864, greenbacks, 55. (*Lincolniana*)

Had Confidence in Him—"But"—

"General Blank asks for more men," said Secretary of War Stanton to the President one day, showing the latter a telegram from the commander named, appealing for re-enforcements.

"I guess he's killed off enough men, hasn't he?" queried the President. "I don't mean Confederates—our own men. What's the use in sending volunteers down to him if they're only used to fill graves?"

"His dispatch seems to imply that, in his opinion, you have not the confidence in him he thinks he deserves," the War Secretary went on to say, as he looked over the telegram again.

"Oh," was the President's reply, "he needn't lose any of his sleep on that account. Just telegraph him to that effect; also, that I don't propose to send him any more men." (*"Abe" Lincoln's Anecdotes*)

Uncle Abe Boss of the Cabinet

A prominent Senator was remonstrating with Uncle Abe a few days ago about keeping Mr. Chase in his Cabinet, when it was as well known that Mr. C. is opposed, tooth and nail, to Uncle Abe's re-election.

"Now, see here," said Uncle Abe, "when I was elected I resolved to hire my four Presidential rivals, pay them their wages and be their 'boss.' These were Seward, Chase, Cameron and Bates; but I got rid of Cameron after he had played himself out. As to discharging Chase or Seward, don't talk of it. I pay them their wages and am their boss, and wouldn't let either of them out on the loose for the fee simple of the Almaden patent." (*Lincolniana*)

Has It "Gin Out?"

We do not know what joke Uncle Abe made when he heard the news of the surrender of Plymouth. In regard to the Fort Pillow affair he made a Bunsby speech, but no joke. His last joke, of which we have any knowledge, occurred when Secretary Chase was starting on his trip to New York. Uncle Abe is like Cromwell without his military genius, and is very fond of playing practical jokes on his associates. It is said that after Cromwell had signed the warrant for the execution of King Charles he turned round to one of his colleagues and smeared his face with the ink. This he thought capital fun. Uncle Abe's jokes are of about the same quality. When Chase called upon him to say good-bye, the Secretary of the Treasury asked for some information about the probable end of the war, saying it would help him greatly in getting more money in Wall Street. "Do you want more money?" asked Lincoln, and then quickly added, "What! has the printing machine gin out?" This joke is fully equal to Cromwell's. (*Lincolniana*)

Lincoln on His Cabinet "Help"

A prominent senator was remonstrating with Mr. Lincoln a few days ago about keeping Mr. Chase in his Cabinet, when it was well known that Mr. C. is opposed, tooth and nail, to Mr. Lincoln's reelection.

'Now, see here,' said the President, 'when I was elected I resolved to hire my four Presidential rivals, pay them their wages, and be their 'boss.' These were Seward, Chase, Cameron and Bates; but I got rid of Cameron after he had played himself out. As to discharging Chase or Seward, don't talk of it. I pay them their wages and am their Boss, wouldn't let either of them out on the loose for the fee simple of the Almaden patent.' (*Old Abe's Jokes*)

At It With a Will

The President and Secretary of State were closeted together, over-whelmed by the affairs of the nation.

'Seward, you look puzzled,' said Secretary Chase as he entered and found that able functionary half buried among papers, scratching his head and biting his pen.

'Never fear,' quoth Old Abe, laughing gaily and slapping the Secretary of State approvingly on the back. 'Where there's a Will there's a way!' (*Old Abe's Jokes*)

Lincoln Saw Stanton About It

Mr. Lovejoy, heading a committee of Western men, discussed an important scheme with the President, and the gentlemen were then directed to explain it to Secretary of War Stanton.

Upon presenting themselves to the Secretary, and showing the President's order, the Secretary said: "Did Lincoln give you an order of that kind?"

"He did, sir."

"Then he is a d—d fool," said the angry Secretary.

"Do you mean to say that the President is a d—d fool?" asked Lovejoy in amazement.

"Yes, sir, if he gave you such an order as that."

The bewildered Illinoisian betook himself at once to the President and related the result of the conference.

"Did Stanton say I was a d—d fool?" asked Lincoln at the close of the recital.

"He did, sir, and repeated it."

After a moment's pause, and looking up, the President said: "If Stanton said I was a d—d fool, then I must be one, for he is nearly always right, and generally says what he means. I will slip over and see him." (*"Abe" Lincoln's Anecdotes*)

Has No Influence with the Administration

Judge Baldwin, an old and highly respectable and sedate gentleman, called a few days since on Gen. Halleck, and presuming upon a familiar acquaintance in California formerly, solicited a pass outside of our lines, to see a brother in Virginia, not thinking that he would be met with a refusal, as both his brother and himself were good Union men.

"We have been deceived too often," said General Halleck, "and I regret I can't grant it."

Judge B. then went to Stanton, and was very briefly disposed of with the same result. Finally he obtained an interview with Uncle Abe, and stated his case.

"Have you applied to Gen. Halleck?" inquired the President.

"And met with a flat refusal," said Judge B.

"Then you must see Stanton," continued Uncle Abe.

"I have, and with the same result," was the reply.

"Well, then," said Uncle Abe, with a smile of good humor, "I can do nothing; for you must know that I have very little influence with this Administration." (*Lincolniana*)

Hard on Butler

"Mr. Welles," inquired Old Abe of the venerable Secretary of in the Navy at a Cabinet Council, "What does the affair at Fort Fisher remind you of?"

"Another of your jokes, Mr. President," replied Father Welles. "How should I know?"

"Well, then, I will tell you. It reminds me of a Porter who opened the door, and of a Butler who declined to go in." (*Book of Anecdotes*)

That Reminds Me

Mr. John H. Littlefield, who studied law under Mr. Lincoln, is responsible for the following:—

Several men urged Mr. Lincoln to remove Secretary of the Treasury Chase. They said that he was in the way of the administration, and hampered the President. A smile played around the corners of the President's mouth, and he said,—

"That reminds me of a farmer out West. He was ploughing with his old mare Nance one hot summer day, and his son was following another plough in an adjoining furrow. A horse-fly got on Nance's nose, and the son kept yelling to his daddy to stop and get the fly off the mare's nose. The father paid no attention to his vociferous son for a while. Finally the son kept yelling about the fly on Nance's nose until the old man answered,—

"'Now, low-a-here, jist keep quiet; that ere fly on Nance's nose makes her go faster.'"

There was a sudden collapse on the part of those who wanted Secretary Chase removed. (*Scissors*)

One War at a Time

Nothing in Lincoln's entire career better illustrated the surprising resources of his mind than his manner of dealing with "The Trent Affair." The readiness and ability with which he met this perilous emergency, in a field entirely new to his experience, was worthy of the most accomplished diplomat and statesman. Admirable, also, was his cool courage and self-reliance in following a course radically opposed to the prevailing sentiment throughout the country and in Congress, and contrary to the advice of his own Cabinet.

Secretary of the Navy Wells hastened to approve officially the act of Captain Wilkes in apprehending the Confederate Commissioners Mason and Slidell, Secretary Stanton publicly applauded, and even Secretary of State Seward, whose long public career had made him especially conservative, stated that he was opposed to any concession or surrender of Mason and Slidell.

But Lincoln, with great sagacity, simply said, "One war at a time." (*Wit and Humor*)

Lincoln's Modesty

Secretary Chase, when Secretary of the Treasury, had a disagreement, and the Secretary had resigned.

The President was urged not to accept it, as "Secretary Chase is today a national necessity," his advisers said. "How mistaken you are!" he quietly observed. "Yet it is not strange; I used to have similar notions. No! if we should all be turned out to-morrow, and could come back here in a week, we should find our places filled by a lot of fellows doing just as well as we did, and in many instances better.

"As the Irishman said, 'In this country one man is as good as another; and, for the matter of that, very often a great deal better.' No; this Government does not depend upon the life of any man." (*Wit and Humor*)

One Bullet and a Hatful

Lincoln made the best of everything, and if he couldn't get what he wanted he took what he could get. In matters of policy, while President he acted according to this rule. He would take perilous chances, even when the result was to the minds of his friends, not worth the risk he had run.

One day at a meeting of the Cabinet, it being at the time when it seemed as though war with England and France could not be avoided, Secretary of State Seward and Secretary of War Stanton warmly advocated that the United States maintain an attitude, the result of which would have been a declaration of hostilities by the European Powers mentioned.

"Why take any more chances than are absolutely necessary?" asked the President.

"We must maintain our honor at any cost," insisted Secretary Seward.

"We would be branded as cowards before the entire world," Secretary Stanton said.

"But why run the greater risk when we can take a smaller one?" queried the President calmly. "The less risk we run the better for us. That reminds me of a story I heard a day or two ago, the hero of which was on the firing line during a recent battle, where the bullets were flying thick. Finally his courage gave way entirely, and throwing down his gun, he ran for dear life.

"As he was flying along at top speed he came across an officer who drew his revolver and shouted, 'Go back to your regiment at once or I will shoot you!'

"'Shoot and be hanged,' the racer exclaimed. 'What's one bullet to a whole hatful?'" (*Wit and Humor*)

LINCOLN AND HIS FAMILY

Lincoln's Love Affairs

Previous to his marriage Mr. Lincoln had two love affairs, one of them so serious that it left an impression upon his whole future life. One of the objects of his affection was Miss Mary Owen, of Green County, Kentucky, who decided that Mr. Lincoln "was deficient in those little links which make up the chain of woman's happiness." The affair ended without any damage to Mr. Lincoln's heart or the heart of the lady. (*Wit and Humor*)

It Tickled the Little Woman

Lincoln had been in the telegraph office at Springfield during the casting of the first and second ballots in the Republican National Convention at Chicago, and then left and went over to the office of the State Journal, where he was sitting conversing with friends while the third ballot was being taken.

In a few moments came across the wires the announcement of the result. The superintendent of the telegraph company wrote on a scrap of paper: "Mr. Lincoln, you are nominated on the third ballot," and a boy ran with the message to Lincoln.

He looked at it in silence, amid the shouts of those around him; then rising and putting it in his pocket, he said quietly: "There's a little woman down at our house would like to hear this; I'll go down and tell her." (*"Abe" Lincoln's Anecdotes*)

His "Glass Hack"

President Lincoln had not been in the White House very long before Mrs. Lincoln became seized with the idea that a fine new barouche was about the proper thing for "the first lady in the land." The President did not care particularly about it one way or the other, and told his wife to order whatever she wanted.

Lincoln forgot all about the new vehicle, and was overcome with astonishment one afternoon when, having acceded to Mrs. Lincoln's desire to go driving, he found a beautiful barouche standing in front of the door of the White House.

His wife watched him with an amused smile, but the only remark he made was, "Well, Mary, that's about the slickest 'glass hack' in town, isn't it?" (*"Abe" Lincoln's Anecdotes*)

Old Abe Occasionally Browses Around

A party of gentlemen, among whom was a doctor of divinity of great comeliness of manner called at the White House, to pay their respects to the President. On inquiring for that dignitary, the servant informed them that the President was at dinner, but he would present their cards. The doctor demurred to this, saying they would not disturb Mr. Lincoln, but would call again. Michael persisted in assuring them it would make no difference to the President, and bolted in with the cards. In a few minutes, the President walked into the room, with a kindly salutation, and a request that the friends would take seats. The doctor expressed his regret that their visit was so ill-timed, and that his Excellency was disturbed while at dinner. 'O! no consequence at all,' said the good-natured Mr. Lincoln: 'Mrs. Lincoln is absent at present, and when she is away, I generally browse around.' (*Old Abe's Jokes*)

Dignifying the Statute

Lincoln was married—he balked at the first date set for the ceremony and did not show up at all—November 4, 1842, under most happy auspices. The officiating clergyman, the Rev. Mr. Dresser, used the Episcopal church service for marriage. Lincoln placed the ring upon the bride's finger, and said, "With this ring I now thee wed, and with all my worldly goods I thee endow."

Judge Thomas C. Browne, who was present, exclaimed, "Good gracious, Lincoln! the statute fixes all that!"

"Oh, well," drawled Lincoln, "I just thought I'd add a little dignity to the statute." (*Wit and Humor*)

Why She Married Him

There was a "social" at Lincoln's house in Springfield, and "Abe" introduced his wife to Ward Lamon, his law partner. Lamon tells the story in these words:

"After introducing me to Mrs. Lincoln, he left us in conversation. I remarked to her that her husband was a great favorite in the eastern part of the State, where I had been stopping.

"'Yes,' she replied, 'he is a great favorite everywhere. He is to be President of the United States some day; if I had not thought so I never would have married him, for you see he is not pretty.

"'But look at him, doesn't he look as if he would make a magnificent President ?'" (*Wit and Humor*)

Lincoln as a Dancer

Lincoln made his first appearance in society when he was first sent to Springfield, Ill., as a member of the State Legislature. It was not an imposing figure which he cut in a ballroom, but still he was occasionally to be found there. Miss Mary Todd, who afterward became his wife, was the magnet which drew the tall, awkward young man from his den. One evening Lincoln approached Miss Todd, and said, in his peculiar idiom:

"Miss Todd, I should like to dance with you the worst way."

The young woman accepted the inevitable, and hobbled around the room with him. When she returned to her seat, one of her companions asked mischievously:

"Well, Mary, did he dance with you the worst way?"

"Yes," she answered, "the very worst." (*"Abe" Lincoln's Anecdotes*)

Entered the Colt

Mr. Lincoln was seen coming away from church, unusually early one Sunday morning. "The sermon could not have been more than halfway through," says Mr. Alcott. "'Tad' was slung across his left arm like a pair of saddle-bags, and Mr. Lincoln was striding along with long, deliberate steps toward his home. On one of the street corners he encountered a group of his fellow-townsmen. Mr. Lincoln anticipated the question which was about to be put by the group, and, taking his figure of speech from practices with which they were only too familiar, said: 'Gentlemen, I entered this colt, but he kicked around so I had to withdraw him.'" (*Wit and Humor*)

"Tad" Got His Dollar

No matter who was with the President, or how intently absorbed, his little son "Tad" was always welcome. He almost always accompanied his father.

Once, on the way to Fortress Monroe, he became very troublesome. The President was much engaged in conversation with the party who accompanied him, and he at length said:

"'Tad,' if you will be a good boy, and not disturb me any more until we get to Fortress Monroe, I will give you a dollar."

The hope of reward was effectual for a while in securing silence, but, boylike, "Tad" soon forgot his promise, and was as noisy as ever. Upon reaching their destination, however, he said, very promptly: "Father, I want my dollar." Mr. Lincoln looked at him half reproachfully for an instant, and then, taking from his pocketbook a dollar note, he said: "Well, my son, at any rate, I will keep my part of the bargain." (*"Abe" Lincoln's Anecdotes*)

Lieutenant Tad Lincoln's Sentinels

President Lincoln's favorite son, Tad, having been sportively commissioned a lieutenant in the United States Army by Secretary Stanton, procured several muskets and drilled the men servants of the house in the manual of arms without attracting the attention of his father. And one night, to his consternation, he put them all on duty, and relieved the regular sentries, who, seeing the lad in full uniform, or perhaps appreciating the joke, gladly went to their quarters. His brother objected; but Tad insisted upon his rights as an officer. The President laughed but declined to interfere, but when the lad had lost his little authority in his boyish sleep, the Commander-in-Chief of the Army and Navy of the United States went down and personally discharged the sentries his son had put on the post. (*Wit and Humor*)

Short, but Exciting

William B. Wilson, employed in the telegraph office at the War Department, ran over to the White House one day to summon Mr. Lincoln. He described the trip back to the War Department in this manner:

"Calling one of his two younger boys to join him, we then started from the White House, between stately trees, along a gravel path which led to the rear of the old War Department building. It was a warm day, and Mr. Lincoln wore as part of his costume a faded gray linenduster which hung loosely around his long gaunt frame; his kindly eye was beaming with good nature, and his ever-thoughtful brow was unruffled.

We had barely reached the gravel walk before he stooped over, picked up a round smooth pebble, and shooting it off his thumb, challenged us to a game of 'followings,' which we accepted. Each in turn tried to hit the outlying stone, which was being constantly projected onward by the President. The game was short, but exciting; the cheerfulness of childhood, the ambition of young manhood, and the gravity of the statesman were all injected into it.

"The game was not won until the steps of the War Department were reached. Every inch of progression was toughly contested, and when the President was declared victor, it was only by a hand span. He appeared to be as much pleased as if he had won a battle." (*Wit and Humor*)

Old Abe and His Tod

'For occasional sallies of genuine original wit, give us a country grocery on winter evenings and rainy days, and the bar rooms of country hotels. As an instance take the following, which occurred in a bar-room. There was quite a collection, and our friend S., who is a democrat, and friend M., who is a republican, had been earnestly but pleasantly discussing politics; and as a lull took place in the conversation, S. spoke up as follows:

'M., how many public men are there who are really temperance men?'

'Oh, I don't know,' replied M.

'Well,' said S., 'I don't know of but one that I can speak positively of on our side, and that is General Cass.'

'Well,' said M., promptly, 'there is President Lincoln on our side, certain.'

'Guess not,' said S., incredulously.

'Guess yes,' replied M., warmly.

'But you don't pretend to say that President Lincoln is a temperance man?' asked S.

'Yes, I do,' answered M., 'and can maintain the statement.'

'Well, now I tell you that Abraham Lincoln is as fond of his tod as any man living,' replied S. earnestly, 'and I can prove it to you.'

'Well, I tell you that he isn't,' replied M., who began to get excited; 'that he is as pure and strict a temperance man as there is in the country.'

'I contend,' replied S. with provoking coolness, 'that Abraham Lincoln is so fond of his tod that it is the last thing he thinks of when he goes to bed, and the first when he wakes in the morning.'

'It's a confounded locofoco lie!' exclaimed M., springing to his feet.

'Hold on, friend M.,' said S, 'what was Lincoln's wife's name before she was married?'

'*Todd, by thunder*!' exclaimed M., jumping more than a foot from the floor; 'boy's let's adjourn to the other room.' (*Old Abe's Jokes*)

LINCOLN AND THE NEGRO

The Negro and the Crocodile

In one of his political speeches, Judge Douglas made use of the following figure of speech: "As between the crocodile and the negro, I take the side of the negro; but as between the negro and the white man—I would go for the white man every time."

Lincoln, at home, noted that; and afterward, when he had occasion to refer to the remark, he said: "I believe that this is a sort of proposition in proportion, which may be stated thus: 'As the negro is to the white man, so is the crocodile to the negro; and as the negro may rightfully treat the crocodile as a beast or reptile, so the white man may rightfully treat the negro as a beast or reptile.'" (*Wit and Humor*)

The Niggers and the Small Pox

I dropped in upon Mr. Lincoln and found him busily counting greenbacks. "This, sir," said he, "is something out of my usual line; but a President of the United States has a multiplicity of duties not specified in the Constitution or acts of Congress. This is one of them. This money belongs to a poor negro who is a porter in one of the Departments (the Treasury), and who is at present very bad with the small pox. He did not catch it from me, however; at least I think not. He is now in hospital, and could not draw his pay because he could not sign his name.

"I have been at considerable trouble to overcome the difficulty and get it for him, and have at length succeeded in cutting red-tape, as you newspaper men say. I am now dividing the money and putting by a portion labeled, in an envelope, with my own hands, according to his wish"; and his Excellency proceeded to endorse the package very carefully. No one who witnessed the transaction could fail to appreciate the goodness of heart which would prompt a man who is borne down by the weight of cares unparalleled in the world's history, to turn aside for a time from them to succor one of the humblest of his fellow creatures in sickness and sorrow." (*Old Abe's Jokes*)

Mr. Lincoln and the Barber

The other day a distinguished public officer was at Washington, and in an interview with the President, introduced the question of slavery emancipation. "Well, you see," said Lincoln, "we've got to be mighty cautious how we manage the negro question. If we're not we shall be like the barber out in Illinois, who was shaving a fellow with a hatchet face and lantern jaws like mine. The barber stuck his finger in his customer's mouth to make his cheek stick out, but while shaving away he cut through the fellow's cheek and cut off his own finger! If we don't play mighty smart about the nigger we shall do as the barber did." (*Old Abe's Jokes*)

One of Abe's Anecdotes

"Well," said a gentleman to Old Abe, "we had the nigger served up in every style last session."

"Yes," broke in the Executive, as his eyes twinkled, "ending off with the *fire-cussee* style."

"I hope," resumed the gentleman, "I hope we shall have something new now."

"There was a man down in Maine," said the President, "who kep' a grocery store, and a lot of fellows used to loaf around there for their toddy, Well, he only gave 'em New England rum, and they drinked a pretty considerable of it. But after a while they. began to get tired of that, and kep' asking for something New—something New; all the time. Well, one night, when the whole crowd was around, the grocer, he sot out his glasses, and says he, 'I've got something New for you to drink, boys.' 'Honor bright,' says they. 'Honor bright,' says he; and with that he sot out a jug. 'Thar,' says he, 'that's something New; it's *New*-England rum!' says he. "Now," remarked Abraham, shutting one eye, "I guess we're a good deal like that crowd, and Congress is a good deal like that store-keeper!" (*Old Abe's Jokes*)

Crossing a River When He Got to It

Lincoln's reply to a Springfield (Illinois) clergyman, who asked him what was to be his policy on the slavery question was most apt:

"Well, your question is rather a cool one, but I will answer it by telling you a story:

"You know Father B., the old Methodist preacher? and you know Fox River and its freshets?

"Well, once in the presence of Father B., a young Methodist was worrying about Fox River, and expressing fears that he should be prevented from fulfilling some of his appointments by a freshet in the river.

"Father B. checked him in his gravest manner. Said he:

"'Young man, I have always made it a rule in my life not to cross Fox River till I get to it.'

"And," said the President, "I am not going to worry myself over the slavery question till I get to it."

A few days afterward a Methodist minister called on the President, and on being presented to him, said, simply:

"Mr. President, I have come to tell you that I think we have got to Fox River!"

Lincoln thanked the clergyman, and laughed heartily. (*Wit and Humor*)

The Negro in a Hogshead

Abe often laughs over the following:

A curious incident, which escaped general attention at the time of its occurrence, happened at police headquarters during the riot. While President Acton was giving some final orders to a squad of men who were just leaving to combat the crowd in First avenue, a wagon containing a hogshead was driven rapidly up to the Mulberry street door, by a lad who appeared much excited and almost breathless.

"What have you there, my lad?" said the President.

"Supplies for your men," was the answer.

"What are they?"

"It is an assorted lot, sir; but the people says it's contraband."

Being exceedingly busy, the President ordered the wagon to be driven round to the Mott street entrance, where an officer was sent to look after the goods. When the wagon arrived the officers were about to tip the cask out, but were prevented by the boy, who exclaimed:

"Wait a minute, bring me a hatchet." A hatchet was brought, and the little fellow set to work unheading the cask, and as he did so the officers were astonished to see two full grown negroes snugly packed inside. Upon being assured by the lad that they were safe they raised their heads, took a long snuff of fresh air, and exclaimed, "Bress de Lord!"

The boy stated that the rioters had chased the poor unfortunates into the rear of some houses on the west side of the town, and that they had escaped by scaling a fence and landing in a grocer's yard; that the grocer was friendly to them, but feared his place might be sacked if they were found there. He accordingly hit upon this novel plan of getting them out, and while he kept watch in front the boy coopered the negroes up. The cask was then rolled out like a hogshead of sugar, placed in the wagon and driven off to Mulberry street. The colored heroes of this adventure may still be found at police headquarters, thankful to the ingenuity and daring of those who suggested and carried out this singular method of saving them from violence. (*Old Abe's Jokes*)

Too Cussed Dirty

The following story is often told of Father Abraham about two contrabands, servants of General Kelly and Capt. George Harrison. When the General and his staff were on their way up the mountains they stopped at a little village to get something to eat. They persuaded the occupant of the farm-house to cook them a meal, and in order to expedite matters, sent the two contrabands mentioned to assist in preparing the repast. After it was over the General told the negroes to help themselves. An hour or two afterward he observed them gnawing away at some hard crackers and flitch.

"Why didn't you eat your dinner at the village?" asked the General of one of them.

"Well, to tell the God's trufe, General, it wos too cussed dirty!" was the reply. (*Old Abe's Jokes*)

Identified the Colored Man

Many applications reached Lincoln as he passed to and from the White House and the War Department. One day as he crossed the park he was stopped by a negro, who told him a pitiful story. The President wrote him out a check, which read: "Pay to colored man with one leg five dollars." (*Wit and Humor*)

Rough on the Negro

Mr. Lincoln, one day, was talking with the Rev. Dr. Sunderland about the Emancipation Proclamation and the future of the negro. Suddenly a ripple of amusement broke the solemn tone of his voice. "As for the negroes, Doctor, and what is going to become of them: I told Ben Wade the other day, that it made me think of a story I read in one of my first books, *Aesop's Fables*. It was an old edition, and had curious rough wood cuts, one of which showed three white men scrubbing a negro in a potash kettle filled with cold water. The text explained that the men thought that by scrubbing the negro they might make him white. Just about the time they thought they were succeeding, he took cold and died. Now, I am afraid that by the time we get through this war the negro will catch cold and die." (*"Abe" Lincoln's Anecdotes*)

LINCOLN AND SOUTHERNERS

Even Rebels Ought to be Saved

The Rev. Mr. Shrigley, of Philadelphia, a Universalist, had been nominated for hospital chaplain, and a protesting delegation went to Washington to see President Lincoln on the subject.

"We have called, Mr. President, to confer with you in regard to the appointment of Mr. Shrigley, of Philadelphia, as hospital chaplain."

The President responded: "Oh, yes, gentlemen. I have sent his name to the Senate, and he will no doubt be confirmed at an early date."

One of the young men replied: "We have not come to ask for the appointment, but to solicit you to withdraw the nomination."

"Ah!" said Lincoln, "that alters the case; but on what grounds do you wish the nomination withdrawn?"

The answer was: "Mr. Shrigley is not sound in his theological opinions."

The President inquired: "On what question is the gentleman unsound?"

Response: "He does not believe in endless punishment; not only so, sir, but he believes that even the rebels themselves will be finally saved."

"Is that so?" inquired the President.

The members of the committee responded, "Yes, yes."

"Well, gentlemen, if that be so, and there is any way under Heaven whereby the rebels can be saved, then, for God's sake and their sakes, let the man be appointed."

The Rev. Mr. Shrigley was appointed, and served until the close of the war. (*Wit and Humor*)

Let Jeff Escape, I Don't Want Him

When Grant saw that Lee must soon capitulate, Grant asked the President whether he should try to capture Jeff Davis, or let him escape from the country if he would. The President said:

"About that, I told him the story of an Irishman, who had the pledge of Father Matthew. He became terribly thirsty, and applied to the bartender for a lemonade, and while it was being prepared he whispered to him, 'And couldn't ye put a little brandy in it all unbeknown to myself?' I told Grant if he could let Jeff Davis escape all unbeknown to himself, to let him go, I didn't want him." (*Wit and Humor*)

A Dry Drop

A refugee from Richmond was telling Uncle Abe of the sad state of affairs reigning there. Among other things he said liquor was so scarce that the rebel President himself could scarcely get a drop to drink.

He ought not to have a drop to *drink* in this world or the next," said Uncle Abe.

"You are rather severe," replied the refugee.

"Well," said Uncle Abe, "if you think a drop would do him good, let it be a drop from the scaffold." (*Lincolniana*)

Wished Jeff Would Skip

At an informal Cabinet meeting, at which the disposition of Jefferson Davis and other prominent Confederates was discussed, each member of the Cabinet gave his opinion; most of them were for hanging the traitors, or for some severe punishment. President Lincoln said nothing.

Finally, Joshua F. Speed, his old and confidential friend, who had been invited to the meeting, said, "I have heard the opinion of your Ministers, and would like to hear yours."

"Well, Josh," replied President Lincoln, "when I was a boy in Indiana, I went to a neighbor's house one morning and found a boy of my own size holding a coon by a string. I asked him what he had and what he was doing.

"He says, 'It's a coon. Dad cotched six last night, and killed all but this poor little cuss. Dad told me to hold him until he came back, and I'm afraid he's going to kill this one too; and oh, "Abe," I do wish he would get away!'

"'Well, why don't you let him loose?'

"'That wouldn't be right; and if I let him go, Dad would give me h—. But if he got away himself, it would be all right,'

"Now," said the President, "if Jeff Davis and those other fellows will only get away, it will be all right. But if we should catch them, and I should let them go, 'Dad would give me h—!'" (*Wit and Humor*)

Jeff Davis and Charles the First

Jefferson Davis insisted on being recognized by his official title as commander or President in the regular negotiation with the Government. This Mr. Lincoln would not consent to.

Mr. Hunter thereupon referred to the correspondence between King Charles the First and his Parliament as a precedent for a negotiation between a constitutional ruler and rebels. Mr. Lincoln's face then wore that indescribable expression which generally preceded his hardest hits, and he remarked: "Upon questions of history, I must refer you to Mr. Seward, for he is posted in such things, and I don't profess to be; but my only distinct recollection of the matter is, that Charles lost his head." (*Wit and Humor*)

"Yankee" Goodness of Heart

One day when the President was with the troops who were fighting at the front, the wounded, both Union and Confederate, began to pour in.

As one stretcher was passing Lincoln, he heard the voice of a lad calling to his mother in agonizing tones. His great heart filled. He forgot the crisis of the hour. Stopping the carriers, he knelt, and bending over him, asked: "What can I do for you, my poor child?"

"Oh, you will do nothing for me," he replied. "You are a Yankee. I cannot hope that my message to my mother will ever reach her."

Lincoln, in tears, his voice full of tenderest love, convinced the boy of his sincerity, and he gave his good-by words without reserve.

The President directed them copied, and ordered that they be sent that night, with a flag of truce, into the enemy's lines. (*Wit and Humor*)

Who Commenced This Fuss?

President Lincoln was at all times an advocate of peace, provided it could be obtained honorably and with credit to the United States. As to the cause of the Civil War, which side of Mason and Dixon's line was responsible for it, who fired the first shots, who were the aggressors, etc., Lincoln did not seem to bother about; he wanted to preserve the Union, above all things. Slavery, he was assured, was dead, but he thought the former slaveholders should be recompensed.

To illustrate his feelings in the matter he told this story:

"Some of the supporters of the Union cause are opposed to accommodate or yield to the South in any manner or way because the Confederates began the war; were determined to take their States in out of the Union, and, consequently, should be held responsible to the last stage for whatever may come in the future. Now this reminds me of a good story I heard once, when I lived in Illinois.

"A vicious bull in a pasture took after everybody who tried to cross the lot, and one day a neighbor of the owner was the victim. This man was a speedy fellow and got to a friendly tree ahead of the bull, but not in time to climb the tree. So he led the enraged animal, a merry race around the tree, finally succeeding in seizing the bull by the tail.

"The bull, being at a disadvantage, not able to either catch the man or release his tail, was mad enough to eat nails; he dug up the earth with his feet, scattered gravel all around, bellowed until you could hear him for two miles or more, and at length broke into a dead run, the man hanging onto his tail all the time.

"While the bull, much out of temper, was legging it to the best of his ability, his tormentor, still clinging to the tail, asked, 'Darn you, who commenced this fuss?'

"It's our duty to settle this fuss at the earliest possible moment, no matter who commenced it. That's my idea of it." (*Wit and Humor*)

Honest Old Abe

"An old man hailing from Mississippi, dressed in plain homespun, came to our city Saturday. He mingled freely with the Republican Representatives, got their news, and seemed to think we are not quite so black as we are represented.

"He called on Mr. Lincoln talked freely with him, and heard the President-elect express his sentiments and intentions. He learned that Mr. Lincoln entertained none but the kindest feelings towards the people of the South, and that he would protect the South in her just rights.

"He had a long conversation, and went away delighted. He left the office of Mr. Lincoln in company with a friend, who communicated this to us, and when outside the door he remarked, while the tears stole down his furrowed cheeks: 'Oh! if the people of the South could hear what I have heard, they would love and not hate Mr. Lincoln. I will tell my friends at home; but,' he added sorrowfully, 'they will not believe me.' He said that he did wish that every man in the South could be personally acquainted with Mr. Lincoln." (*Wit and Humor*)

The President Shaking Hands with Wounded Rebels

A correspondent, who was with the President on the occasion of his recent visit to Frederick, Md., tells the following incident:

'After leaving Gen. Richardson, the party passed a house in which was a large number of confederate wounded. By request of the

President, the party alighted and entered the building. Mr. Lincoln, after looking, remarked to the wounded confederates that if they had no objection he would be pleased to take them by the hand. He said the solemn obligations which we owe to our country and posterity compel the prosecution of this war, and it followed that many were our enemies through uncontrollable circumstances and he bore them no malice, and could take them by the hand with sympathy and good feeling. After a short silence the confederates came forward, and each silently but fervently shook the hand of the President. Mr. Lincoln and Gen. McClellan then walked forward by the side of those who were wounded too severely to be able to arise, and bid them to be of good cheer; assuring them that every possible care should be bestowed upon them to ameliorate their condition. It was a moving scene, and there was not a dry eye in the building, either among the nationals or confederates. Both the President and Gen. McClellan were kind in their remarks and treatment of the rebel sufferers during this remarkable interview.' (*Old Abe's Jokes*)

Rebuking a Doctor

Dr. Jerome Walker, of Brooklyn, told how Mr. Lincoln once administered to him a mild rebuke. The doctor was showing Mr. Lincoln through the hospital at City Point.

"Finally, after visiting the wards occupied by our invalid and convalescing soldiers," said Dr. Walker, "we came to three wards occupied by sick and wounded Southern prisoners. With a feeling of patriotic duty, I said: 'Mr. President, you won't want to go in there; they are only rebels.'

"I will never forget how he stopped and gently laid his large hand upon my shoulder and quietly answered, 'You mean Confederates!' And I have meant Confederates ever since.

"There was nothing left for me to do after the President's remark but to go with him through these three wards; and I could not see but that he was just as kind, his hand-shakings just as hearty, his interest just as real for the welfare of the men, as when he was among our own soldiers." (*Wit and Humor*)

Lincoln on Slave Dealers

President Lincoln, having been applied to pardon a repentant slave-trader who had been sentenced to prison, answered the applicant: "My friend, if this man had been guilty of the worst murder that can be conceived of, I might, perhaps, have pardoned him. You know the weakness of my nature—always open to the appeals of repentance or of grief; and with such a touching letter, and such recommendations, I could not resist. But any man who would go to Africa and snatch from a mother her children, to sell them into interminable bondage, merely for the sake of pecuniary gain, shall never receive pardon from me." (*Civil War in Song and Story*)

A Southern Anecdote

An English officer, who passed some time with the air of General Lee, writes the following, in the pages of Blackwood:

"As we were riding back to Hagerstown, we fell in with Colonel Wickham, who commands a brigade of Stuart's cavalry, in connection with whom the following story was told me:—

"It will be remembered that Virginia was one of the last States to secede, and did not do so until she had exhausted every effort to effect a compromise; and when she did so, the few Southern States that were still hesitating followed her example, and the war became inevitable.

"Matters were coming to a crisis, when the leading men of Virginia sent a deputation of three of their number to wait on the President, Mr. Lincoln. They tried to impress him with a sense of the gravity of the situation, and urgently entreated that he would do something to calm the excitement amongst the people, whose irritation at the threats of the Administration, and of the Northern States, was getting beyond control.

"It was just after the taking of Fort Sumter and Lincoln's having called out seventy-five thousand men to coerce the South.

"'But what would you have me do?' said Mr. Lincoln.

"'Mr. President,' replied one of the deputation, 'I would beg you to lend me your finger and thumb for five minutes'—meaning, of course, that he wished to write something that should allay the prevailing excitement.

"But Mr. Lincoln did not choose to understand him. 'My finger and thumb!' he repeated. 'My finger and thumb! What would you do with them? Blow your nose?'

"The deputation retired in disgust, and Virginia seceded!" (*Civil War in Song and Story*)

Old Abe on Bayonets

'You can't do anything with them Southern fellows,' the old gentleman at the table was saying. 'if they get whipped they'll retreat to them Southern swamps and bayous along with the fishes and crocodiles. You haven't got the fish-nets made that'll catch 'em.' 'Look here, old gentleman!' screamed old Abe, who was sitting alongside. 'We've got just the nets for traitors, in the bayous or anywhere.' 'Hey?—what nets?' '*Bayou nets*' and Abraham pointed his joke with a fork, spearing a fishball savagely. (*Old Abe's Jokes*)

President Lincoln Presented with a Pair of Socks

At the Presidential reception on Saturday, Major French presented to the President a pair of woolen socks, knit expressly for the President by Miss Addie Brockway, of Newburyport, Mass. On the bottom of each was knit the secession flag; and near the top the glorious stars and stripes of our Union, so that when worn by the President he will always have the flag of the rebellion under his feet. These socks were sent by the maker to Mrs. Wm. B. Todd, of this city, and at her request Major French presented them with a few appropriate remarks. They were most pleasantly and graciously received by the President. (*Uncle Abe's Jokes*)

The Old Lady and the Pair of Stockings

An old lady from the country called on the President, her tanned face peering out from the interior of a huge sunbonnet. Her errand was to present Mr. Lincoln a pair of stockings of her own made a yard long.

Kind tears came to his eyes as she spoke to him, and then, holding the stockings one in each hand, dangling wide apart for general inspection, he assured her that he should take them with him to Washington, where (and here his eyes twinkled) he was sure he should not be able to find any like them. The amusement of the company was not at all diminished by Mr. Boutwell's remark, that the lady had evidently made a very correct estimate of Mr. Lincoln's latitude and longitude. (*Wit and Humor*)

Take Your Choice, Madam

At Nashville the ladies have been peculiarly spiteful and bitter against the hated rival which waves victorious over the stars and bars. It sometimes happens, however, that they are compelled to render a formal obedience at least to the spangled folds.

Over the large gate at the Provost Marshal's splendid headquarters—Eliot's Female School—waves a Union flag. A very ardent secesh lady, who wished to see Col. Matthews, was about to pass through the gate, when looking up she beheld the proud flag flapping like an eagle's wing over his eyrie. Starting back horror struck, she held up her hands and exclaimed to the guard:

"Dear me! I can't go under that dreadful Lincoln flag. Is there no other way for me to enter?"

"Yes, madam," promptly replied the orderly; and turning to his comrade, he said:

"Here, orderly, bring out that rebel flag and lay it on the ground at the little gate, and let this lady walk over it!"

The lady looked bewildered, and after hesitating a moment, concluded to bow her head to the invincible Goddess of Liberty, whose immaculate shrine is the "Star Spangled Banner." The rebels may all just as well conclude to follow her example. (*The Picket Line*)

Southern "Happiness"

Old Abe declares, in epigrammatic phase, 'the only happy people in the Confederacy are those who have black hearts or black skins.'

Reduced to plainer English, this confession means that the rebel rulers and the rebel speculators are all rascals together, and that the blacks are never happy until they begin to run away from such contaminating influences. (*Old Abe's Jokes*)

Old Abe on the "Compromise"

When the conversation turned upon the discussions as to the Missouri Compromise, it elicited the following quaint remark from the President: 'It used to amuse me some (sic) to find that the slave holders wanted more territory, because they had not room enough for their slaves, and yet they complained of not having the slave trade, because they wanted more slaves for their room.' (*Old Abe's Jokes*)

The Devil and the Rebels

Uncle Abe says there is a good deal of the devil in the Rebels. They sometimes fight like him, frequently run like him, and always lie like him. (*Lincolniana*)

Secesh Lady

A secesh lady of Alexandria, who was ordered away into Dixie by the Government, destroyed all her furniture and cut down her trees, so that the 'cursed Yankees' should not enjoy them. Lincoln hearing of this, the order was countermanded, and she returned to see in her broken penates, the folly of her conduct. (*Old Abe's Jokes*)

Rival of Uncle Abe

Old Abe has got off many good things since he left Springfield, but the following equals anything which has proceded from that veteran joker.

"In the Georgia Legislature, Mr. Linton Stephens, brother of the rebel Vice President, introduced a resolution in the House of Representatives declaring that peace be officially offered to the enemy after every Confederate victory." (*Lincolniana*)

A Useless Dog

When Hood's army had been scattered into fragments, President Lincoln, elated by the defeat of what had so long been a menacing force on the borders of Tennessee, was reminded by its collapse of the fate of a savage dog belonging to one of his neighbors in the frontier settlements in which he lived in his youth. "The dog," he said, "was the terror of the neighborhood, and its owner, a churlish and quarrelsome fellow, took pleasure in the brute's forcible attitude.

"Finally, all other means having failed to subdue the creature, a man loaded a lump of meat with a charge of powder, to which was attached a slow fuse; this was dropped where the dreaded dog would find it, and the animal gulped down the tempting bait.

"There was a dull rumbling, a muffled explosion, and fragments of the dog were seen flying in every direction. The grieved owner, picking up the shattered remains of his cruel favorite, said: 'He was a good dog, but as a dog, his days of usefulness are over.' Hood's army was a good army," said Lincoln by way of comment, "and we were all afraid of it, but as an army, its usefulness is gone." (*"Abe" Lincoln's Anecdotes*)

Ran Away When Victorious

Three or four days after the battle of Bull Run, some gentlemen who had been on the field called upon the President.

He inquired very minutely regarding all the circumstances of the affair, and, after listening with the utmost attention, said with a touch of humor:

"So it is your notion that we whipped the rebels and then ran away from them!" (*"Abe" Lincoln's Anecdotes*)

Five-Legged Calf

President Lincoln had great doubt as to his right to emancipate the slaves under the War power. In discussing the question, he used to liken the case to that of the boy who, when asked how many legs his calf would have if he called its tail a leg, replied, "five," to which the prompt response was made that calling the tail a leg would not make it a leg. (*Wit and Humor*)

A Very Brainy Nubbin

President Lincoln and Secretary of State Seward met Alexander H. Stephens, Vice-President of the Confederacy, on February 2nd, 1865, on the River Queen, at Fortress Monroe. Stephens was enveloped in over-coats and shawls, and had the appearance of a fair-sized man. He began to take off one wrapping after another, until the small, shriveled old man stood before them.

Lincoln quietly said to Seward: "This is the largest shucking for so small a nubbin that I ever saw."

President Lincoln had a friendly conference, but presented his ulti-matum—that the one and only condition of peace was that Confederates "must cease their resistance." (*Wit and Humor*)

Lincoln's Rejected Manuscript

On February 5th, 1865, President Lincoln formulated a message to Congress, proposing the payment of $400,000,000 to the South as compensation for slaves lost by emancipation, and submitted it to his Cabinet, only to be unanimously rejected.

Lincoln sadly accepted the decision, and filed away the manuscript message, together with this indorsement thereon, to which his signature was added: "February 5, 1865. To-day these papers, which explain themselves, were drawn up and submitted to the Cabinet and unanimously disapproved by them."

When the proposed message was disapproved, Lincoln soberly asked: "How long will the war last?"

To this none could make answer, and he added:

"We are spending now, in carrying on the war, $3,000,000 a day, which will amount to all this money, besides all the lives." (*Wit and Humor*)

Incident in Lincoln's Last Speech

Edward, the conservative but dignified butler of the White House, was seen struggling with Tad and trying to drag him back from the window from which was waving a Confederate flag captured in some fight and given to the boy. Edward conquered and Tad, rushing to find his father, met him coming forward to make, as it proved, his last speech.

The speech began with these words, "We meet this evening, not in sorrow, but in gladness of heart." Having his speech written in loose leaves, and being compelled to hold a candle in the other hand, he would let the loose leaves drop to the floor one by one. Tad picked them up as they fell, and impatiently called for more as they fell from his father's hand. (*Wit and Humor*)

LINCOLN'S TENDER HEART

How "Jake" Got Away

One of the last, if not the very last story told by President Lincoln, was to one of his Cabinet who came to see him, to ask if it would be proper to permit "Jake" Thompson to slip through Maine in disguise and embark for Portland.

The President, as usual, was disposed to be merciful, and to permit the arch-rebel to pass unmolested, but Secretary Stanton urged that he should be arrested as a traitor.

"By permitting him to escape the penalties of treason," persisted the War Secretary, "you sanction it." "Well," replied Mr. Lincoln, "let me tell you a story. There was an Irish soldier here last summer, who wanted something to drink stronger than water, and stopped at a drug-shop, where he espied a soda-fountain. 'Mr. Doctor,' said he, 'give me, plase, a glass of soda-wather, an' if yez can put in a few drops of whiskey unbeknown to any one, I'll be obleeged.' "Now," continued Mr. Lincoln, "if 'Jake' Thompson is permitted to go through Maine unbeknown to any one, what's the harm? So don't have him arrested." (*"Abe" Lincoln's Anecdotes*)

He "Skewed" the Line

When a surveyor, Mr. Lincoln first platted the town of Petersburg, Ill. Some twenty or thirty years afterward the property-owners along one of the outlying streets had trouble in fixing their boundaries, They consulted the official plat and got no relief. A committee was sent to Springfield to consult the distinguished surveyor, but he failed to recall anything that would give them aid, and could only refer them to the record. The dispute therefore went into the courts. While the trial was pending, an old Irishman named McGuire, who had worked for some farmer during the summer, returned to town for the winter. The case being mentioned in his presence, he promptly said: "I can tell you all about it. I helped carry the chain when Abe Lincoln laid out this town. Over there where they are quarreling about the lines, when he was locating the street, he straightened up from his instrument and said: 'If I run that street right through, it will cut three or four feet off the end of —'s house. It's all he's got in the world and he could never get another. I reckon it won't hurt anything out here if I skew the line a little and miss him.' "

He handed this card to her advocate, saying, "Give this to Betsy Ann."

"But, Mr. President, couldn't you write a few words to the officers that would insure her protection?"

"No," said Mr. Lincoln, "officers have no time now to read letters. Tell Betsy Ann to put a string in this card and hang it around her neck. When the officers see this, they will keep their hands off your Betsy Ann." (*"Abe" Lincoln's Anecdotes*)

The Other One Was Worse

It so happened that an official of the War Department had escaped serious punishment for a rather flagrant offense, by showing where grosser irregularities existed in the management of a certain Bureau of the Department. So valuable was the information furnished that the culprit who "gave the snap away" was not even discharged.

"That reminds me," the President said, when the case was laid before him, "of a story about Daniel Webster, when the latter was a boy.

"When quite young, at school, Daniel was one day guilty of a gross violation of the rules. He was detected in the act, and called up by the teacher for punishment.

"This was to be the old-fashioned 'feruling' of the hand. His hands happened to be very dirty.

"Knowing this, on the way to the teacher's desk, he spit upon the palm of his right hand, wiping it off upon the side of his pantaloons.

"'Give me your hand, sir,' said the teacher, very sternly.

"Out went the right hand, partly cleansed. The teacher looked at it a moment, and said:

"'Daniel, if you will find another hand in this school-room as filthy as that, I will let you off this time!'

"Instantly from behind his back came the left hand.

"'Here it is, sir,' was the ready reply.

"'That will do,' said the teacher, 'for this time; you can take your seat, sir.'" (*"Abe" Lincoln's Anecdotes*)

He Couldn't Wait for the Colonel

General Fisk, attending a reception at the White House, saw waiting in the anteroom a poor old man from Tennessee, and learned that he had been waiting three or four days to get an audience, on which probably depended the life of his son, under sentence of death for some military offense.

General Fisk wrote his case in outline on a card and sent it in, with a special request that the President would see the man. In a moment the order came; and past impatient senators, governors and generals, the old man went.

He showed his papers to Mr. Lincoln, who said he would look into the case and give him the result next day.

The old man, in an agony of apprehension, looked up into the President's sympathetic face and actually cried out:

"Tomorrow may be too late! My son is under sentence of death. It ought to be decided now!"

His streaming tears told how much he was moved.

"Come," said Mr. Lincoln, "wait a bit and I'll tell you a story"; and then he told the old man General Fisk's story about the swearing driver, as follows:

"The general had begun his military life as a colonel, and when he raised his regiment in Missouri he proposed to his men that he should do all the swearing of the regiment. They assented; and for months no instance was known of the violation of the promise.

"The colonel had a teamster named John Todd, who, as roads were not always the best, had some difficulty in commanding his temper and his tongue.

"John happened to be driving a mule team through a series of mud-holes a little worse than usual, when, unable to restrain himself any longer, he burst forth into a volley of energetic oaths.

"The colonel took notice of the offense and brought John to account.

"'John,' said he, 'didn't you promise to let me do all the swearing of the regiment?'

"'Yes, I did, colonel,' he replied, 'but the fact was, the swearing had to be done then or not at all, and you weren't there to do it.'"

As he told the story the old man forgot his boy, and both the President and his listener had a hearty laugh together at its conclusion.

Then he wrote a few words which the old man read, and in which he found new occasion for tears; but the tears were tears of joy, for the words saved the life of his son. (*"Abe" Lincoln's Anecdotes*)

Lincoln's Last Afternoon

During the afternoon the President signed a pardon for a soldier sentenced to be shot for desertion, remarking as he did so, "Well, I think the boy can do us more good above ground than under ground."

He also approved an application for the discharge on taking the oath of allegiance, of a rebel prisoner, in whose petition he wrote, "Let it be done."

This act of mercy was his last official order. (*Wit and Humor*)

"Abe" Recites a Song

Lincoln couldn't sing, and he also lacked the faculty of musical adaptation. He had a liking for certain ballads and songs, and while he memorized and recited their lines, someone else did the singing. Lincoln often recited for the delectation of his friends, the following, the authorship of which is unknown:

The first factional fight in old Ireland, they say,
Was all on account of St. Patrick's birthday;
It was somewhere about midnight without any doubt,
And certain it is, it made a great rout.
On the eighth day of March, as some people say,
St. Patrick at midnight he first saw the day;
While others assert 'twas the ninth he was born—
'Twas all a mistake—between midnight and morn.
Some blamed the baby, some blamed the clock;
Some blamed the doctor, some the crowing cock.
With all these close questions sure no one could know,
Whether the babe was too fast or the clock was too slow.
Some fought for the eighth, for the ninth some would die;
He who wouldn't see right would have a black eye.
At length these two factions so positive grew.
They each had a birthday, and Pat he had two.
Till Father Mulcahay who showed them their sins,
He said none could have two birthdays but as twins.
"Now, boys, don't be fighting for the eight or the nine;
Don't quarrel so always, now why not combine."
Combine eight with nine. It is the mark;
Let that be the birthday. Amen! said the clerk.
So all got blind drunk, which completed their bliss,
And they've kept up the practice from that day to this. (*Wit and Humor*)

LINCOLN AND THE SPIRITS

Kept His Courage Up

The President, like old King Saul, when his term was about to expire, was in a quandary concerning a further lease of the Presidential office. He consulted again the "prophetess" of Georgetown, immortalized by his patronage.

She retired to an inner chamber, and, after raising and consulting more than a dozen of distinguished spirits from Hades, she returned to the reception-parlor, where the chief magistrate awaited her, and declared that General Grant would capture Richmond, and that "Honest Old Abe" would be next President.

She, however, as the report goes, told him to beware of Chase. (*Wit and Humor*)

A Fortune-Teller's Prediction

Lincoln had been born and reared among people who were believers in premonitions and supernatural appearances all his life, and he once declared to his friends that he was "from boyhood superstitious."

He at one time said to Judge Arnold that "the near approach of the important events of his life were indicated by a presentiment or a strange dream, or in some other mysterious way it was impressed upon him that something important was to occur." This was earlier than 1850.

It is said that on his second visit to New Orleans, Lincoln and his companion, John Hanks, visited an old fortune-teller—a voodoo negress. Tradition say's that "during the interview she became very much excited, and after various predictions, exclaimed: 'You will be President, and all the negroes will be free.'"

That the old voodoo negress should have foretold that the visitor would be President is not at all incredible. She doubtless told this to many aspiring lads, but Lincoln, so it is avowed, took the prophecy seriously. (*Wit and Humor*)

Fascinated by the Wonderful

Lincoln was particularly fascinated by the wonderful happenings recorded in history. He loved to read of those mighty events which had been foretold, and often brooded upon these subjects. His early convictions upon occult matters led him to read all books tending to strengthen these convictions.

The following lines, in Byron's "Dream," were frequently quoted by him:

"Sleep hath its own world,
A boundary between the things misnamed
Death and existence: Sleep hath its own world
And a wide realm of wild reality.
And dreams in their development have breath,
And tears and tortures, and the touch of joy;
They leave a weight upon our waking thoughts,
They take a weight from off our waking toils,
They do divide our being."

Those with whom he was associated in his early youth and young manhood, and with whom he was always in cordial sympathy were thorough believers in presentiments and dreams; and so Lincoln drifted on through years of toil and exceptional hardship—meditative, aspiring, certain of his star, but appalled at times by its malignant aspect. Many times prior to his first election to the Presidency he was both elated and alarmed by what seemed to him a rent in the veil which hides from mortal view what the future holds.

He saw, or thought he saw, a vision of glory and of blood, himself the central figure in a scene which his fancy transformed from giddy enchantment to the most appalling tragedy. (*Wit and Humor*)

Mr. Lincoln and the "Mediums"

'There is a secret, known only to a few, in reference to the manner in which our armies are commanded,' says a New York writer. 'Mr. Lincoln has mediums in constant communication with the spirit world. Each military hero has a special medium. Not a battle has been fought, except under the direct command, not of McClellan, Scott, McDowell, Pope, Burnside, Hooker, and modern generals, but they have acted merely as lieutenants for the master war-spirits of the other world! All the generals in the other world were consulted by the spirits previous to Hooker's defeat, and the old adage proved true that 'too many cooks spoil the broth.' Napoleon and Ellington, and Generals Washington and Jackson, were not at the council: Napoleon, because he did not understand Lincoln's English communications, and the Duke of Wellington, because of his contempt for them, or that anybody in supreme power should ask military advice. Generals Washington and Jackson would not give advice, because, though they were extremely annoyed at the dissolution of the Union, yet, as such a miserable fact had occurred, their friendly feelings were enlisted with their descendants on the side of the South. That Mr. Lincoln is guided altogether by spiritual advisers is now well known.' (*Old Abe's Jokes*)

Old Abe Consulting the Spirits

A Washington correspondent of the Boston *Saturday Evening Gazette*, gives the following account of a *spiritual* manifestation at the White House:

A few evenings since Abraham Lincoln, the President of the United States, was induced to give a Spiritual soiree in the Crimson Room at the White House, to test the wonderful alleged supernatural powers of Mr. Charles E. Shockle. It was my good fortune as a friend of the medium to be present, the party consisting of the President, Mrs. Lincoln, Mr. Welles, Mr. Stanton, Mr. L., of New York, and Mr. F., of Philadelphia. We took our seats in the circle about eight o'clock, but the President was called away shortly after the manifestations commenced, and the spirits, which had apparently assembled to convince him of their power, gave visible tokens of their displeasure at the President's absence, by pinching Mr. Stanton's ears and twitching Mr. Welles' beard. The President soon returned, but it was some time before harmony was restored, for the mishaps to the Secretaries caused such bursts of laughter, that the influence was very unpropitious. For some half hour the demonstrations were of a physical character—tables were moved, and a picture of Henry Clay, which hangs on the wall, was swayed more than a foot, and two candelabras, presented by the Dey of Algiers to President Adams, were twice raised nearly to the ceiling.

It was nearly nine o'clock before Shockle was fully under spiritual influence, and so powerful were the subsequent manifestations that twice during the evening restoratives were applied, for he was much weakened, and though I took no notes, l shall endeavor to give to you as faithful an account as possible of what took place.

Loud rappings about nine o'clock were heard directly beneath the President's feet, and Mr. Shockle stated that an Indian desired to communicate.

'Well, sir,' said the President, 'I should be happy to hear what I should like if possible, to hear what Judge Douglas says about this war.'

'I'll try to get his spirit,' said Mr. Shockle, 'but it sometimes happens, as it did to-night in the case of the Indian, that though first impressed by one spirit, I yield to another more powerful. If perfect silence is maintained, I will see if we cannot induce General Knox to send for Mr. Douglas.'

Three raps were given, signifying assent to the proposition. Perfect silence was maintained, and after an interval of perhaps three minutes, Mr. Shockle rose quickly from his chair and stood behind it, resting his left arm on the back, his right thrust into his bosom. In a voice such as no one could mistake who had ever heard Mr. Douglas, he spoke. I shall not pretend to quote the language. It was eloquent and choice. He urged the President to throw aside all advisers who hesitated about the policy to be pursued, and to listen to the wishes of the people, who would sustain him at all points, if his aim was, as he believed it was, to restore the Union. He said there were Burrs and Blenderhassetts still living, but that they would wither before the popular approval, which would follow one or two victories, such as he thought must take place ere long. The turning point in this war will be the proper use of these victories; if wicked men in the first hours of success think it time to devote their attention to party, the war will be prolonged, but if victory is followed up by energetic action *all will be well*.

'I believe that,' said the President, 'whether it comes from spirit or human.'

Mr. Shockle was much prostrated after this, and at Mrs. Lincoln's request it was thought best to adjourn the seance *sine die*. (*Old Abe's Jokes*)

Two Quaker Ladies on Lincoln

Lincoln's ability to withstand life's jolts apparently grew with age and he was less and less compelled to take refuge in humor. He came more and more to recognize the possible cost of seeming to slip into laughter when others fell into tears. He began to see himself as others saw him. According to Merrill D. Peterson (*Lincoln in American Memory* 1994, p. 98) one of Lincoln's favorite stories was about two Quaker women in a conversation Lincoln overheard on the train:

"I think that Jefferson will succeed," one said.
"Why does thee think so?" asked the other.
"Because Jefferson is a praying man."
"And so is Abraham a praying man."
"Yes, but the Lord will think Abraham is only joking."

Chapter 2

Lincoln

and the

Scriptures

Introduction

Some of the most interesting items of Lincolniana are the re-writings of the Bible and the use of Bible-like books and religious rites to praise or curse the President. In general these pieces were long. But at the time they had great appeal.

They wove a web on sanctity around Lincoln, making him Father Abraham, or they stripped him of all humanity and turned him into Tyrant Abraham. Usually the authors turned the United States into Bible-land, and the parallel between the countries was pushed as far as possible.

According to the reviewers of the time, by far the most artistic and successful of these works was *The New Gospel of Peace*, re-printed for the first time. Published pseudonomously in four books from July 24, 1863, to May 19, 1866, it may have been written by Richard Grant White. But in an advertisement to the four books in one, White said that although the work had been attributed to him he was not the author. The publisher claimed, in fact, that he printed the book from and old "ancient, faded, torn and much defaced manuscript" which was found and translated from "the langkie language."

One reviewer said the work was "Probably the greatest literary success of its kind ever achieved." "On an average," the reviewer went on, "within a fraction of forty-five thousand copies of each book have been sold, making the sale of the three books nearly one-hundred and thirty-five thousand copies!" There is no reason to believe that the fourth book was received less enthusiastically. Such was a phenomenal sale for the time and the type of work.

Harper's Weekly called it "one of the cleverest political squibs of the war." "It is a broad, popular, humorous burlesque upon the Copperhead faith and practice." According to the Boston *Transcript* the work "did Copperheadism more harm than even its own folly and malignity could do."

Despite these praises for this work, I have included only a small portion in this volume. It is too general, too broad in scope, to be reprinted in a book on Lincoln. Further, it is so topical that most of the references are too obscure and lifeless for us. I have, however, reprinted the sections in it which deal with Lincoln in particular.

126

THE NEW GOSPEL OF PEACE
BY BENJAMIN THE SCRIBE

Chapter IV

1. The Armies of Unculpsalm (Uncle Sam) rest. 3. Ben Hit the Scribe. 6. Ulysses made Chief Captain over all the Armies of Unculpsalm. 9. Abraham hath familiar Spirits. 15. Micege Nation. 29. John See of Mah Rippozah. 31. What he did. 32. And what he did not do. 46. The outlandish men set up John See to be chosen Chief Ruler. 54. Who they were that called the Assembly to set him up. 58. Pshawdee joineth himself unto them that set up John See.

1. And after these things the winter came on, and the armies of Unculpsalm rested in their camps.

2. And the time drew nigh when the people should choose again their chief ruler.

3. And a certain scribe named Ben Hit (Bennett) who was not of the men of Unculpsalm, but who came from the land of Psawknee, which is a province of the land of Jonbool (John Bull), said, Let us make Ulysses chief ruler. For, Ben Hit said, If I name Ulysses and he is chose, he will be gracious unto me.

4. But Ulysses would not, saying, Let me serve in the armies of Unculpsalm until the government is restored throughout the land. Moreover, Ulysses said within himself, Let me not be set up by Ben Hit to be chief ruler, for whomsoever he setteth up the people do put down; and he remembered how when the Phiretahs (Fireeaters) first made war upon the government of Unculpsalm at Tshawlstn (Charleston), Ben Hit was on their side, but turned against them in one night because he feared the people.

5. For Ben Hit sought to please the people, and especially the Pahdees (Parties), and to say what he thought they would have him say. Wherefore many. listened to him, but no man regarded him.

6. And the people said, Let Ulysses be made Chief Captain of all the armies of Unculpsalm, and be lieutenant unto Abraham. And it was so.

7. And the people saw that Abraham had become wise, and that his knees were strong, and that he was a just man and kept his soul un-spotted from corruption; and they saw that in the first year of his rule they had judged him foolishly because of their own ignorance how great a matter this war was, and because they considered not that he had been made ruler of a great nation, and of a land larger than the land of any other nation, which was divided by a war the like of which no man hath told or written of for its greatness.

8. And they saw that Abraham, although he had set his face like a flint against all them that would use the Great Covenant to protect and to justify the Phiretahs in their rebellion and to hold the Niggahs in everlasting bondage, was a discreet man, and walked warily; not setting himself up for a prophet, or the son of a prophet, or seeking to become a preacher of new doctrine, which he was not chosen to be, but to rule the land, and to defend it, and to maintain the government thereof.

9. And it began to be noised abroad that Abraham had two familiar spirits, Euman Aytsher [Human Nature] and Kawmunz Entz [Common Sense], and that these and the mighty spirit Bak Bohn [Back Bone] were in league with him.

10. And whoever taketh counsel of these spirits, Euman Aytsher and Kawmunz Entz, if he have also the mighty spirit Bak Bohn to help in the doing, there is little that he may not accomplish.

11. Forasmuch, therefore, as Abraham had these spirits and hearkened unto them, he divined the thoughts of the hearts of the people, and they felt that he was like unto themselves, and they had faith in him that he would do what was acceptable unto them. (For such was the law in the land of Unculpsalm.)

12. Wherefore all they that longed chiefly for the preservation of the land of Unculpsalm, and the maintenance of the honor and the glory of the nation, and that men might be no more held in bondage within its borders, wished that Abraham should again be chosen chief ruler.

13. But the Kopur-Hedds, which looked for the triumph of the Phiretahs, while they yet professed to be faithful to the government of Unculpsalm, and the Knsuvvutivs, which would have kept the nation in hot water lest it should be scalded, and all they that said in their hearts, If this nation cannot be saved by the rule of the Dimmichrats (Democrats) of our faction, let it perish, and be broken up into little provinces, wished that Lituimak (McClellan) the Unready should be chosen.

Chapter VII

Book Three (July 22, 1864)

47. And it was told unto Abraham that the Kopur-Hedds and the outlandish men, and the men that thought only of the everlasting Niggah, had joined themselves together to judge him in this matter. And Abraham said, Behold now this remindeth me of a parable. (For he often spake in parables; and the people said He learneth these parables of Euman Aytsher and Kawmunz Entz, his familiar spirits; but others called them Eumah [Humor] and Muthah-ouit [Mother-wit].)

48. A certain man had a large household which was at strife within itself. And some of the members said, We will no longer be of this household; but we will depart, and we will destroy the house and the barns and the buildings, and will divide the household stuff and carry off our part thereof, so that there shall no longer by the same household.

49. Now, these were all of one mind. But the remainder were at strife among themselves; and it was chiefly about the manner of serving and the payment and receipt of money, and the treatment of strangers; and some said one thing and some another.

50. Then the master of that household said, What shall I do? I will withstand them that would destroy the household, but I must also reconcile the remainder one with another, else I cannot do the former thing, and we shall all perish.

51. And he did so; and he withstood the destroyers, and day by day he reconciled some of the remainder one with another; and they that were reconciled held up their hands. But the others said, Not so; for we will not have this household reconciled, except the serving and the money and the treatment of strangers be as it seems good to us; and these hated each other day by day more and more, and feared more and more that they should be reconciled. And they each sought to cast out the master of the household; but they could not.

Lincoln's Assassination—Book Fourth, May 19, 1866

28. And it came to pass that while the men-players and women-players played before Abraham as he sat in the little room, and before the people as they sat in the hall, one of the liers-in-wait entered the room privily and slew him by the side of his wife;....

(Footnote: Abraham was slain as he sat looking upon men-players and women-players. This good man was betrayed into going to what was very plainly something like what we now call a theatre. Having yielded to the temptation, and stepped aside from the path of duty, he met his death. If he had not gone to see the players, he would not have been killed in a theatre. A fruitful example and an awful warning to the wordly in these latter days . . . .)

Revelations

Chapter I

1. The Revelation. 2. The War. 3. The Patriarch. 4. The Brigadiers. 5. Shoddee. 8. The Patriarch clothes his Brigadiers. 12. Temple of High Shoddee. 14. The Patriarch's little story.

1. BEHOLD! O my Patriots, the mystery is revealed; even unto babes and sucklings.

2. In the reign of the Patriarch horrid war filled the land with wailing, even the fair land of Jonathan.

3. From morn till night, and from night till morn, there was no rest for the people; for did not the voice of the Patriarch continually cry, "Raze it, raze it; there's nobody hurt, there's nobody hurt."

4. So the Brigadiers went up and down the land, seeking whom they might devour.

5. In that never-to-be-forgotten reign there arose in the city of the Gothamites many who were possessed of a *devil* (the word *devil* means Niggero in the original), who were denominated in the census of the mighty city, Ripuplicanas, which signifies the followers of Beelzebub, alias Shoddee.

6. And they were not like other men; for they believed *black* was *white*, only a little more so.

7. But they cried unto the Patriarch, and the Patriarch was their friend.

8. Now as the Patriarch grew plucky, he summoned his brave Brigadiers, and answered unto them and said: "Behold! my valiant cocks, your seedy toggery; your shocking bad 'ats; your hungry soles. I, even I, the Patriarch, will cover your nakedness. Ye shall stand adorned with the blue of the skies, and stars shall bedeck your shoulders."

9. When the Patriarch had "dried up," the assembled throng gave him a Tigahah, and went their way rejoicing.

10. Then there was naught heard throughout the land, save the noise of the shearers as they sheared their sheep, and the buzz of the wheels

within wheels of the mighty works, until the martial hosts the Patriarch had summoned were equipped as their worshipful lord had commanded.

11. So when all this was accomplished, the Ripuplicanas, the followers of Beelzebub, alias Shoddee, were full of glee and gold; for did not they *shear* the *sheep*; and did not they move the wheels; and were not they the priests of the new order of Shoddee; and theirs the *blood* of the *prophets*?

12. Then did the Ripuplicanas, followers of Beelzebub, alias Shoddee, wax fat and saucy, and they said one to another, Let us up and build us an altar even in the place of our High Shoddee, called Fifthavynew. There let us build it, and place upon it the figure of our god, even a molten Niggero, and fall down and worship it in the sight of all the people; for we shall thereby find favor with our father the Patriarch.

13. So they straightway went and did according to their counsel. And, behold, an altar of brown stone richly, carved, and above it the figure of the idol of the great Shoddee, which may be seen there even at this day.

14. And the noise of their rejoicing reached the ears of the Patriarch, and he was exceeding glad. And unto his chief priest and scribe he answered and said, "That reminds me of a little story." Thereupon he related the following narrative: "In the days of the Lawgiver, certain of the people, forgetting that it was because of their observance of the Compact they had been brought in safety out of the land of Egypt, did with malice prepense gather themselves together unto Abraham, and said, Be thou our ruler. And Abraham "saw it," and did as they desired. Then did the spirit of the Lawgiver cry: "The people have corrupted themselves." But Abraham answered and said, "The Compact is played out. I have put my foot down; and when I raise it again it will be felt in the seat of war."

15. Here the laugh of the Patriarch's chief priest and scribe came in, upon which the Cabinet of the Patriarch was adjourned

16. Behold! O my patriots, the end of First Chapter.

Chapter II

1. The Wail. 2. Webfoot. 3. Morgahno. 7. The Gourd Story. 11. The Brigadiers down on Webfoot. They desire a seafaring man. 13. The Cottonade. 14. Loyalty.

1. After these things there came a wail from the great deep; for mighty was the damage the foe had done thereon.

2. Then the Patriarch clapped his hands, and summoned unto his presence his Seacretary called Webfoot, and answered unto him and said. "Buy me ships wherewith I may float my Brigadiers to the battle-field to crush the Cottonade."

3. And when the Patriarch had ended his speech, his Seacretary Webfoot clapped his hands, and summoned unto his presence his faithful Morgahno, whose name was great "on change," and answered unto him and said, "Buy me ships wherewith I may, or may not, float my brave Brigadiers to the battle-field to crush the Cottonade."

4. So his faithful Morgahno did as he was commanded, and the wail returned to the deep, and many were the ships that the faithful Morgahno bought, so that soon did he jostle the crowd of devotees at the altar of High Shoddee, and great was the stir in their midst as he counted out his gold-offering.

5. Then did the Seacretary Webfoot go straightway into the presence of the Patriarch, and unto his majesty did say: ('Look out, O Patriarch, upon the deep, and tell me what thou seest.'! And the Patriarch rose up and gazed upon the face of the waters, until a mighty storm arose and floated his brave Brigadiers from his sight.

6. And the Patriarch cried with a loud voice unto his chief priest and scribe: "O Seaword! cover me with a gourd."

7. Then unto his Seacretary Webfoot he answered and said, "That reminds me of a story: There was a certain man named Jonah, who cried unto the people, saying: 'Let them turn every one from his evil way, and from the violence that is in their hands.' They turned; and Jonah was angry." Hence the gourd story.

8. Now, my Webfoot, which of us resembles Jonah the most?

9. Echo answered, Who!

10. So when the Ripuplicanas, followers of Beelzebub, alias Shoddee, heard of all the great things that had been done upon the sea, they were filled with rejoicing, and said: Who so great as the Patriarch; and Webfoot is his prophet.

11. But the brave Brigadiers were down on Webfoot and his faithful Morgahno; and they prayed the Patriarch to grant them another Seacretary, even a sea-faring man.

12. Moreover, notwithstanding, nevertheless, the Patriarch disturbed his Cabinet furniture; and he did continue to declare to the people the wisdom and greatness of his Seacretary Webfoot.

13. Then did it come to pass that the Ripuplicanas, followers of Beelzebub, alias Shoddee, seeing the mind of the Patriarch, did take and load many ships with merchandise and sail them to the Cottonade, and there barter the merchandise for the treasure of Niggero, and return with

their vessels heavy laden, to bow the knee anew at the shrine of the great Shoddee.

14. And thus did the Ripuplicanas, followers of Beelzebub, alias Shoddee, testify their loyalty to the land of their fathers.

15, And continually did they cry unto the Patriarch, and the Patriarch was their friend.

16. Behold, O my patriots, the end of the Second Chapter.

Chapter III

1. The War. 2. The needy Brigadiers. 4. The Patriarch's tears. 6. Another story. 13. Achancammerone. 15. The uneasy Brigadiers. 20. The Reason of their Disquiet. 24. The Remedy. 27. The Spoils. 29. The Scribes and Pharisees murmur. 30. They disturb the Patriarch. 41. The cause of their murmurings. 43. The Remedy. 53. Achancammerone goeth abroad. 56. A great Feast.

1. AND the war was grievous in the land.

2. And it came to pass that there was sore need among the hosts of the Patriarch, go that the brave Brigadiers cried aloud unto the Patriarch.

3. O most Lengthy Potentate! didst thou not command the heavens to clothe us, and the stars to glitter on us? Alas! alas! No sooner was thy command obeyed than our toggery vanished like the baseless fabric of a vision, leaving no rag behind. Be merciful unto thy servants, even as Scotchplaidy was merciful unto thee.

4. And the spirit of the Patriarch was stirred within him. He arose and viewed his brave Brigadiers,—and wept.

5. Then with a loud voice he cried unto them: "This reminds me of a little story."

6. There was a certain king, who had an honest minister.

7. One day the spirit moved the king to command his minister to tell his mind concerning him.

8. Whereupon the minister fell upon his face, and Said: O thou Mighty One! thy servant must speak the words of truth and soberness! "Thou art weighed in the balances, and found wanting," "Thy kingdom is divided."

9. And when the Patriarch had made an end of speaking, the multitude shouted: Long live the Patriarch, our Great Potentate!

10. And every man went his way.

11. And the Patriarch entered into the Palace of the Whiteman, even into the innermost chamber.

12. There did the Patriarch remain fasting many days and nights, until the shadow of the Patriarch had nearly disappeared.

13. Then summoned he unto him his familiar, yclept Achancammerone, surnamed Bellicose,

14. And thus did he discourse:

15. I pray thee tell me, my familiar, why all this disquiet among my brave Brigadiers?

16. Why do they rage, and imagine a vain thing?

17. Whereupon, Achancammerone, the Patriarch's familiar, surnamed Bellicose, answered him, and said:

18. It becometh not thy servant, O, thou Wisest of Mortals, to show thee what thou already seest.

19. Rather let me be numbered with those who have merited thy displeasure.

20. But, O Patriarch, I make me bold to say, thy brave Brigadiers imagine *not* a vain thing. They rage; but there is method in their raging:

21. The Patriarch bade his familiar speak on.

22. Now know, Most Elevated One, that the children of this world are wise in their generation. Therefore do I declare unto thee my whole counsel.

23. The Patriarch bade his familiar speak on.

24. Give thou, O Dispenser of Patronage, unto these men to plume themselves with the spoils, as becometh the victors to do. Bid them feather their nests with the fat things which are the pride of the foe. Say unto them: Gather the gold and precious stones, and bedeck ye yourselves and your wives, your children and servants; and clothe ye your households in fine linen, even in the royal purple.

25. Speak thus unto them, O thou Most Honest Ruler, and as thy servant liveth, thou shalt no more be vexed.

26. And the Patriarch said—nary a word.

27. However, there was great spoil taken; of gold, and silver, and precious stones; linen and royal purple; and great was the prey that was taken, both of man and of beast.

28. And great was the rejoicing of the people; and gayly did the brave Brigadiers drive their fast horses in the broad ways before the temple of High Shoddee.

29. But certain of the scribes and pharisees, who dwelt in the city of the temple of High Shoddee, murmured against the Patriarch's familiar, Achancammerone, surnamed Bellicose.

30. And the noise of their murmurings reached the ears of the Patriarch.

31. So it came to pass that the Patriarch hid himself as before in his most secret chamber.

32. And, after much fasting, he clapped his hands, and summoned again unto him

33. Achancammerone, his familiar, surnamed Bellicose.

34. And thus did he discourse.

35. I pray thee, my familiar, tell me why the money-changers quarrel in the place of High Shoddee?

36. Why do the scribes write bitter things against their ruler?

37. Why do the pharisees put on airs?

38. And the Patriarch's familiar answered him and said:

39. Behold, O Sagacious Sage, as thy servant liveth I will speak the truth.

40. The Patriarch bade his familiar speak on.

41. Do thou, O Warrior of the White House, bid them gather weapons of war for thy brave Brigadiers.

42. Do thou bid them lay up of the treasure which thou controllest.

43. Do thou create new posts of honor for them, which shall fill them to repletion with the great mammon.

44. And as thy servant liveth, they shall no longer vex thee, O most Amiable Sovereign.

45. And the Patriarch was—mum.

46. Then there arose a great shout in the palace of High Shoddee.

47. And the scribes sang the praises of the Patriarch throughout the length and breadth of the land.

48. The pharisees forgot the Samaritans in their glee.

49. And all the people united in the shout: Long live the Patriarch, and Achancammerone his *prophet!*

50. So the fame of Achancammerone spread abroad; and he was known far and near.

51. Thereupon the Patriarch bethought him to send his familiar, Achancammerone, surnamed Bellicose, to foreign lands; that the name and fame of the Patriarch might be known throughout the earth.

52. For the Patriarch was ambitious.

53. So the Patriarch sent his familiar to a far distant country, to tell the heathen of the great Patriarch who ruled the western hemisphere.

54. And the Patriarch saw what he had done, and was satisfied.

55. But his familiar, Achancammerone, surnamed Bellicose, said nary a word.

56. Then there was a great feast in the place of the High Shoddee; and the air rang with the shouts of the multitude; and the great idol Niggero glittered and glistened in the sun:

57. For the scribes and pharisees were as an army with banners.

58. And the people cried unto the Patriarch, and the Patriarch was their friend.

59. Behold, O my Patriots, the end of the Third Chapter.

Chapter IV

1. Horace the Grilleyte and Henry the Raymite. 5. "I am here." 7. Herod-bar-Stantine. 8. The Acts of Achancammerone. 9. His record.

1. In those days. there were two scribes, one Horace the Grilleyte and Henry the Raymite, who gave the Patriarch no peace, neither day nor night.

2. Then was the Patriarch greatly troubled. And hid himself from the sight of men for many days.

3. And it came to pass that the Patriarch opened his mouth and said:

4. Oh that my familiar, even Achancammerone, surnamed Bellicose, were not in my thoughts.

5. Then, as it were in the twinkling of an eye, he heard the voice of his familiar saying, "I am here."

6. So Horace the Grilleyte and Henry the Raymite gave the Patriarch no peace, neither day nor night.

7. And the Patriarch's familiar was thrust from his presence, and Herod-bar-Stantine was chosen from among the people to minister unto the Patriarch in his stead, for did he not out-Herod Herod.

8. Thus endeth this record of the deeds of Achancammerone, surnamed Bellicose.

9. But are not his mighty. acts written in the pages of the archives in the temple of Beelzebub in the palace of the High Shoddee!

10. Behold, O my Patriots, the end of the Fourth Chapter.

Chapter V

1. Chason the Treasurer. 2. His skill in Metallurgy and Astrology. 3. Star gazing. 4. He soliloquizes, 7. A graven image, and what he will do with it. 12. A No. 1. 14. The Patriarch's disturbers.

1. Now there was one of those who stood in high places before the Patriarch, who was called Chason the Treasurer, whose duty it was to look after the Patriarch's money-bags in the fair land of Jonathon.

2. This Chason the Treasurer was skilled in metallurgy and astrology. And daily did he study the one, and nightly did he delight in the other.

3. So it came to pass one night, as he sat gazing at the stars, that a lucky thought struck him, and thus did he soliloquize:

4. "Am I not A No. 1? Do I not rule on change and control the sinews of war? Am I not alone worthy to receive the mantle of the Patriarch?

5. O Stars! how shall I obtain the prize?

6. Ah! I have it!

7. I will make unto myself a graven image of my patron Beelzebub, alias Shoddee, and this will I imprint in living green on fairest linen bands.

8. And on the face thereof will I put the likeness of Chason the Treasurer, the successor of the Patriarch.

9. These linen bands will I scatter broadcast among the people. Then will the Patriarch be forgotten, and Chason the Treasurer be remembered in the land forevermore."

10. And straightway went Chason the Treasurer, and did as he had devised.

11. And he scattered the fair linen bands with backs of living green up and down the highway , so that there was no man to be found in the land that had not one of the fair linen bands.

12. Then Chason the Treasurer stood A No. 1 before the people.

13. But the Patriarch was from that day no longer before the people as A No. I.

14. And Horace the Grilleyte and Henry the Raymite gave the Patriarch no peace neither day nor night.

15. Behold, O my Patriots, the end of the Fifth Chapter.

Chapter VI

1. Confiscation. 4. Bootyler. 5. Bearfremount. 6. The Wailing of the Women and Children. 8. Bootyler's Deeds. 12. Bearfremount's Ambition. 13. The Patriarch's Indignation. 17. The Perseverance of the Patriarch's Messengers. 21. The Patriarch's Latest Joke.

1. Now it came to pass that certain leaders of the brave Brigadiers, who had buckled on their armor at the eleventh hour, because of the tidings of the great spoil their brethren had taken from the foe, did beseech the Patriarch to declare unto the people the statute known as "Confiscation."

2. For, said they, if thou doest but this, O most Illustrious Ruler, thy brave Brigadiers shall be as the sands of the sea for multitude, and *we*, most noble Patriarch, will lead them on to victory.

3. And in an evil hour the Patriarch raised his foot.

4. So the brave Brigadiers returned to the war: and they were led in the way of the Cottonade by him whom the Patriarch called Bootyler;

5. And in the way of the Niggero by him whom the Patriarch called Bearfremount.

6. And great was the wailing of the women and children at the Cottonade.

7. And the spoil of Bootyler was more than the ships of the Patriarch could transport.

8. And his deeds, if they should be all written, I suppose that even the temple of High Shoddee itself could not contain the books that should be written.

9. But Bearfremount looked not alone to spoil, for was he not lord of Mariposa?

10. Therefore did he seek occasion to gain the favor of the false god, Niggero, that he might betray the Patriarch into the hands of the Philistines.

11. So he bade his heralds declare to the people wheresoever he tarried, the new dispensation of which he was the sole originator and dispenser.

12. And he did establish his court, and issue his decrees, as though the Patriarch had deceased and was gathered to his fathers.

13. But a bird did carry the news to the house of the Whiteman, and to the ear of the Patriarch; and he became exceeding wroth, even foaming at the mouth in his great indignation.

14. For the Patriarch read the thought that was in the breast of Bearfremount, as though Bearfremount had said: Oh that I were made judge in the land, that every man which hath any suit or cause might come unto me, and I would do him justice!

15. So the Patriarch dispatched his messengers to bid Bearfremount to come unto him.

16. But sorely vexed were the Patriarch's messengers.

17. Yet did they persevere, until, by wonderful strategy, they placed the Patriarch's command before the dread Bearfremount.

18. Then did the tidings of their success thrill the heart of the Patriarch, like as it were the tidings of a great victory.

19. So when Bearfremount was come unto the house of the Whiteman, the Patriarch rushed forth, and fell upon his neck and embraced

him, saying, Never more, my beloved Bearfremount, shalt thou hazard thy life for *my* sake; sit thou here at my right hand.

20. And there was great rejoicing throughout the land

21. And the meeting of the Patriarch and Bearfremount was recorded in the pages of Seaword's book as "the Patriarch's latest joke."

22. Behold, O my Patriots, the end of the Sixth Chapter.

Chapter VII

1. The Spoil. 2. Contention. 5. The Captives. 7. Emancipation. 8. The Patriarch a Planter. 10. Another Story.

1. AND the spoil, both of men and beasts, was very great.

2. So that there was much contention touching the division thereof.

3. And the noise of the contentious ones ascended to the ear of the Patriarch.

4. And he said unto the contentious ones, Why quarrel ye concerning the captives, even in the face of the foe?

5. And they answered him, and said, It is for the *good* of the captives we do this thing.

6. But the Patriarch read their thoughts afar off.

7. Therefore did he declare unto the people a new statute, called "Emancipation," which caused all such spoil to fall to the share of the Patriarch.

8. For, behold! my people, said the Patriarch, I will take possession of the fairest lands of the foe, and I will cause these my captives to till the soil thereof, and great shall be the gain to the Patriarch.

9. And the Patriarch was well pleased with "Emancipation."

10. Then said the Patriarch to the assembled multitude, That reminds me of a story:

11. A certain man named Abram went up out of Egypt, he, and his wife, and all that he had, and Lot with him, into the south.

12. And Abram was very rich in cattle, in silver and in gold.

13. And he went on his journeys from the south even to Bethel, unto the place where his tent had been at the beginning, between Bethel and Hai;

14. Unto the place of the altar, which he had made there at the first: and there Abram called on the name of the Lord.

15. And Lot also, which went with Abram, had flocks, and herds, and tents.

16. And the land was not able to bear them, that they might dwell together: for their substance was great, so that they could not dwell together,

17. And there was a strife between the herdmen of Abram's cattle and the herdmen of Lot's cattle: and the Canaanite and the Perizzite dwelt then in the land.

18. And Abram said unto Lot, Let there be no strife, 1 pray thee, between me and thee, and between my herdmen and thy herdmen; for we be brethren.

19. Is not the whole land before thee? Separate thyself, I pray thee, from me: if thou will take the left hand, then I will go to the right; or if thou depart to the right hand, then I will go to the left.

20. And Lot lifted up his eyes, and beheld all the plains of Jordan, that it was well watered everywhere, before the Lord destroyed Sodom and Gomorrah, even as the garden of the Lord, like the land of Egypt, as thou comest unto Zoar.

21. Then Lot chose him all the plain of Jordan; and Lot journeyed east: and they separated themselves the one from the other.

22. And when the Patriarch had made an end of speaking, the assembled multitude sent up a shout in praise of the Patriarch, for the Patriarch was their friend.

23. And Horace the Grilleyte and Henry the Raymite were among the multitude, and they remembered the Patriarch's story.

24. Behold, O my patriots, the end of the Seventh Chapter.

Chapter VIII

1. The War. 4. The Patriarch's Speech. 18. And there was a Pause. 20. The only Speaker left.

1. YET did the war desolate the land, and the prophets saw no signs of peace.

2. So the Patriarch summoned all the wise men of the land to the house of the Whiteman, that they might take counsel together concerning the war.

3. And when they were assembled in the presence of the Patriarch, he spoke unto them, saying,

4. Ye men of the fair land of Jonathan, I appear before you on this august occasion that I may see you and be seen by you. Although I summoned you hither, it was but for this great purpose—to see and be seen.

5. And that I might call your attention, in particular and public manner, to the only clause of the Compact that I decreed should be permitted to stand.

6. O ye men of the fair land of Jonathan, have you forgotten that these immortal words were the first your Patriarch uttered in your ears?

7. Have you forgotten how often your Patriarch has since their first utterance repeated them to you?

8. And now I again say that the great privilege you enjoy as my subjects, and the only one left you from the Compact, is—*to see and be seen*! (Sensation.)

9. Oh that you would live up to the spirit of these words.

10. If you would but see and be seen there would be an end to war.

11. If you would but see and be seen I could bid adieu to my bodyguard.

12. If you would but see and be seen, I could remain your Patriarch, and live and die seeing and being seen.

13. But ye are a stiff-necked and perverse people, therefore have I caused a new statute to be promulgated, to be called the "Expatriation," which my brave Burnsydy will declare unto you.

14. So that hereafter, ye men of the fair land of Jonathan, do ye naught else, but see and be seen.

15. Then did the wise men depart in silence,

16. And no one durst speak; for, to be loyal, he must only see and be seen.

17. And it came to pass that silence brooded over the once fair land of Jonathan; and there was no sound heard throughout the length and breadth thereof save the clicking of the instruments called Telegraphs, which carried the Patriarch's immortal proclamation—*See and be seen*—from pole to pole.

18. In the place of the High Shoddee not a word was heard; and men bowed the knee in silence.

19. By the river of Patome the brave Brigadiers saw, and were seen by the foe; and all was quiet there.

20. Now there was but one speaker left in the land, and he, the Patriarch.

21. Behold, O my Patriots, the end of the Eighth Chapter.

Chapter IX

1. Silence. 2. The Patriarch reasons. 6. The Patriarch reads. 34. The Patriarch muses. 37. The Patriarch soliloquizes. 41. The Patriarch's Policy. 43. The Patriarch's Preachers.

1. AND it came to pass that while silence reigned in the fair land of Jonathan, the Patriarch bethought him of the saying,—Wisdom is better than strength.

2. And thus to himself he spake: What hindereth now?

3. Yea, I will search the books of the wise and holy of the earth, that peradventure I may find therein written the thing I desire to know, even the way of deliverance for my people.

4. And he straightway sought far and near in the fair land of Jonathan, and he found the books he desired.

5. Then sat he himself down in the innermost chamber of the house of the Whiteman;

6. And he gave himself no rest neither day nor night, that he might find the precious words.

7. And Horace the Grilleyte and Henry the Raymite were filled with confusion.

8. Then the Patriarch opened a book, and with a loud voice did he utter:

9. "The words of wise men are heard in quiet more than the cry of him that ruleth among fools."

10. The Patriarch turned on.

11. "There is an evil which I have seen under the sun, as an error which proceedeth from the ruler."

12. The Patriarch closed that book, and opened another.

13. "Christianity quite annihilates the disposition for martial glory."

14. "To sacrifice our lives for the liberties, and laws, and religion of our native land, are undoubtedly high-sounding words:—but who are they that will do it? Who is it that will sacrifice his life for his country? Will the senator who supports a war? Will the writer who declaims upon patriotism? Will the minister of religion who recommends the sacrifice? Take away glory—take away *war*, and there is not a man of them who will do it."

15. The Patriarch threw that book down in disgust, and opened another.

16. "You would, perhaps, die to save your country; but this is not the question. A soldier's death does not save his country. The question is,

whether, without any of the circumstances of war, without any of its glory or its pomp, you are willing to resign yourself to the executioner. If you are not, you are not willing to die for your country."

17. The Patriarch mused a moment, then turned on.

18. "Christianity does not encourage particular patriotism, in opposition to general benignity."

19. "As long as mankind shall continue to bestow more liberal applause on their destroyers than on their benefactors, the thirst of military glory will be the vice of the most exalted characters.

20. "The safety of nations is not to be sought in arts or in arms. War reverses, with respect to its objects, all the rules of morality. It !is nothing less than a temporary repeal of all the principles of virtue. It is a system, out of which almost all the virtues are excluded, and in which nearly all the vices are incorporated. In instructing us to consider a portion of our fellow-creatures as the proper objects of enmity, it removes, as far as they are concerned, the basis of all society, of all civilization, and virtue; for the basis of these is the good will due to every individual of the species."

21. The Patriarch shook his head, and turned on.

22. "There is but one community of Christians in the world, and that, unhappily, of all communities one of the smallest, enlightened enough to understand the prohibition of war by our Divine Master, in its plain, literal, and undeniable sense; and conscientious enough to obey it, subduing the very instinct of nature to obedience."

23. The Patriarch grew red in the face, slung the book behind him, and opened another.

24. "They who defend war, must defend the dispositions which lead to war."

25. The Patriarch adjusted his spectacles, read the passage again, and—turned on.

26. "I am persuaded that when the spirit of Christianity shall exert its proper influence over the minds of individuals, and especially over the minds of public men in their public capacities, over the minds of men constituting the councils of princes, from whence this happy period shall arrive, war will cease throughout the whole Christian world."

27. "Morality and religion forbid war in its motives, conduct, and consequences."

28. The Patriarch's countenance assumed a grave cast. He laid the book carefully down, and took up another.

29. "Be at peace among yourselves. See that none render evil for evil to any man. God hath called us to peace."

30. "*Avenge* not yourselves. If thine enemy hunger, feed him; if he thirst, give him drink. Recompense to no man evil for evil. Overcome evil with good."

31. "It has been said, Thou shalt not kill, and whosoever shall kill, shall be in danger of the judgment; but I say whosoever is angry with his brother without a cause, shall be in danger of the judgment."

32. The Patriarch was disturbed.

33. "All they that take the sword shall perish with the sword."

34. The Patriarch could read no farther; but fell back upon his couch in a deep and painful revery.

35. For a long time he remained silent.

36. Then he arose, and paced the chamber with a firm step, and an air of resolution.

37. And thus did he soliloquize:

38. If these things that I have read be true; if it be true that there is a "*new commandment*" which is to be obeyed instead of "an eye for an eye, a tooth for a tooth," then I must at last adopt a—Policy. What shall it be?

39. At that moment the Patriarch's eye fell upon a page of the book as it lay open before him, and read these words:

40. "The Preacher sought to find out acceptable words: and that which was written was upright, even words of truth."

41. Ah! happy thought, the Patriarch cried, I have found a policy.

42. And thus did he reason within himself.

43. Are not my preachers called to declare the things I this day have read? Is it not their mission to proclaim "peace on earth, and good will to men?" Is it not their duty to tell the people of the "*new commandment?*"

44. This very day (the Patriarch continued) will I publish my Policy; and it shall be known in the land as—"The Conscription."

45. Behold! O my Patriots, the end of the Ninth Chapter.

Chapter X

1. The Summons. 3. The Patriarch's Speech. 12. The People rejoice. 16. The Patriarch's Wisdom. 18. Conscription. 22. The Beecherite. 24. The Cheeverite. 26. Philip the Amalgamator. 30. "I will be the Leader." 31. The Patriarch's Satisfaction. 32. The Great Commission. 33. The End not Yet.

1. THEN it came to pass that the Patriarch did summon every man throughout the length and breadth of the land to the Palace of the Whiteman.

2. And when the people had assembled themselves before the Patriarch, thus did he address them:

3. Ye men of the western hemisphere, give ear unto your Patriarch.

4. Your Patriarch is well pleased with your obedience to his mandate,—*See and be seen.*"

5. He is well pleased with your obedience to it, that he has directed this mandate to continue in force until the end of the war. (Applause.)

6. Your Patriarch summoned you here to-day in, order that he might say this to you; and that he might see you, and be seen by you on this glorious occasion.

7. He has also something new to make known unto you,—he has a Policy. (Sensation.)

8. This policy is called, "The Conscription." (Breathless silence.)

9. The Patriarch thus understands this Policy. The brave Brigadiers are to be called back from the Cottonade, and their places are to be supplied from the ranks of the clergy!

10. Thus will the Patriarch place his preachers where they may give practical effect to their teachings; and to their labors does the Patriarch look for the return of *blessed peace.*

11. (The Patriarch here became too much affected to prolong his remarks, and the multitude returned to their respective abodes.)

12. And there was great rejoicing among the people, because the preachers were chosen to go against their enemies; For, said every man, are they not called to proclaim "the glad tidings of salvation, and to publish Peace!"

13. Blessed peace-makers!

14. They shall deliver our unhappy land from the scourge of the sword.

15. Then did all the people speak one with another of the great things the preachers should do.

16. And greatly did they magnify the wisdom of the Patriarch, saying, Behold a wiser man than Solomon.

17. But the preachers were—mum.

18. And the Patriarch caused the preachers to be gathered together according to the Conscription.

19. And when they were assembled without the camp, the Patriarch with his body-guard, and the chiefs among his brave Brigadiers, went forth to meet them.

20. And when the Patriarch drew near, every man of them was debating with his fellow touching the war, and great was the confusion of their tongues, for as yet they had no leader.

21. So it came to pass that, when the Patriarch saw they had no leader, he waxed exceeding wroth.

22. And the Patriarch said unto them, Where is he who did so loudly proclaim the Gospel of Sharp's Rifles? He, even the Beecherite shall lead you.

23. But the Beecherite could not be found, for aforetime had he taken counsel with himself, and said: "I will get me to the far distant Angleland, and there will I tarry till this cruel war is over."

24. And the Patriarch said unto them, Where is he who calleth Niggero his better? He, even the Cheeverite shall lead you.

25. But the Cheeverite could not be found, for he had fled for safety to the temple of the Woolly-heads.

26. And the Patriarch said unto them, Where is Philip the Amalgamator? He shall lead you.

27. And some answered him, and said, Behold, O Patriarch, we have sent messengers unto Philip, the Amalgamator, to bid him be one with us, but he hath replied, Your banner is not my banner, therefore will I not go.

28. And other some answered him, and said, We pray thee, O Patriarch, to be charitable unto Philip, the Amalgamator, for per-chance he may have taken him a wife from among the daughters of Niggero, and therefore he cannot come.

29. Then did the Patriarch again address them, saying, Tell me which one from among you shall be your leader.

30. And the assembled preachers, as with the voice of one man, each for himself, did cry, I will be the leader.

31. And the Patriarch saw what was in their mind, and he was satisfied.

32. So he commanded them to go forth upon their mission, taking naught with them but their Great Commission.

33. *And the end was not yet come.*

Chapter 3

Abraham Africanus I

Introduction

Of all the extended attacks on Lincoln, probably the cleverest and most interesting is this work, *Abraham Africanus I*, which changes the President into King. Published anonymously in 1861 by J.F. Feeks, New York, who specialized in violent anti-Administration distribes, it exploited outstanding or prominent characteristics of the President and his Administration. Typically, Lincoln is pictured, like Faust before him, as having trafficked with Satan. Naturally such a long and unprincipled character as Lincoln would try to outsmart the arch Demon. The fact that he did not succeed undoubtedly represents a profound hope on the part of the author and his fellows. As was usual in this kind of attack, the names of Lincoln and his Cabinet members were only thinly disguised.

I include the complete work.

Abraham Africanus I. (New York: J.F. Feeks, 1861)

To the Reader

Immortal Truth! thy power essay
To lash the morals of the day,
And should the Muse's efforts claim
Small honor for an humble name,
Her aim is gained, by thee directed,
If but one rascal be detected.

Great knaves deserve thy lash the most,
Because they sin at greatest cost,
And every sin thou dost forgive,
Will in a hundred, meaner live,
Till multitudes will boldly ape
The greater one, should he escape.

Man is my theme, yet when I choose
A playful measure for my Muse,
Forget not, Reader, I design
To make the graver censure thine;

Forget not, as I paint for you
Revolting scenes as droll as true,
I claim this judgment still for them,
That; tho' you smile, you do condemn.

Chapter I

The Great Man's Friend

One stormy night in chill November,
As cold a night as folks remember,
'Twas ten o'clock and every street
Was cold and damp with rain and sleet

Old chimneys rocked and tiles were cast
At mercy of the fitful blast;
And houses shook and shutters slammed,
And stray curs yelpt and hackmen damned;
And tavern signs were heard to creak
As if their very hearts would break,
And leafless trees swayed to and fro
As if they'd nothing else to do.
Still grew the darkness, deep, profound,
O'er roof and dome and all around,
And froze the rain, and moaned the blast
Like gibbering spirits as it passed.
Each straggler hugged his friendly cloak,
As home his lonely way he took,
While all the smiles which blessed his home
Seem'd brighter 'mid the deep'ning gloom;
And oft he started as he passed,
At shadows which the street lamp cast;—
The sleeping watchman snug and tight
Forgot to hail the passing night;
And wind and rain and driving sleet
Soon held possession of the street.

Within his arm-chair, snug and warm,
Brain, dozing sat, nor heard the storm,
Or, if he heard, he thought, no doubt,
How very cold it must be, out.
The warm full bed and cozy curtain
Made pleasant rest and slumber certain;
And the warm arm chair, as you'll suppose,
Seemed almost courting him to doze.
Within the broad hearth where he gazed,
A gladsome fire creaked and blazed,
And rose and fell with cheering sound,
Dispensing light and heat around.
The clothes he wore and all his pride,
Were both together laid aside,
And in his night gown, at his ease,
He felt his comfort much increase;

Small case had he for rain or snows;
His Excellency viewed his toes,

And took his punch, as grateful heat
Came running through his lanky feet.
Bram warmed his toes and sipped his liquor,
Until his thoughts and tongue grew thicker;
Nor could he think, small brains he boasted,
Whether his feet were warmed or roasted.
Thus in his mind confusion grew
Until he neither thought nor knew;
Yet, tho' he slept, his master mind,
(These common folks are always blind)
Beheld what passed. "What's that I see?
The very andiron bows to me!"
And so it was; the andiron grew
Beneath his Excellency's view,
And as it grew he could but note
Its brass arms stuck beneath its coat;
He wondered if 'twould next have wings,
For rum and dreams can do strange things.
"Great God!" quoth Bram, "what do I see?
The very andiron bows to me!"

"Yes, Bram," quoth it, "I bow; you'll find
A fellow feeling makes us kind.
I am the Devil, and I feel
Of all the rogues who wrong, who steal,
Who murder, intrigue, violate,
I love the rogue who rules a State,
Because, when he does wrong or says it,
A thousand knaves and fools must praise it,
And all the efforts preachers make
Will not avail, *'tis bound to take*;
I love you Bram, your high position
Gives hope to knaves of mean condition,
When gazing on your strange success,
They think their own fate can't be less
Make 't easy men should find a flaw
In codes of morals and of law;
And on their wits in firm reliance,
Set all of virtue at defiance;
They think that he who like yourself,
Concentres all and all in self,
Will find that fate and luck conspire,

> Both, that the knave may rise the higher,
> Both, that a strange success in life,
> May be of knave, fool, fortune, rife;
> That Justice, being blind, must lag;
>
> That Luck's by far the fastest nag,
> And on her back in hope they'll vault,
> To carry Fortune by assault.
> This serves my ends. It proves when past,
> Knave, fool, and fortune, all won't last,
> And while it hides the sure defeat,
> Mine is the profit and the cheat;
> I've ruled the world and still must rule
> As long as there's a knave and fool."

> "Stop, stop," cried guilty Bram, "suppose
> Instead of jingling verse we chat in prose."

> "Agreed," said Satan, "though it's my conviction
> You'll find the prose as difficult to face as fiction."

"Well, the fact is," said Abraham, handing old Nick a chair and pushing the decanter towards him, "it comes more natural I can defend myself a good deal easier; your word to the contrary notwithstanding. This reminds me of a western story."

"Ah," said Satan, pouring himself out a pretty stiff horn and gazing at the fire through its amber transparency with the air of a connoisseur, "a joke?"

"Yes, what I should call a d—n good joke, for it served my purpose elegantly."

"Don't swear it;" interrupted Nick, "forget your old habits for once, and behave yourself while in the presence of a gentleman *as* a gentleman"

Twas a big thing on Douglas, though; I assure you," continued Abe.

"Douglas, Douglas," said the Devil reflectively, "don't know him."

"What! not the Little Giant of the West? I thought he had gone to — *you*, long ago."

"Mistake, my dear boy; he must have gone the other way, for I haven't seen him in our direction."

"Well, well," said Abraham, "no matter. Here's the story: During the electioneering campaign I hid with Douglas in Illinois, we agreed to debate our differences in public. On the occasion of the first debate which took place at Ottowa, the Judge asked me a number of questions which he had written down on a piece of paper. Among them were the following:

[Q, 2.] I desire Lincoln to answer whether he stands *pledged* to-day as he did in 1854 against the admission of any more slave States into the Union, even if the people want them?

[Q. 3.] I want to know whether Lincoln stands pledged against the admission of a new State into the Union, with much a Constitution as the people of that State may see fit to make?

[Q. 4.] I want to know whether he stands to-day pledged to the abolition of slavery in the District of Columbia?"

"Pretty good for the Judge," cried Satan, polishing off the end of his tail with his pocket-handkerchief. "I don't see how you managed to get round them."

"Easy enough, my boy," says Abraham, tipping his friend the wink, "I didn't answer them at all!"

"Then he defeated you in the debate?"

"Not at all. I *promised* to answer them at the next debate at Freeport."

"Ha! ha! very good," cried Satan, "promises are an easy means to appease. You promised to end the war in ninety days for instance. *The walls of my abode are covered with them.* But how did you manage the Judge at Freeport?"

"You shall hear," said Abe, exultingly. "When I appeared on the stand I had my answers all ready in writing. They were as follows:

[Ans. 2.] I do not now, nor ever did, stand *pledged* against the admission of any more slave States into the Union.

[Ans. 3.] I do not stand *pledged* against the admission of a new State into the Union, with such a Constitution as the people of that State may see fit to make.

[Ans. 4.] I do not stand *to-day pledged* to the abolition of slavery in the District of Columbia."

Bram was silent. The Devil twitched nervously on his chair, turning over the blade of his tail with a troubled air, as though by so doing he hoped to find the point.

"I confess," said Nick, "I don't see the *point!*"

"Plain enough;" said Bram, putting his arms round his friend's neck and speaking in a tone of exultation. "I said, 'my friends, the Judge shall be answered strictly in accordance with the interrogatories he has put to me. *I do not stand* PLEDGED *to anything!*'"

"Bully for you," cried Satan, enraptured, "you are the smartest pupil I ever had! I am afraid people will find you out after a while, though."

"Devil a fear, Old Boy. *As long as I'm called 'Honest Old Abe,' the people will swallow anything. There's nothing like having an honest name. It is a cloak for everything.*"

"True," said Beelzebub. He forbore to say any more. His mind was filled with uneasy suspicions. What if the cute Bram should slip out of his bargain with *him*? "True," he continued, rolling this idea over in his mind; "if I hadn't tacked this name to you, you would have been no-where to-day. It gave *confidence*, and you've profited well by it. But how about *our* arrangement. You don't expect to argue *me* out of *that*, do you?"

"Come, come, brother," said Bram with an affected air of honest indignation. "You don't suspect my *intentions* do you?"

"Hell is paved with them," said the Father of Lies, sententiously. "I want something more palpable than your assurances, Abe. Suppose we draw up a little memorandum of our agreement?"

So saying, he whipped out a little scroll of parchment, and tapping a hole in Bram's arm before he was sufficiently aware of his intention to prevent it, used his blood for ink. Then scribbling furiously for a few minutes, he covered the scroll with fine writing, and read the contract to his *confrere*:

"'I hereby pledge to elevate Abraham Lincoln to a life Presidency of the United States of America—'"

"Stop, stop!" cried Bram," you promised a Monarchy, or at least a First Consulship."

"Fool!" said the Devil. "Don't you perceive that if you call yourself a King or First Consul, the whole people will rise upon you?"

"Let them rise," said Bram, "I have my army. Every officer has been selected and appointed with that view. They are all men who believe the government needs to be *strengthened*."

"Your army wouldn't be worth a straw if you proceed so rudely. There are democrats enough in the country to eat up your army."

"But they're not organized," urged Bram," and what's more, I don't intend to let them organize."

"Very strongly put, brother; but still there's nothing like doing things smoothly. My word for it, the easiest way is the best. You owe all your present success to four things, *First*, MY NOMINATION. *Second*, Your Sobriquet of 'Honest,' *Third*, Those weak points of the Constitution which a little management converted into flaws, and a little stretching widened into fissures wide enough to drive a train of cars through. 'Military necessity' did the rest. *Fourth*, DOING THINGS QUIETLY. All these things combined have given you what I promised you in our first contract, POWER. In return you brought on a war which has made, taking both belligerents together, something like a million of victims."

"And out of that million," chuckled Abe, "of course, you reaped a plentiful harvest."

"Not so, Bram. I never was more deceived in my life. I GOT MY SHARE; but the majority of them were poor ignorant fools, infused with a false patriotism. I did well with the Abolitionists, and the men who accepted bounties; but the former were very scarce and the latter were hardly worth picking up. But to our contract. If you'r elected for another term, you can easily get a law passed declaring the country in a state of permanent insurrection, and demanding more power to put it down. The first thing will be, a law to make the Presidency perpetual while the war lasts; the next, another making it perpetual during your life. Thus you will have got over the hardest part of it. The rest is easy enough. You can then have it entailed on your posterity, and change the title whenever you please. I should advise you to stick to that of President, though. there's nothing like a mild name. To continue:

'I hereby pledge to elevate Abraham Lincoln to a life Presidency of the United States of America, and to stand by him and assist him to subvert the liberties of the American people and debauch their civic aspirations; to impose upon them in every imaginable form of low cunning, and cheat them with words of double meaning and with false promises, until by these, and kindred means, that end is accomplished, and his dynasty firmly established.' "

While Satan was writing the contract, Bram held out his arm very patiently by way of inkstand; but now he withdraw it hastily, and looking at his watch, exclaimed:

"All right, my boy, I'll sign that, and then you'll please to consider this interview at an end, for some of my generals have been advancing too quickly, and if I don't relieve them of their commands the war will be over in a jiffy, and good-bye to my plans."

"You forget," said Beelzebub meaningly, and fixed his burning eyes upon Bram's, till the latter winced and wiggled as though he was on a toasting fork, "you forget, my dear Bram."

"What?" stammered Bram, fearing that he had been detected, yet hoping to escape, "What do I forget?"

"What!" roared the Evil One, "Do you pretend you don't know! you low, cunning, pettifogging, cringing, artful, Illinois stump lawyer! Would you cheat *me*? You know very well *there's no consideration expressed in that deed*, or you wouldn't have been in such a hurry to sign it, and run to look after your major-generals. But come, let us remain friends. I admire you the more for your dishonesty; only you musn't think to 'beat the Devil round a stump.' Honor amongst thieves, you know."

So saying, the worthy pair shook hands and smiled. The elder one then proceeded to finish the agreement:

"'In consideration whereof my friend promises, (no—pledges,) pledges to render unto me what he possesses (it ain't much, any how,) of a MORTAL SOUL, the same to be MINE forever!

(Signed)   BAAL."

(Signed)   BRAM."

"Now," said Baal, as Old Abe with trembling fingers and face white as a sheet, signed the bond; "now, my dear Abe, if you want any advice, just let me know, for like yourself, I've other matters to attend to."

"Don't be in a hurry," said Abe, looking with regret upon the parchment which Baal had suffered to remain on the table, "what shall I do with the Abolition party? Nothing I do seems to please them. Phillips is constantly abusing me."

"Issue a Proclamation of Emancipation. You remember you said at Chicago, July 10, 1858, 'I hate, and have always hated slavery as much as any other Abolitionist.' It will run well with your words."

"You've such a good memory, Nick; but your advice is rather late. I've issued such a Proclamation already."

"The deuce you have! who put you up to that, Abey?"

"It was original, old fellow, original, every line of it."

"Come, come, friend," said Old Nick reproachfully, "you know you haven't brains enough to stretch a clothes line. Somebody must have put you up to it or you never could have done it. Who was it? Sumner?"

"No."

"Hale?"

"No."

"Wilson?"

"Well, Wilson gave me a hint or two."

"Exactly, and upon that hint you spoke."

"Wasn't a bad idea, was it?"

"No! Still you may lose the support of the Conservatives."

"I've provided against that. I issued secret instruction to Banks and others, to pay no attention to the proclamation, and to order the negroes in their respective departments, to remain on their plantations."

"Well, what good will that do?"

"Don't you see? By compelling them to remain, they will be *obliged to work*—."

"But that's slavery again."

"True, but it won't appear so. We say it is necessary to the public peace that the negroes shall not be roaming about the country. That keeps them at work, and while their labor benefits the men I have appointed to cultivate the plantations, all of whom are creatures of mine, the measure will give assurance to the Conservatives that I am not in a hurry to emancipate."

"Not so bad. I trace brother Seward's mind in that arrangement. But to the Abolitionists again. I don't exactly see what you can do for them, although I understand the value of their support at the elections. How would a draft for half a million more men do?"

"You frighten me. What! half a million more?"

"Yes. It would have a threefold advantage. *1st*, Please the radicals. *2d*. Draw away so many votes from the opposition. *3d*, Convert enemies into friend, for once in the army they'd have no chance for Democratic sentiments."

Bram here slyly covered the scribbled parchment with his long bony hands, but the Devil had been watching him, and caught it up in time. Bram appeared not to be aware of the manoeuver, but continued the subject of a proposed draft.

"I like your advice, and shall act upon it. But wouldn't such an act be treachery to the States that have filled up the last quota, and treachery to those that were given to suppose there would be no other draft?"

"Bram," said the Devil with a curse,
And dropping prose—relapsing into verse,
"It little becomes either you or I,
To pause at acts of treachery,
Since in the end if there be shame,
We both of us have often been to blame.
Your treason but extends to States,
Mine to a Higher cause relates.
You grasp at POWER; I did the same;
The treason differs but in name."

The Devil vanished as he spoke,
While clouds of ashes and of smoke,
Flew up the chimney in delight,
As if to aid his sudden flight.
Bram rubbed his eyes, and looked to see
The Devil in reality.
Could he have dreamed, or was it true?
The old brass andiron met his view,
And in the hearth burned dim and low,
The fire which was flick'ring, now;
A strange dull feeling in his head,

Warned him 'twas time to go to bed,
With tottering steps he sought his rest,
Where soon he snored as 't may be guessed;
He snored away, and any fellow
Might do the same, who got as mellow

Chapter II

The Conspiracy

SCENE.—*The Smoking Room in the White House.*—Cheeze *and* Stentor
discovered in conversation.
        Enter, BRAM *and* SOO (*the great Irrepressible Magician.*)

BRAM
Good friends, to banish public cares,
The mighty Soo with us appears,
And hath engaged to please us so,
In that he purposes to do:
We have consented he shall steep
Our senses in mesmeric sleep,
So that the past and future rise,
As he may will, before our eyes;
And by clairvoyance clearly view,
Each scene or transit we pass thro'.

CHEEZE AND STENTOR, TOGETHER
Haste thou, great Soo, your power essay,
In feats not furnished every day.
For us who know your skill in feats,
Of vaultings, tumblings, somersets,
There's little fear that we may doubt,
Should you turn Bram just inside out.

SOO
Great Sirs, I do not seek to addle,
Your brain with long unmeaning twaddle,
Nor by abstractions infinite,
Your minds to puzzle or benight;
But by some strong unchallenged facts,
Give truth and credence to my acts,

So that the science and the man,
May challenge doubt, if you can.
Till then, we all must silence keep,
The while I charm Great Bram to sleep.
Then seating Bram upon a chair,
The might Soo began to stare,
Whilst watching both with anxious eye,
The other two stood wondering by.
Thus, long they stood, till Soo advancing,
His eye with magic meaning glancing,
He stood beside, then wildly throwing
His arms about, began pow-wowing;
Till Bram's great eyes were seen to wink,
His head to nod and forward sink—
Then with a smile to those around,
Great Soo announced the sleep profound.
Invited both to touch and scan,
And then to this effect began;—

You see that all's not what 't appears,
To smell, touch, taste, or eyes, or ears,
And many wondrous things may be,
Which baffle our philosophy;
So Mesmer's magic sleep defies
Hands, nose, and mouth, and ears, and eyes.
He sleeps, and forthwith I'll commence
To act upon his slumbering sense,
And thro' each phrenologic bump,
Act on the brain with moral pump;
By touching each we'll make appear,
The trait that's hid beneath each hair;
Of good or ill, we'll have it shown,
And first we'll place our touch on 'Tune.'

Soo here proceeded where he said,
To place his hand upon Bram's head,
Who answering to the magic touch,
Straightway broke out into this snatch:

BRAM
Retrospectivo piu alleghressimo

AIR—"John Brown."
"We'll hang Jeff Davis on a sour apple tree,
We'll hang Jeff Davis on a sour apple tree,
We'll hang Jeff Davis on a sour apple tree,
 As we go marching along!"

Hold! hold! cried Cheeze and Stentor; hold!
That song grows hateful as 't grows old!
For party purposes it had its day—
We pray thee, wondrous Soo, to change the lay.

BRAM
Prospectivo fortissimo
"Oh carry me back,
Oh carry me back,
 To ole Virginny shore;
I'll change my ways,
And reappoint Mac,
And never do so no more!"

Then shifting his position on the chair,
Great Abram cleared his throat and changed the air:—

BRAM
Andante jollisimo
"Come back! come back! we'll vote for Mac,
 Success where'er he goes,
We'll drink to-day as well we may,
 Confusion to his foes!"
The greenback Chief with threatening frown,
Upon the sleeping Bram looked down—
While Soo himself, perplexed and puzzled,
Pow-wowed in vain to get him muzzled;
Nor did succeed 'till one or two
More jolly songs were thus got thro'.
Great sirs, quoth the Magician, grinning,
I fear my art, not I's been sinning,
In calling secret feelings forth,
Of doubtful use and little worth.
But if forgiven, I'll instead
Proceed again to touch his head.

The Greenback Chief with smile resigned,
And willing ear his head inclined,
And trembling Stentor dreading worse,
Expressed himself as not averse.
With this the skillful conjurer struck
On "Self-esteem," when forth he broke.

BRAM

Thrice lucky Bram, thy destiny,
The Fates have made for ever high,
As upwards still thy fate to rise,
Success for e'er shall glad thine eyes.
Heaven's own especially favorite thou,
Called Honest Bram where'er you go;
Gaze on the past and learn from thence,
How well thou'st earned thy recompense;
Gaze on the future still as kind,
In promise to thy master mind.
From western flat-boats, doomed to toil,
Thy back to bend, thy hands to soil,
Thy fitness for this occupation
Inspired thee to rule the nation;
And what if nature's freak denied thee brains,
Thou had'st the tact to use thy friend.
To have thyself dubbed "Honest," thy reign a "Mission,"
By simple advocating Abolition.

CHEEZE

Something too much of this, great Soo,
I cry thee quits, we've something more to do;
These vaunting boasts can profit naught,
Nor serve in any way our thought;
But if by arts possessed you can,
In any way confess this man,
Take from him in his slumbering state,
His mental guards, and make him prate;
Tell whom he trusts and whom he doubts,
What his designs towards "INS" and "OUTS;"
Whom he will favor, who oppose,
Who thinks his friends, and who his foes,
Who he will aid and who refuse,

And what his own ambitious views—
I'm free to say, my friends and I,
Will be obliged eternally.

SOO

To do this well upon compunction,
I'll put yourself in close conjunction;
By proxy make thee act magician,
And touch the bump of his Ambition;
Which having done, ask what you can, Sir,
The obedient tongue won't fail to answer.
And quickly was it done as said,
The Greenback touch was on Bram's head.

CHEEZE

Has thou reliance, hope, and trust
In thy own Cheezey?

BRAM

Well, I must.

CHEEZE

Dost think him honest as he's great,
What e'er betide?

BRAM

He'd sell the state.

CHEEZE

Why then by thee is he caressed?
Why not discard?

BRAM

'Tis not my interest.

CHEEZE

How can this be; art thou content
To leave thy Cheezey to his bent?
You know his object is by paper circulation,
To lay down pipe for next year's nomination—

BRAM—(*interrupting him*)

Your rhyme's played out, my dove. I ain't no such fool as to give up this berth to Salmon P. Cheezey or any other man. I ain't here for nothing, and I just tell you I'm going to stay here.

CHEEZE—(*blandly*)

But the people, my dear Bram, the people. You know if the people say your time's up, you must go.

BRAM—(*excitedly*)

The people be d—d! Do you suppose I've been playing the Fool and the Honest Man all this time for your benefit. No, gentlemen! 'Tis time we understood one another. The Honest role I have undertaken was to further my own ends, not yours.

CHEEZEY—(*soothingly*)

My dear Bram, you know we made you what you are. But for us you would still have been the obscure, uncouth, Illinois rail-splitter, "unwept, unhonored and unsung."

BRAM

I want to hear no more of this. You nominated me for your own ends. I jumped at the officer and was elected, and sometimes I shudder at the great sin I committed; for, to be elected, I had to pledge myself to your views and those of Soo, Stentor, and the whole party. Now look at the consequences.

CHEEZE

But the Union, my dear friend, the Union. Your forget that. See the strength of our own party to-day, by simply changing the name from Black Republican to Union.

BRAM

Stuff and bosh! and you know it too. What is all this talk about the Union. You want no Union—neither to the rest. You want what I want, but I'll be hanged if I am going to let you get ahead of me at it.

CHEEZE—(*suspiciously*)

What do you mean?

BRAM

I MEAN EMPIRE! *That's what I mean, and that's what you mean, and that's what all of you mean*; but I've got the advantage of you in the race, and intend to keep it.

CHEEZE—(*aside to Soo and Stentor,
each with his forefinger to his nose*)

The vile toad! He's wide awake. This comes of elevating such trash.

STENTOR

I didn't suspect him of such ideas. It reminds me of Tittlebat Titmouse and his patron.

SOO

My friend, suspect every man. No one is too humble to be ambitious—none too 'honest' to take that which has no owner, and EMPIRE is one of those things—and none too ignorant to grasp that which has been thrust at him. Cheezey, suppose we vary the entertainment by touching him upon the subject of "Buffoonery."

CHEEZE

Good. We'll talk about that other matter anon. [*Advances to the sleeping Bram, and touches his bump of "jokes."*] What's the biggest joke you ever heard of, Bram?

BRAM

Your legal tender!

CHEEZE—(*viciously*)

Bram, your jokes always put me in mind of a ball.

BRAM

Why?

CHEEZE

Because they never have any point!

BRAM

You never laugh when I say a good thing.

CHEEZE

Don't I? You'd better try me with one!

BRAM

When does the House of Representatives present a ridiculous appearance?

CHEEZE

When it discusses my finance bills.

BRAM

No. When its ayes (eyes) are on one side, and its noes (nose) one the other.

CHEEZE

Pretty good. Now tell me why is Dick Busteed like Necessity?

BRAM

That's old, Cheezey. *Because he knows no law.* But speaking of law reminds me of a good thing I heard the other day on old Breezy Welles. A fellow down in Ohio exhibited him a plan for making ships out of india-rubber. Old Periwinkle wouldn't listen to him, though, because he was afraid that such ships in crossing the line, might rub it out!

"The law entitles me to be heard," said the Buckeye.

"Go to Gov. Morgan," said the Secretary.

"But he's your brother-in-law," urged the inventor.

"Then go to Captain So-and-so."

"But he's your nephew."

"Then go to Commissioner So-and-so."

"But he's your cousin."

"Then go to the devil."

"Ah, that's a still closer connection." said the fellow, pitching an inkstand at the Secretary's head and consoling him with the parting reflection that "All's well as ends Welles."

CHEEZE

You said 'twas not your interest to discard your Cheezey. Have you no fears his power over the treasury will carry him into the presidential chair?

SOO—(*to Cheese*)

You're out of order, Cheezey. He cannot reply to that question. It's not a funny one.

CHEEZE—(*to Bram*)

Well then Bram, you said my legal tenders were the biggest joke you ever heard of. Ain't you afraid the joke may be carried too far for your chances of re-election?

BRAM

No. When the time comes I'll put a stop to them. They remind me of a story I heard out west at one time. There was an old farmer who had an old mare called Greenbacks. He took her out one day to plow. But the old mare wouldn't go, no how. He coaxed her and coaxed her, then he whipped her and whipped her, and finally he set his gal SUE at her with a big stick to beat the hide off of her. She wouldn't go though, and the old man was in a tarnation fix. "Calkerlate I'll swap the mare off," says he, " or what's better, I'll sell her to Uncle Sam for cavalry purposes;" when jist as he was gettin' kinder soft on her, up she starts and goes off at a canter that threatened to knock the wind out of her in tarnal short time. After her goes the old man, tumbling over the furrows, and risking his neck at every step. "Halloa!" says Sue, and she strikes after old Greenbacks, and runs up to his neck with her cudgel a hitting him right smart in the *tender* parts. "What are you about there Sue," said the ole man. "Trying to get that all-fired green-bottled fly off his neck," said Sue. "Don't do no such thing!" screamed the old man, "that green-bottled fly is all that makes her go and if you brush that off she'll bust her biler and collapse straightway!" Now that green-bottled fly is Cheezy's hopes for the Presidency. As long as I leave that on, the machine will run easy, but the moment it is taken off the critter stops and devil a foot of land will be reclaimed.

CHEEZE

Then you believe in Greenbacks?

BRAM

As I believe in steam. Useful while under control; but sure to bust up if used expansively.

SOO

We ought to have old Welles here on the subject of expansive steam.

STENTOR

Or Isherwood. He might give us the benefit of his Lake Erie experiments. But let us change the theme. What do you say to a touch of biography.

SOO AND CHEEZEY

Agreed. Suppose you take him in hand, Stentor.
'Twas done. The crafty Stentor passed the drinks around
'Till Abram's slumbers grew more profound;
Then mounting high his categoric stump,
He tapped Bram's auto-biographic bump.

Chapter III

Bram's Biography

"I was first elected," commenced Bram, "to the Illinois legislature in 1834."

"Stop, stop," cries Soo, "if you've no objection Bramy, we'll go back a little earlier."

"Come, come, gentlemen," said Stentor, "you don't want the man to tell us all his flat boating and wood-sawing adventures in Illinois."

"Yes we do," said Soo, "we want to know how such a man ever emerged from obscurity, and in doing so perhaps elicit some beneficial hint for our private benefit."

"Well then, I was born," continued Bram speaking still with his eyes closed and between his teeth, as though against his will "on the 12th of February, 1809, in La Rue county, Kentucky."

"Oh we know all that," interrupted Soo; "your mother's name was Nancy Hanks and your father's Tom Lincoln, a rail splitter, stump extractor, swamp clearer, root burner, and cow breeder."

"That's true," said Bram, "but he was of aristocratic descent. We can trace our lineage to the times of Robin Hood, who had about him men in Lincoln green."

A sarcastic smile and a movement towards his LITTLE BELL, betokened the rising contempt in Soo's great breast. The others interposing, he resigned himself to Bram's genealogical rhapsody.

"One of my ancestors was the noble Earl of Lincoln, who emigrating to America along with Wm. Penn to escape the displeasure of Charlemagne the great, brought with him a stump of the rod of Aaron and a copy of the *Habeas Corpus*."

"Which you have since lost," suggested Stentor.

"Exactly," said Bram, with a chuckle "which ain't no whar to be found. The firs thing they did was to make a treaty with the Indians who were in rebellion against the infant colony and couldn't be put down under ninety days. The treaty was as follows:

Motto—The PENN is mightier than the Sword:
Art. 1. The Indians agree to give up all their lands.
Art. 2. All their medicine men.
Art. 3. All their squaws.
Art. 4. Everything else.
Art. 5. And to accept a bottle of bad whisky in return.

"Well, the natives stuck to this arrangement with commendable honor until they got their whisky, when the broke into open revolt. Penn was for peaceable measures, but Lincoln advised coercion. Said Penn, 'you cannot fight always.'

'But Lincoln showed that if the war was conducted with sufficient ferocity, the aborigines would soon be wiped out and the country would be their own. So they went in and slaughtered without mercy, giving no quarter, making no exchanges, no sparing even the women, and burning and confiscating everything in their path. In a very short time the country was cleared and Penn and Lincoln not agreeing about a proper division of the spoils the latter with the aid of his soldiery, took the best part of it and leaving the avaricious and envious Penn, settled on the best farming lands and established himself supreme in the western part of the country. His posterity eventually became attracted to the new state of Kentucky and removing their immense capital thence, invested it in the lumber business."

"Not so fast, mighty Bram," cried Soo, "what do you mean by 'capital' and 'lumber business?' "

"Well, their capital consisted of a rifle and a broad ax and the lumber business was the trees standing all round them ready to be cut down."

"Rather a falling off," suggested Cheeze.

"They quarreled a good deal with one another, and that was all there was left. My immediate ancestor there met and wooed the lovely Hanks, and in proper time I made my appearance. I grew so fast that my father used to be in the habit of making chalk marks on my legs to see how much I gained over night. He had to raise the top of our shanty on three occasions to make room for my increasing altitude, and even then I had to put my head through the smokehole in the roof, to comb my hair.

"From Kentucky we moved to Indiana, generously leaving out stock of standing lumber—"

"Which you couldn't take with you," hinted Cheeze.

"Exactly. Leaving our stock of lumber to the next man that came along, we squatted in Indiana near what is now called Gentryville. As we were intent upon remaining there, we didn't need a log cabin—"

"How so?" asked Stentor.

"Because we were as I said *in tent*."

"But how did you provide for your farm stock, your pigs and chickens?" persisted his interrogator.

"Well, as for the pigs, we tied their tails in a knot and so provided each of them with a *pigs tie*, and as for the poultry, we inherited our great ancestors' genius for a *coup de etat*.

"The reasons why we left our old Kentucky home I need not go into. Suffice to say in the words of one of my biographers: 'We have at least the fact, that though painfully, and with an exile's sadness, he turned his back forever on a State that tolerated slavery, to seek a new home where free labor had been sacredly and assured exclusive rights and honors.'

"After receiving my education I was elected to the Illi—"

"Stop, stop, stop," cries Stentor, "you appear to be in a great hurry to get that the legislature. Let's hear a little more of your Indiana life. What kind of an education did you get?"

"Well, the first thing I learnt was the dignity of labor. That consisted in twenty-deck poker, and handling a gad, thus:

> Plowing, sans shoes or socks on,
> With snake pole and a yoke of oxen.

"I stumped a twenty acre field with immense success. I learnt my statesmanship from a comic almanac, and got my jokes from an old Joe Miller."

"How long were you at school?" asked Cheeze.

"I'd rather not answer that question, gentlemen," pleaded the sleeping Bram.

"You must!" replied Stentor.

"Well then, about a year altogether. But you mustn't judge me from that. I learnt a good deal from A FRIEND in Illinois."

"If you only went to school a year, what's the meaning of this passage in your 'authentic biography:'

'His *last teacher* was a Mr. Dorsey, who has had the satisfaction, in later years, of taking his former scholar by the hand, rejoicing to recognize the once obscure boy as the foremost LEADER OF THE PEOPLE.' "

"Oh! that meant OFFICE" said Bram.

At this magical word the conspirators were observed to lose their sportive humor and become much more taciturn. Bram continued:

"The name of *honest*, which was afterwards bestowed upon me by A FRIEND, is popularly attributed to the following incident of my life:

"I borrowed a book from a man named Crawford, and as books were very scarce in those parts, *I lost half of it.* Carrying the ruined book to my friend, I offered to pull fodder for him for two days, to make it square. As he didn't have any fodder to pull, he took me, and I pulled it, and so made the matter square. So my biographer put it in this shape: 'The offer was accepted and the engagement literally fulfilled. As a boy, *no less than since* Abraham Lincoln had an honorable conscientiousness, a constitutional integrity, a miscellaneous industry, and an ardent love of knowledge.'

'When I was nineteen years old, I went a flat boating. Now gentlemen, people are very fond of calling me a flat boatman, a rail splitter, and so forth. I assure you I never made but one voyage on a flat boat and never split but one rail and that's the *rail* truth. Pass the bottle over here, Cheezey."

"*Really*, Lincoln," commenced Soo, "you are the meanest li—."

"Hush," said Cheeze, plying the President with a gallon of contract whisky.

Chapter IV

Paying Debts

About this time I made the great discovery that "it is easier to pay a large debt than a larger one. That it is easier to pay a small debt than a small one; and that it is easier to pay nothing than even a small debt."

"The events that occurred during my absence, were of such a nature that I deemed another voyage would benefit my health, so I bade good bye to all hands and braved the western wave once more."

"I thought you only made one voyage!" said Soo.

"The only one at *that time*. Ha! ha! a good joke. Well I made my second voyage down the river and picked up a good deal of money by dancing jigs and singing nigger songs."

"I don't see any notice of that in any of your numerous biographies," interrupted Stentor, referring to a stack of books on the shelves, all labeled, 'Abraham Africanus, his life and services.'"

"Yes," returned Abe, "it's all writ down; only in different language. Just refer to Jim Barret's Life, Page 35, and you will see: 'It is reported by his eminent friends that His Excellency refers with much pleasant humor to this early experience, some of its incidents affording abundant amusement to his auditors.'"

"On my third voyage, I sang so much that my jaws have remained widened ever since. On my fourth voyage, I told so many yarns that my neck got stretched over four inches. From some I got the sobriquet of "Clam mouth"—from others that of "Scraggy," perhaps in allusion to the proportions of my neck. On my eleventh voyage—"

"Hold!" cried Stentor. "These voyages are getting tedious. There is no end to them."

"There's only one more," replied Cheeze; "then we'll get him on the subject of rail splitting."

"If he's as good at rail splitting as he is at Union splitting," rejoined the warrior, "we shall have some rare amusement. But let us end these voyages. It's evidence he has a tedious succession of them to relate for the fool is only *half seas over* as yet."

"Pretty good," said Soo, lighting a cigar, "I agree with you, Stentor. Drop these *flat* boat yarns, and let's have some *rail* anecdotes."

"Agreed, gentlemen," said Bram, "but in leaving the water for the land I'm afraid you find my stories rather *dry*."

"*Tell that to the marines*," cried Stentor.

"Moisten them with a little 'forty-rod,'" suggested Cheeze.

Chapter V

Rail Stories

"After thirteen voyages, I went in on my old grounds and re-occupied them. I took a laborer with me by the name of Johnny Hanks and we together split 3,000 rails."

"Stop one moment," cries Soo. "How long did you take to split them."

"In a day, I take it," says Cheeze.

"No interruption, gentlemen. I want to get at the truth of this. Well, how long, Abe?"

"About six years!" replies Abe.

"And how many of you were there?"

"There was Hanks, and me, and —"

"Never mind, that'll do. If you can't amuse us without lying, my friend, we'll have to let Cheeze take the chair in 1865, and leave you out in the draft."

"Don't, *don't*! Soo, my friend," cried the sleeping Bram, with sudden energy. "I'll do anything you wish—Let me only be President for four years more! I thought it would be no harm to romance a little. It's so popular with the people, dear creatures, they'll believe anything."

"All very fine, your Excellency," rejoined Soo, "but just remember you can't stuff *us* quite so readily."

"Gentlemen," said Bram, turning to his auditors one by one and exhibiting his great lanky face blanched with fear and working with petty cunning—"whatever is done, I don't want you to leave me out in the cold. I'd sacrifice everything to be re-elected. I've got a million of money at command and can produce more if wanted!"

"Where from!" asked Cheeze.

"Oh never you mind," replied Abe, with a knowing air. "It's none of your shabby greenbacks, Master Cheeze, but good SOLID GOLD. I've got friends that have the chink, gentlemen."

At the word "gold" they all pricked up their ears.

Taking advantage of their attention, Bram broke forth:

Oh friends of my bosom, I've made up my mind
And to miss re-election I don't feel inclined,
To you a large fortune I'd gladly give o'er
If you let me be in office just four or five years more.

"Gentlemen, I repeat my request. *Don't* leave me out in the draft. I had enough of that once."

"Let's hear about it," said Senator.

"Promise to keep me in office, then. Do, my dear Stentor," said Bram with a cringing air, and trying to get on his knees and clasp Stentor's legs, "you know how much I've done for you—made you chief of the war department when you never knew anything of war, given you million after million of profits on contracts—bigger spoils than Cameron ever earned or Morgan and Cummings ever dreamed of; and you, Cheeze, I've given you every chance—you must have made largely on all them revenue cutters, besides what you laid by in gold contracts and stock operations."

The humility of the creature was disgusting. He dragged himself towards Soo and exclaimed in pitying accents:

"Soo, I've given you every chance, kept you in office after your blundering allowed the Sumpter and the Alabama to get out—after you let Mason and Slidell escape—after you gave up the mails of the Peterhoff—after you truckled to every power in Europe and permitted France to ignore the Monroe doctrine. I've let you lock up all your private enemies in Forts Lafayette, Delaware and Warren, and many of them in dungeons from whence they will never emerge. Surely, you can't be so ungrateful as to throw me, after all that?"

The three conspirators began to dislike the turn affairs had taken.

They soothed him, promised him everything, got him in his chair again, and started him on the subject of the Black Hawk War.

Chapter VI

Modesty

The modesty of a soldier forbids that I recount the valorous deeds performed by me during this campaign; this I leave to Barret, whom I have rewarded with a fat office for his pains. On my way back to Illinois, and while separated on the road from my companions, I met and defeated, single handed, twenty of the natives, and left their dead bodies on the road.

"WHAT!" cried Cheeze and Stentor, in stentorian chorus, "Twenty-five—and single handed, too!"

"On my honor," said Bram, with an air of modest merit.

"Oh! oh!"

"Gentlemen, allow me to explain," interposed Soo. "I think I can give you the clue to this in a moment. Meanwhile, let us hear what became of Black Hawk."

Bram thus reminded, continued his tale:

"It seems that TAYLOR came upon him at the bluffs of the Wisconsin, and after one of the most absurd battles ever fought, he defeated Black Hawk and took him prisoner. For the sake of getting hold of this man and putting an end to the war, he absolutely sacrificed several of his own."

"How many of the enemy did he kill?" asked Stentor.

"About sixty-eight. Only think of it. It makes one's blood run cold to think of it."

"Remarkable instance of a sensitive nature," said Cheeze, in a bland tone, putting his fat white hand approvingly upon Bram's head and smiling at his confreres. "Now, Soo, let's hear the sequel of the twenty-five natives killed by my friend, (you'll permit me to call you my friend, Bram?)

"Certainly, Cheezey, here it is. I shall read an extract from a Congressional speech of Mr. Lincoln, delivered during the canvass of 1848."

"By the way, Mr. Speaker, did you know I am a military hero? [Derisive laughter from the galleries.] Yes, sir, in the days of the Black Hawk War, I fought, bled, and came away. Speaking of General Cass's career, reminds me of my own. I was not at Stillman's defeat, but I was about as near it as Cass to Hall's surrender; and like him, *I saw the place very soon afterwards.* It is quiet certain I did not break my sword, for I had none to break; *but I often drew the long bow*. If Cass broke his sword, the idea is, he broke it in desperation; I drew my bow for amusement. If General Cass went in advance of me in picking huckle-berries, I guess I surpassed him in charges upon the wild onions. If he saw any live fighting Indians, it was more than I did, but *I had a good many blood struggles with the mosquitos*, and on one occasion I remember to have *killed twenty-five of them single handed!*"

"This, gentlemen," said Soo, "is a verbatim extract from the *Daily Globe*; and what is more it was in this momentous struggle the great Bram first realized that immortal saying—"Nobody Hurt!"

Chapter VII

Palmam Qui Meruit Ferat

Bram felt so indignant at the laughter raised by this sally of Soo, that he refused to answer any more questions. The confederates petted and soothed him to no purpose. He was as obstinate as a mule.

Soo then proposed, in order that the amusement should not flag, to continue Bram's biography from Barret's pages, and meanwhile Stentor should ply the sleeper well with 'forty rod,' until he got him in good humor again. This being agreed upon, and Bram well nourished with the 'star-spangled-striped-pig,' Soo opened the book, and commencing at page 47, read:

"We now approach the period in the life of this exalted personage which he was destined by nature to attain—we meant the career of a statesman. Still it must not be concealed that Mr. Lincoln's own preferences were in favor of a military life. The adventurous career he had just passed through in the desolating warfare with Black Hawk, and the heroic deeds which make his name illustrious in the annals of the State of Illinois, in connection with this now famous campaign, made him feel that Providence had not intended him to be a mere private in the great battle of life, but that he had certain qualities which could place him at the head of a column, or of a brigade, if he were so minded.

He came home from the Black Hawk War with the high and noble determination of working for his own living thereafter, provided he would get nobody else to do it for him.

His tact at wire pulling, his acquaintance with the long shore men and other roughs of the place, and his faculty of sticking at nothing to gain power, obtained its legitimate reward, in his election to the State Legislature.

He was so exhausted of funds after getting into the legislature that his surveying instruments were sold under the hammer.

His appearance in the legislature was not very dignified it is true—but he made up for that by the quickness he soon displayed of making money. He possessed the rare art of assuming an extra uncouthness of rusticity of manner and outward habit, for the purpose of securing particular favor with the masses.

He seldom or never spoke during the session, but found means to have himself appointed on the Committee of Public Accounts and Expenditures, which he managed so well that nobody ever suspected him.

On both subsequent occasions that he was elected to the Legislature—he always managed to get himself on Committees that had the management of Money Affairs—and in this respect showed obvious wisdom.

He had thus (p. 63) honorably acquitted himself on the battlefield, in defending our border settlements against the ravages of the savage foe, and in the halls of the legislature had an eye to the main chance.

His eloquence was so scathing and withering, that that which at first would appear plain and probable, he made to look crooked as a serpent's path; and that which was tortuous and involved, he straightened out and made it plausible to the simplest minds.

This talent stood him in so well, that when in 1860, the Presidential convention met at Chicago and gave on first ballot, 173 votes for Seward, 50 for Cameron, 49 for Chase, 48 for Bates, 14 for Dayton, and 12 for McLean, he managed matters in such a way, that on the second, Cameron's name was not voted for and on the third, he (Lincoln) got the nomination himself by 231 votes. It is said he rather got the best of both Seward and Chase."

"Fool!" cried the Premier, throwing away the book and *touching his little bell*, "I'll teach the knave to write us simpletons, eh, Cheezey?"

"Fool," said Cheeze.

An officer entered.

"Search for a man named Barret, who wrote a life of Lincoln and convey him under a strong guard to Fort Lafayette! No charge. Instruct Col. Burke not to obey writes of *Habeas Corpus*."

"Excuse me, your honor," said the officer, "but if I'm not mistaken this same gentlemen you refer to is one of the President's ministers now on foreign stations."

"What political services did he perform to deserve that post," demanded the lofty Soo.

"He wrote the very book, your worship," replied the marshal.

"Ah I see. You may go."

The officer retired.

The Confederates looked serious. This little incident alone, convinced them they had no child to deal with. Bram was evidently up to snuff. And when they came to think for what a small mess of pottage they had bargained away their own nominations, they wondered how this flatboatman of long shanks and little brains had managed to outwit them all.

All three fell into a brown study.

Chapter VIII

The Friend

A long time elapsed before either of them spoke.

It was a singular scene. Upon a chair reclining at his greatest length, his feet on upon the hearth, his hands in his pockets, his head resting heavily on his chest, his hair dishevelled, his cravat awry, and a general air of smuttiness, and a general odor of liquor pervading him, sat Bram; still dreaming, still snoozing, still in the mesmeric state, and yet so strong in his self concentration, so fixed in his self estimation, as to be capable of being indifferent, in spite of his stupor, at the exposure his own words had made of his ridiculous boasts and his miserable inconstancy.

There sat Soo, turning the keys over in his trousers pocket, thinking what a fool he had been to lift such a man into power, and at his own expense, and to his own great shame.

There Stentor, too, weighed uneasily the poor chances that remained of his longer holding officer, and stretching his legs out under the table, put one hand to his waist-coat arm, and with the other fumbled at his watch guard.

Cheeze lustily rattled a pocket full of specie (he was the only once that had any hard money about him, though the others didn't lack paper,) and passed the time with glancing uneasily at his three companions, probably distrustful of them all.

Stentor was the first to break silence.

"Soo," said he," tell us a story to while away the time."

"Don't ask me, Stentor, my boy, I've told so many different stories in my time, and none of them seemed to answer, that I despair of ever succeeding with another. Ask Cheezey to give you a song. He has a fine rich voice, sweet as a syren's. He sung so sweetly to the New York bankers two years ago, that they haven't got over it yet."

Cheeze, thus called upon, begged to be excused—said he was no singer—only knew one song, and didn't like to sing that on account of its disunion tendencies—and so on.

"Pooh, pooh," said Soo and Stentor in a breath," we don't care anything about its disunion tendencies, as you call it. You don't suppose we are such asses as to believe in the political nursery trash we preach, do you?"

"It's a *nursery song*," said Cheeze

"Go ahead, then, my boy," said Soo.

Stentor nodded an additional approval, and thus fortified, Cheeze cleared his bag-pipe and thus began:

Air—*A Song of Sixpence*

Sing a song of Greenbacks,
    Pockets full of trash,
Over head and ears in debt
    And out of ready cash;
Heaps of Tax Collectors,
    As busy as a bee;
Ain't we in a preety fix
    With gold at sixty-three.

Bram in the White House,
    Proclamations writing;
Grant on the Rapidan
    Afraid to do the fighting,
Seward in the cabinet
    Surrounded by his spies;
Halleck with the telegraph
    Busy forging lies.

Cheeze in the treasury,
    Making worthless notes;
Curtin at Harrisburg,
    Making shoddy coats;
Dahlgren at Charleston,
    Lost in a fog;
Forney under Bram's chair
    Barking like a dog.

Schenck down at Baltimore,
    Doing dirty work;

Butler at Norfolk,
    As savage as a Turk;
Sprague in Rhode Island,
    Eating apple sass;
Everett at Gettysburg,
    Talking like an Ass.

Banks out in Texas,
    Trying to cut a figure;
Beecher in Brooklyn,
    Howling for the Nigger;
Lots of Abolitionists,
    Making such a yell,
In comes Parson Brownlow,
    And sends them all to hell.

Burnside at Knoxville,
    In a kind of fix;
Gilmore at Sumter,
    Pounding at the bricks;
Grant at Chattanooga
    Trying Bragg to thrash:
Is it any wonder
    The Union's gone to smash?

"Bravo! bravo" encored the friends. "Cheezey, my boy, you've a mellow voice and a fine vein of humor."

"You'd say, I had altogether too much humor if you knew, how cheaply I let that countryman there," pointing to Bram, "choice me out of the nomination on last election," returned Cheeze, secretly flattered at the compliment, but chagrined at the reflections it suggested.

At those words, Soo began to pick his teeth. Stentor commenced spitting tobacco juice at a key hole.

"It seems to me as though that man had the DEVIL at his side," continued Cheeze.

Soo here arose from his chair and advanced towards Cheeze.

"Cheeze," said the Secretary," I have the same belief myself and I have more than one reason for it."

Stentor who had been crossing himself with pious vehemence now got up and turning to Cheeze said: "And I, too, have heard strange stories about Bram's Friend."

"And I," chimed in Cheeze. "Suppose we exchange ideas and tell each other what we know about it."

To this they all agreed, and resuming their old postures, they first wet their whistles, then satisfied themselves that Bram was still unconscious, and Soo, setting the example, began telling what he knew of Bram's Mysterious Friend and Patron.

Chapter IX

Devilish Strange

"I have heard it related by a party that Mr. Lincoln has seen fit to incarcerate in Fort Warren, that on a certain occasion when Bram was very hard up and had to sell his furniture out there in Illinois, in order to keep the pot boiling, he wandered out into the prairie, unconscious of where he was, so deeply was he engrossed with the difficulties that beset him on all sides. He hadn't a friend in the world, and didn't know what to turn his hands to, to earn a living. Thus moodily engaged he came near to a spot where my informant was trapping prairie hens and then he sat down and gave vent to this pent up miseries in these words:

"Calkerlate I'd better bust these parts and emigrate right smart, or maybe I'll come to grief. Mother's cove in and father's looking arter other critters; flat-boatin is too all-fired fatiguing, rail-splitting is played out, 'cause Hanks throwed me,, and singing nigger songs is gone to smash. I could dance right smart on a spring board; but what's the use when you can't get nuthin for it but a shock or two o' corn and a pull of forty rod. I'd a heap sight rather go a canallin' if I could git aboard one of them craft; but even them is no go. There ain't no canals in this section of the country. 'Taint no use speculatin' on father's kickin' the bucket, so the only thing left is to dig a hole here in the prairie, and just expire right off."

So saying, he proceeded to divest himself of his clothing and boots. The later he hung upon an old ridge pole that stood on the plain and affixed a placard to them. They were odd specimens of foot gear, being nearly eighteen inches long and proportionately wide; the legs or uppers were so near the centre, that it was difficult to determine which the wearer had the most of, heel or toe, and the soles were entirely gone from long wear. The placard read thus:

"These is from Abe Hanks, likewise named Abe Linkun, to the widder Hennepin, her son, likewise named Abe. The eels is fled, the shanks is rather *gone up*, the soul is gone *the other way*, but the uppers is good and will make a pare of boots four him if he's a good boy. Fairwell! my biler is bust, and go I must. ABE HANKS."

And now, said the intended suicide, making a pillow of his clothes, and lying down on the earth in a posture of determined sleep, "I don't care what the *devil* becomes of me."

He had no sooner s

Curiosity getting the better of judgment, he crept cautiously towards them until he heard the stranger say:

"On this condition, sign thaid the word DEVIL, than up jumps a man as it were from the very earth itself, and advances very politely towards the recumbent Abe. In a few moments they became very intently engaged in conversation, but in such low tones that my informant could not catch a word.e bond and you shall not only get all you ask but I'll make you a member of the Legislature."

"What!" cried Abe, "Have you any interest with the Legislature."

"I should think I had," returned the other. "I'm personally acquainted with every man of them, and besides that, keep a boarding house *down below* for all the ex-members."

"Suppose I stir up this all-fired nigger question, kinder cussed brisk, what'll you do in that case, old boy?"

"Keep you in for two terms."

"Couldn't you make it Washington instead of Vandalia," insinuated Abe.

"What!" cried the other. "Are you so ambitious as all that? Why, man, you haven't ability enough to keep two listeners in their seat."

"Never mind that" returned Abe. "Just you help me a little when I falter, and have the name of "Honest" well stuck to me, and I'll go through it easier than you imagine."

"Well then, agreed," said the other, "and if any success attends the plan and any certain indications of civil war appear, I will be willing perhaps to enter into a new contract with you. *You know war contracts are very profitable.*"

"What do you mean?" enquired Abe, evidently not understanding his friend correctly.

"I mean *I'll give you the first contract under the war*—YOU AGREE TO BRING TO DEATH ONE MILLION OF HUMAN BEINGS; and I'll agree to give you the Presidency."

"The PRESIDENCY!" exclaimed Abe, rising from the earth in his agitation, and seeming to soar with his long limbs, as high as the ridge pole itself. His emotion was so extraordinary, that words failed to express it. The stranger pleased at this exhibition, extended his hand. Abe grasped it heartily, and pulling the other towards him, threw himself into his arms. They were the tallest pair my informant ever saw, and bore a striking resemblance to each other—sufficient to be brothers. Fearful of discovery, he crept away at this juncture, and turning round at the distance of a couple of miles, beheld them still together, standing hand in hand beside the ridge pole.

Chapter X

The Fiend

The last words of Soo's tale died away into a sort of hoarse whisper, and were heard in dead silence; as the supernatural subject of it fixed itself upon the minds of himself and his listeners.

A long silence followed it.

Soo whittled the arm of his chair, Stentor poked the fire, and Cheeze pulled out a little parchment scroll from his vest bosom and read it over privately; glancing at the others now and then to see if they were watching him.

"All right," he murmured, "it doesn't interfere with my contract. Every man for himself, say I."

At this moment a knock was heard at the door.

"Come in," said Stentor.

The door flew open and a servant in livery disclosed himself.

"The President?" he enquired blandly.

"Not here," returned Soo curtly.

"Excuse me, my Lud—I mean your Excellency—but if I'm not mistaken, the President is before me."

"I tell you he's not here," persisted Soo.

"And I tell you, you lie!" roared the flunkey, pushing past him and rousing the sleeping Bram from his chair.

Soo became livid with rage.

He ran to his *little bell* and hastily put his name to a blank order of arrest. An officer appeared at the door.

"Here!" said he, "arrest that impudent rascal directly and convey him to the vilest dungeon in America."

"Where?" enquired the officer.

"Park Barracks, New York."

The officer advanced and collared his prisoner.

"Come along with me," said he roughly.

But Bram was now fully awake and seeing the danger his Cockney friend was in, quickly interposed his superior authority.

"Let go!" he commanded.

The officer relinquished his hold.

"*Vamous!*" said Bram.

The provost marshal obsquatulated the ranch,

"What's all this about, gentlemen;" said Bram furiously, "can't a friend of mine ask for me without running in danger of being arrested?"

The Confederates hung their heads without daring to say a word. Bram glared furiously upon them."How long have I been to sleep," he demanded.

"Nearly three hours," replied Cheeze.

"Have I been blabbing to you—saying anything I ought not to have said—been indiscreet? Eh?"

Rapid glances passed between the three. Bram caught one of these tell tales, and suspecting all was not right, changed his tone instanter.

"Pardon me, Soo, my boy, I was only joking with you. Let's make up. I'll give you permission to lock up the very next man that comes along. Cheezey and Stentor, I'll make it all square with you when I come back. We'll make up a game of poker, *and play one Southern plantation ante up.* How do you like that? eh?"

"Capital!" they exclaimed.

They shook hands all around, and looked quite delighted; and in the midst of all this happiness, Bram departed, arm-in-arm with his liveried friend. As the door closed upon him, the faces of the Confederates lengthened.

"Who is that flunkey?" asked Senator, "that Bram should feel so soft about him and be so thick with him?"

"Is it possible you don't know?" replied Cheeze.

Stentor shook his head.

"Nor do I," jerked out the mortified Soo, "or I wouldn't have handled the fellow so roughly. Pray enlighten us."

"He is the private and confidential servant of Doctor—," and here Cheeze whispered the name in his friends' ears.

Soo looked serious. Stentor didn't comprehend it.

"Who is Doctor—" he began, bluntly.

"Hush!" said Cheeze. "Don't mention the name for worlds. I'll tell you. Did you never hear of a certain Chiropodist in New York who possessed great mastery over Bram's mind—who could manage him any way he pleased—who cut his corns—went on secret missions—was commissioned to New Orleans to watch Banks and afterwards to Norfolk to overlook Butler—who possessed great influence with all the rich Jews in New York and undertook to get loans of money from them—the H-n-d-r-cks, the J-s-phs, who used to represent the Rothschilds, the B-mh-m-rs, the E-nst-n-rs, and the N-th-ns?—who got up to the Russian Ball, and who danced with Mrs. Bram, at the party last winter?—who doctors him, and writes his speeches?—who advises him and directs him in questions of state? who—"

"Hold!" cried Soo, "I thought I was the man who did all this!"

"The devil you did!" cried Stentor, "I thought I was the man."

"You're both wrong, gentlemen, I was the man till the doctor stepped in and took the wind out of my sails, for which I was not sorry, for I was getting tired of him at that time, and might have missed the opportunity, I soon after had, of forming an alliance with another party."

Soo and Stentor bit their lips till the blood came, and then ran from the room howling, [French style.]

Cheeze smiled complacently and sitting down to the table, penned the following telegram in secret cypher to New York:

"Buy Rock Island at anything under 140 for a 'corner.' Sell 2,000 Erie 'short' and bull the market on gold. Mum."

Chapter XI

A Year Later—The End

How little do the humble know,
What miseries greatness is heir to,
What heart-aches, jealousies and cares,
Beset their anxious hearts with fears,
When high resolves have once elated,
What pain to see them all frustrated.
What hellish passions take their place,
When failure brings with it disgrace;
How stoop their minds beneath the blow,
To everything that's mean and low,
What shifts they make, what agents use,
What'er gives hope they madly choose.
With naught to risk, they spare no cost
To gain position they have lost;
Debased themselves, they seek to find,
A kindred baseness in mankind.
And feeling self-condemned the while,
Would think all others just as vile.

'Twas eve of one eventful day,
As story tellers always say,
The President had far surpassed

His greatest effort and his last;
And all the world went home in thought,
On all the wondrous things he taught.
The day had passed—the crown had gone,
And all that had been said or done,
Were records of the silent past.
Say, will his fleeting triumph last?
The fierce excitements of the day,
Had chased the great man's griefs away;
But now, when all was calm again,
Began the torments of his brain,
And in his silent chamber, there
Awoke the vision of despair.
No longer from his fishy eye,
Shot cunning and shone energy;
But lone and silent, and subdued,
He yielded to his sullen mood.
Long time he sat, convulsed and wrought,
Till words gave utterance to his thought.

"Oh! what a wretched thing am I,
The veriest fool of destiny;
How meanly have I sunk below
The dignity of honest woe.
How have I lost that high estate
I might have held among the great,
And sunk beneath my own approval,
Condemned myself to cringe and grovel;
I grasped at POWER; *fool, fool!* the thought
Now mocks the ruin it has wrought—
Time was when even foes respected,
But now how fallen and neglected;
The stake was POWER for which I cast,
'Twas but its shadow, and it passed;
My friends betrayed—I fondly bowed,
To woo the passions of the crowd;
But failing there, I sought again
My former standing to regain.
All will not answer, on my sight
The future rises to affright,
And in that future will I mark
A Path as devious and as dark!"

AIR—*Brilliante Posterioso*

The Devil took sick,
The Devil a saint would be;
The Devil got well,
The *devil* a saint was he!

"Ha!" cried listening Bram, "'tis thou,
Well hast thou timed to tempt me now!"

Who serves the Devil,
Devil take him;
But will the Devil
E'er forsake him?

"No," cried the Old One of a sudden,
"This jest of yours is not a bad 'un,
You would by joke assume superior,
Whereas, in fact, you are inferior.
And being servant, aye, *don't stir, Sir!*
You must obey; a slave you are Sir.
A slave you are, and though much bigger,
As much a slave as any nigger.
A slave you are, because you'll cheat,
And therfore, you are mine complete.
A slave you are, and now believe me,
You cannot, ikf you would, deceive me;
In all that does relate to sin,
I give the power, you but take in."
"Nay, nay, Your Darkness, pause awhile,
My joke was made to raise a smile;
But since it was misunderstood,
I'll recommence in sober mood."

"'Tis useless," quoth the Devil bowing,
I feel 'tis time I should be going;
Give me than hand; for, Bram, thou art
In thought and art my counterpart;
So like; that if (could such things be,)
You had been kicked from heaven with me,
We snacks had gone—yes, who can tell
And kept a hotel down in hell.

I see you like the joke—you laugh,
But time is up. I must be off,
Yet e'er a friendly leave I take,
I've fancy for a hearty shake.
The great Bram seized the proffered hand,
But—had he grasped a lighted brand,
His quivering nerves and changing look
Had not such sudden torture spoke.
He strove to free his hold—but no,
That scorching grasp would not let go.
*   *   *   *   *

Thus, on the very day before election,
The Devil claimed his great connection;
And hurling Bram to black damnation,
At last relieved the Yankee Nation.

THE END

Chapter 4

Lincoln and Songs

Introduction

On the various levels of the non-political world Lincoln did not become a widespread subject of songs, although as President he could not be ignored, especially by serious composers. A far more widely used personality was General George B. McClellan, or "Little Mac," who although incredibly ineffective as an army man nevertheless caught the fancy of the people. The Negro minstrel stage, the most popular "theater" of the day, significantly did not have a wide repertory about Lincoln. As this volume indicates Lincoln-songs were sung by the minstrels, and there were some skits (apparently all now lost) which discussed Lincoln and aspects of his Administration. Generally he was mentioned in derisive or slighting terms. Most minstrel players made no bones about preferring "Little Mac" to "Old Abe."

But in the political world conditions were the opposite. Ever since 1840 when "Tippecanoe and Tyler Too" floated into the White House on the wings of song, king-makers had realized the importance of singing a man to the Presidency. The chief vehicle for the distribution of these songs was the "songster," or "pocket songster," as they were frequently called. These books were small in format, contained sixty to a hundred songs, sold for a dime or a quarter. By widely popularizing the songs in them, these books exerted an influence much greater than might be apparent.

I have chosen songs which are most representative and most valuable in themselves. In the North as well as in the South, Lincoln was attacked and caricatured widely in song. In the North these songs were often circulated in songsters, as were those which were pro-Lincoln. In the South there were fewer songsters, and songs frequently circulated in newspapers and magazines. Generally these items, both in the North and the South, were less artistic, less clever, less pleasurable than their political opposites. But they are nevertheless interesting as relics of the fierce political battles of the time.

Altogether these songs give a clear and detailed picture of Lincoln in the songs of his day. They constitute a larger and more comprehensive selection than have hitherto been reprinted.

188

PRO-LINCOLN SONGS

Lincoln
Air—Old Dan Tucker

Daniel Decatur Emmett (1815-1904) wrote "Old Dan Tucker" (1843) when he was fifteen years old. This song was sung as a regular song and as play-party and dance piece. It was one of the most popular and widely parodied and varied songs in nineteenth-century America. Here it is parodied to provide another campaign song for Lincoln against Stephen A. Douglas (1813-1861). As the "Little Giant," Douglas provided obvious material for references to his stature.

Old Abe is coming down to fight
And put the Democrats to flight;
He's coming with the wedge and maul
And he will split 'em one and all

Abe he lives in a big log hut;
He can drive the wedge and use the glut—
He swings the maul and when he hits
It goes in the ground, or else it splits!

Get out of the way, you little giant!
Get out of the way, you little giant!
Get out of the way, you little giant!
You can't come in you're too short and pliant.

Old Abe knows how to drive the team
Because he never goes by steam
But now the ox-goad he will use
And dust the giant in his shoes

Look! the prairie's all on fire!
If poor Douglas had grown higher
He might have seen the smoke and stuff
But his short legs can't run fast enough!

189

> Get out of the way, you little giant!
> Get out of the way, you little giant!
> Get out of the way, you little giant!
> You can't come in you're too short and pliant.
> (*Americans and Their Songs*)

'Lincoln Hoss' and Stephen A.

Stephen Foster's famous "De Camptown Races" (1850), widely loved and frequently parodied, provided the tune for one of the Lincoln songs against Stephen A. Douglas. Douglas (1813-1861) had confronted Lincoln in a famous series of debates throughout Illinois as advocate of "Popular Sovereignty," that is that people of a frontier region should decide whether they wanted slavery. Douglas was defeated at the 1860 Democratic convention as candidate for President. With war declared he backed Lincoln's policies. Known as the "Little Giant" he provided ready fodder for disparaging remarks.

> There's an old plow "hoss" whose name is "Dug."
>   Doo-dah, doo-dah,
> He's short and thick—a regular "plug,"
>   Oh! doo-dah day.
>
> *Chorus*: We're bound to work all night,
>   We're bound to work all day,
> I'll bet my money on the "Lincoln hoss,"
>   Who bets on Stephen A.?
>
> The "Little Plug" has had his day,
>   Doo-dah, doo-dah,
> He's out of the ring, by all fair play.
>   Oh, doo-dah day. [*Chorus*]
>
> He tried his best on the Charleston track,
>   Doo-dah, doo-dah,
> But couldn't make time with his "Squatter Jack."
>   Oh, doo-dah day [*Chorus*]
>
> The "Little Dug" can never win,
>   Doo-dah, doo-dah,

That Kansas job's too much for him.
    Oh doo-dah day. [*Chorus*]

His legs are weak, his wind unsound,
    Doo-dah, doo-dah,
His "switch tail's" too near the ground.
    Oh, doo-dah day. [*Chorus*]
          (*Read 'Em and Weep*)

Lincoln and Liberty Too
By F.A.B. Simpkins
Air—Rosin the Bow

One of the most popular nineteenth century songs sung in both the North and the South was entitled "Old Rosin, the Beau," or "...the Bow." The origins of the song are unknown. It may be the same quoted by Moros in Wager's *The Longer Thou Livest the More Fool Thou Art*, dated 1658, which has the lines: "Robin lende to me thy Bow, thy Bow,/Robin the Bow, Robin lende to me thy bow a," in which the reference in the second line "Robin the bow" is a corruption of or pun on using resin on fiddle bows. Regardless of the original text, many singers have preferred the reference to Rosin as a heavy drinker and ladies' man. The song may have originated as English or Scotch or Irish. It appeared in dozens of popular songsters during the last half of the nineteenth century, and served for at least four political songs between 1840 and 1870. The following Lincoln song dates from 1860 and probably was written by a certain F.A.B. Simpkins.

Hurrah for the choice of the nation! Our chieftain so brave and so true;
We'll go for the great reformation, For Lincoln and Liberty too.

We'll go for the son of Kentucky, The hero of Hoosierdom through;
The pride of the Suckers so lucky, For Lincoln and Liberty too.

Our David's good sling is unerring, The Slavocrats' giant he slew;
Then shout for the Freedom preferring, For Lincoln and Liberty too.
          (*American Songbag*)

Old Abe Lincoln Came Out of the Wilderness

Carl Sandburg (*American Songbag* 168) said that torchlight proces-
sions of Republicans sang this song in the summer and fall of 1860.
Proud Illinoisans everywhere sang it. Lincoln even heard his two boys,
Tad and Willie, sing it to him. The tune is that of Negro spirituals,
"When I Come Out of De Wilderness" and "Ol' Gray Mare Come Tear-
ing' Out de Wilderness."

> Old Abe Lincoln came out of the wilderness,
> Out of the wilderness, out of the wilderness,
> Old Abe Lincoln came out of the wilderness,
> Down in Illinois.
>
> (*American Songbag*)

Hurrah for Old Abe of the West
By Cyrus Elder
Air—Vive la Companie:

"Vive la Companie," always popular in the U.S. since its first publication in 1838 consists of traditional French words and music.

> Come all ye bold freemen and join in our song,
> Hurrah for old Abe of the West!
> While millions of voices the strain will prolong,
> Hurrah for old Abe of the West!
> Honest and pure is our champion's name,
> Stainless his scutcheon, noble his fame,
> Hurrah for old Abe, Hurrah for old Abe,
> Hurrah for old Abe of the West.
>
> Ye strong-handed yeoman now tilling the soil,
> Hurrah for old Abe of the West!
> Come chant the loud anthem, ye lovers of toil,
> Hurrah for old Abe of the West!
> Old Abe is the man who can work by your side,
> He too was a farmer and that was his pride,
> Hurrah for old Abe, Hurrah for old Abe,
> Hurrah for old Abe of the West!
>
> And all ye that work in the mine and the mill,
> Hurrah for old Abe of the West!

Come raise your strong voices and shout with a will.
Hurrah for old Abe of the West!
He'll give you the boon of Protection once more,
He'll chase the grim spectre of want from your door,
Hurrah for old Abe, Hurrah for old Abe,
Hurrah for old Abe of the West!

Oh list to the voice of the loud bugle horn,
Hurrah for old Abe of the West!
O'er river and mountains its echoes are borne,
Hurrah for old Abe of the West!
The cheers of the boatmen are mixed with the strain,
They're choosing old Abe for their Captain again.
Hurrah for old Abe, Hurrah for old Abe,
Hurrah for old Abe of the West!

The good and the pure and the learn'd of the land,
Hurrah for old Abe of the West,
Have joined our great army and march hand in hand,
Hurrah for old Abe of the West.
They know that our Farmer and Boatman so true
Is an eloquent Statesman and Patriot too,
Hurrah for old Abe, Hurrah for old Abe,
Hurrah for old Abe of the West.

Soon murder and rapine no more we shall see,
Hurrah for old Abe of the West,
The fair state of Kansas at last shall be free,
Hurrah for old Abe of the West.
Her flowery fields for our sons he will save.
They never shall be dyed by the blood of the slave.
Hurrah for old Abe, Hurrah for old Abe,
Hurrah for old Abe of the West.

J.B. and his crew have about had their day,
Hurrah for old Abe of the West,
They must pack their traps and get out of the way,
For Honest old Abe of the West!
He is worthy to sit in Washington's chair
And the true-hearted people are placing him there,
Hurrah for old Abe, Hurrah for old Abe
Three cheers for old Abe of the West.
(*Lincoln and Hamlin Songster*)

John Anderson, My Jo, John
A Campaign Song

"John Anderson, My Jo John" is one of Robert Burns' famous love poems, with music by Josef Marais in 1824. The tune was widely used in other songs, many in Northern or Southern war songs. The first song below illustrates how the tune was used for straight pro-Lincoln songs. The second piece, "O Johnny Bull My Jo John!" "Air—John Anderson My Jo John" illustrates how the tune was adapted to other kinds of songs. This song was published in the *Richmond Dispatch*, January 22, 1862.

John Anderson, My Jo, John
    When we were first acquaint,
The "farms" of "Uncle Sam," John,
    For freedoms' sons were meant.
But now the powers of slavery
    Have said it shan't be so;
I mourn I live to see this day,
    John Anderson, My Jo.

John Anderson, My Jo, John,
    When thou and I were young,
We hoped to get a farm, John,
    For ilka gallant son.
But the lands are gled to slavery.
    Where can our bairns go?
O must they live in poverty,
    John Anderson, My Jo?

O dinna sab sa sair, dear wife,
    I bring ye joyful news,
"Old Honest Abe's" the man, dear wife,
    The people won't refuse—
He'll lead us on to victory,
    Triumphant oer our foe;
The gallant sons of freedom's soil
    Have sworn it shall be so.

The prairies in the west, dear wife,
    To freedom shall be given;
The "old vile harlot, slavery,"
    Shall from free soil be driven!

Our boys shall get their farms, dear wife,
 And thou and I will go,
And tent their bairns' bairns dear wife,
 Their lads and lassies too.

John Anderson, my Jo, John,
 Ye fill my heart wi' joy.
A farm upon the priarie, John,
 For ilka darling boy!
"Old Abe" will help them split the rails
 To fence them in, ye know.
And ye ken they'll keep out slavery too,
 John Anderson, My Jo.
    (*Lincoln and Hamlin Songster*)

Old Abe, My Jolly Jo
Air—John Anderson, My Jo John

In the anti-Lincoln song below, "Old Abe, My Jolly Jo," it is ironic that "Jo," which in Burns' original means love or sweetheart, is turned around to severe criticism. The reference to the "Spanish cloak" in the song is to the Scottish cloak that Lincoln was incorrectly rumored to have worn in Baltimore when, on his way to Washington for his inauguration, he had to slip through that city because of a threatened assassination.

Old Abraham, my jolly Abe,
 When we were first acquaint,
I thought you were an honest man,
 But nothing of a saint;
But since you wore the Spanish cloak,
 You love the negro so,
And hate the white man, so you do,
 My jolly Abe, my Jo.

Old Abraham, my jolly Abe,
 What do you really mean?
Your negro proclamation is
 A wild fanatic's dream.
The war you did begin, old Abe,
 And that you surely know;

You should have made a compromise,
My jolly Abe, my Jo.

Old Abraham, my jolly Abe,
Your darkey plan has failed,
Ere this you know that cruel war
And taxes you've entailed.
In this unhappy land, old Abe,
Is weeping, wail, and woe,
That you can't cure, nor we endure,
My jolly Abe, my Jo.

Old Abraham, my jolly Abe,
The blindest man can see
The Union you will not restore
Till every negro's free,
And equal with the best of men,
In arm and arm they go
To vote as you may wish them to,
My jolly Abe, my Jo.

(*Copperhead Minstrel*)

Buchanan, He Sate in the White House Chair
From the burlesque of In-go-mar
Air—Lord Lovell

The old English ballad "Lord Lovell" (Child 75) has been common in America sung in many variations. The original ballad and numerous variants and satires appeared in dozens of nineteenth-century songsters. One variant began with the lines "Mansfield Lovell, who commanded the Rebel troops at New Orleans, and who on the approach of the national fleet and army to that place, 'led his forces out of the town'." [as Maj. General C.S.A. he withdrew from New Orleans 25 April 1862] Another was the much more jocular ballad:

Love Lovell's Velocipede
Air—Lord Lovell

Lord Lovell stood by the garden gate
With his shining Velocipede

And whispered farewell to his Lady Bell
Who wished fro his lordship good-speed
Chorus:
Speed, speed, speed,
Who wished for his lordship good-speed.

"When will you be back, Lord Lovell," she said,
But he gave her question no heed.
Placed his feet in the stirrup and galloped away
On his famous Velocipede.

Buchanan, He Sate in the White House Chair

Buchanan once sate in the White House chair,
    In the White House chair sate he:
While Davis and Floyd and the others thieves there,
    With the treasure were making quite free,
        Free, free,
    With the treasure they were making quite free.

When somebody happened to mention the fact,
    "I don't care a darn" says he.
"To me what's the difference however they act,
    For they're very good friends to me,
        Me, me,
    They're very good friends to me.

But the people awoke, to Buchanan they spoke,
    And out of the chair popped he:
He went off in disgrace, and right into his place
    The people put honest Abe,
        Bee, Bee,
    The people put honest Abe.

He went in with a rush the rebellion to crush,
    And mighty successful is he;
And shortly, once more, bright stars thirty-four,
    On our banner the world will see,
        See, see,
    On our banner the world will see.
                (*The Little Mac Songster*)

Abe Lincoln Went to Washington
Air—When Johnny Comes Marching Home

Most Lincoln and Civil War songs were imprecise as to event and detail. Few summarized Lincoln, his role in the War and the War itself, so succinctly as the following, for which no title has been attached but to which I have given the generic title above. It was sung to "When Johnny Comes Marching Home," one of the most popular songs of the period. The reference to "for bales" is to bales of cotton, in which cotton was sold.

1. In eighteen hundred and sixty one,
For bowls, for bowls,
In eighteen hundred and sixty one,
For bowls, says I.
In eighteen hundred and sixty one,
Abe Lincoln went to Washington,
And we'll all drink stone blind,
Johnny fill up the bowl!

2. In eighteen hundred and sixty two
Old Abe he put the rebellion through.

3. In eighteen hundred and sixty three
Old Abe he set the darkies free.

4. In eighteen hundred and sixty four
Old Abe he called for a million more.

5. In eighteen hundred and sixty five
John Wilkes Booth took Lincoln's life.

(Songs of the Civil War 213)

Brave Old Abe
By W. Cutter
Air—Auld Lang Syne

"Auld Lang Syne," adapted from Robert Burns in 1711 and sung to a traditional Scottish song, has always been everybody's favorite. After the Civil War it was sung as "Should Brave Ulysses Be Forgot?" in praise of the General. During the Civil War its tune was frequently used.

From West, from East, from South, from North
    What eager-growing throngs
For brave Old Abe are pouring forth
    Their patriotic songs!
        For brave Old Abe, my boys!
           For brave Old Abe.
        Take up the song, and roll it along
           For Brave Old Abe!

He's just the man for you and me,
    He's just the man for all;
A truer, braver heart than he
    The people cannot call.
        For brave Old Abe, my boys!
           For brave Old Abe.
        Take up the song, roll on the ball
           For brave Old Abe.

Old Abe is made of genuine stuff,
    The sort that never fails:
For Cabinet-work he's good enough—
    First-rate for splitting rails.
        For brave Old Abe, my boys!
           For brave Old Abe.
        We'll split the Democratic rail
           With brave Old Abe.

Old Abe, they say, is not genteel—
    He wears a slouching hat;
But, with a heart as true as steel,
    He's none the worse for that.
        For brave Old Abe, my boys!
           For brave Old Abe.
        As true as steel, with a heart to feel,
           Is brave Old Abe.

The flatboat Abe can navigate—
    At that he's tried his hand;
And now the good old ship of state.
    We'll trust to his command.
        To brave Old Abe, my boys!
           To brave Old Abe.

We'll give the helm of this good realm
To brave Old Abe.

(*The Bobolink Minstrel*)

Old Abe
Air—Auld Lang Syne

Old Abe was a pioneer,
　　His cabin in the wood;
He felled the trees, he shot the deer—
　　The work he did was good.
But other work is to be done,
　　A wilder game to chase;
A farm to clear at Washington
　　And Abram suits the place.
　　　　　Old Abe suits the place, ye men,
　　　　　He'll fill it with a grace;
　　　　　Make way! make way! the people say,
　　　　　Old Abe wins the race.

A blacksmith, too, Old Abe was,
　　A judge of iron he;
He holds that dear, which men make here,
　　Not that brought o'er the sea.
And as he handles well the sledge,
　　So to those laws which keep
Our earth concealed in hill and field,
　　For trade across the deep.
　　　　　Old Abe suits the work, ye men,
　　　　　He'll do it with a grace;
　　　　　Make way! make way! the people say,
　　　　　Old Abe wins the race.

Old Abe is a mauler friends,
　　Good rails he always makes;
He'll fence the nation's treasury in,
　　Full ten rails high with stakes.
No Buck will ever break them down.
　　No Fowler find the pray;
Go make the great Pacific road,
　　He'll save the cash to pay.

        Old Abe suits the place, ye men,
        He'll give the vultures chase
        Make way! make way! the people say,
        Old Abe wins the race.

Old Abe is a working-man.
    He knows the sons of toil;
Nor thinks they should compete with slaves
    Upon a virgin soil.
Old Abe is an honest man,
    All bribes he'll flee and shun;
O what a curiosity
    He'll be in Washington!
        Old Abe suits the place, ye men,
        Behold his honest face;
        Make way! make way! the people say,
        Old Abe wins the race.
            (*Lincoln and Hamlin Songster*)

Hurrah Chorus

(4 stanzas)

Old Abe can maul, or he can thrash,
    Hurrah, hurrah, hurrah!
He'll give it to your Loco trash
    Hurrah, hurrah, hurrah.
Your two-faced man is nought to him,
E'en now his prospects are all dim,
    Abe is the man, an honest man,
    He is the man for me.

Abe is not rich in worldly goods,
    Oh no, oh no, oh no!
But in his thoughts, his works, his words,
    He's true, he's true, he's true.
'Tis he who loves his wife and friends.
And o'er his duty daily bends.
    He is the man, an honest man,
    He is the man for me.
            (*The Bobolink Minstrel*)

Rail Song
Air—Dandy Jim

"The People," with unanimous voice,
For President have made their choice;
And the Fourth of March they will be able
To make clean sweep of the *Augean stable*.
     So we'll cut and split and maul away,
     At the Lincoln rails till election day.

Buchanan's "knees are weak" and limber,
Since the sudden fall of *live oak timber*;
Instead of ships with slave-trade sails,
We'll use the wood for *Homestead* rails.
     So we'll cut and split and maul away,
     At the Lincoln rails till election day.

And for this purpose the Keystone pledges
Twenty thousand mauls and wedges.
Now Loco-focos all, remember,
We'll split those rails by next November.
     So we'll cut and split and maul away,
     At the Lincoln rails till election day.

Then we'll secure protection laws,
To keep our gold from foreign claws;
From Border Ruffians we'll have no alarms
While freemen work their Homestead farms.
     So we'll cut and split and maul away,
     At the Lincoln rails till election day.

In October we will make this certain,
By hiding Foster behind the Curtin;
And in November you may rely,
We'll elect "Old Abe" and not half try.
     So we'll cut and split and maul away,
     At the Lincoln rails till election day.
            (*Lincoln and Hamlin Songster*)

The Bay State Hurrah

(6 stanzas)

Free speech Lincoln will aye defend,
   Hurrah, hurrah, hurrah.
And slavery's curse he'll never extend,
   Hurrah, hurrah, hurrah.
He goes for Freedom's holy cause,
For equal rights and equal laws.
   Hurrah, hurrah, hurrah, hurrah,
   Hurrah, hurrah, hurrah.
(The Bobolink Minstrel)

Campaign Song
Air—Old Zip Coon

"Old Zip Coon" was one of the most popular songs of the nineteenth century. It was one of the early popular songs of minstrelsy and resembled a jig dance called "Nachy under the Hill," named after a spot on the banks of the Mississippi at Natchez where boatmen, gamblers, pirates and river-ladies congregated frequently. There was a version in *The Popular National Songster* (Philadelphia 1845) and another in *Christy's Negro Songster* (New York 1855). Informed opinion suggests that the tune was originally a spiritual. The tune was later used for "Turkey in the Straw."

Everybody, 'tention now, to what I'se gwine to say.
Everybody, 'tention now, to what I'se gwine to say.
Everybody, 'tention now, to what I'se gwine to say.
And vote for Uncle Abram on next election day.
He will sabe de Union, and fotch de rebels to.
He will sabe de Union, and fotch de rebels to.
He will sabe de Union, and fotch de rebels to.
I'll bet you all my greenbacks, what I say am true.
   Tudle, taddle, tudle tadle, tuadellel dump.
   Oh tuadellel, tuadellel dump.
   Oh tuadellel, tuadellel dump
   Ri tum tuadellel, tuadellel dee.

For Gin'ral George McClellan, de Copperheads dey shout.
For Gin'ral George McClellan, de Copperheads dey shout.
For Gin'ral George McClellan, de Copperheads dey shout.
But he can't shine for President, while Uncle Abe am 'bout.
In de city of Chicago dey met de odder day.
In de city of Chicago dey met de odder day.
In de city of Chicago dey met de odder day.
Peace seemed to be deir hobby, but like donkies dey did bray.
    Tudle, taddle, etc.

Dar's no use ob talkin peace, until Secesh am floor'd,
Dar's no use ob talkin peace, until Secesh am floor'd.
Dar's no use ob talkin peace, until Secesh am floor'd.
And Uncle Sam's authority, all ober am restored:
For wicked folks 'tis said, dare am no peace at all.
for wicked folks 'tis said, dare am no peace at all.
For wicked folks 'tis said, dare am no peace at all.
Beware den, all ye Copperheads, your chances dey am small.
    Tudle, taddle, etc.

If I had a thousand greenbacks, I'd bet em every cent,
If I had a thousand greenbacks, I'd bet em every cent,
If I had a thousand greenbacks, I'd bet em every cent,
Dat Uncle Abram Lincoln will be next President.
Stand back, Little Mack, now, stand back, Wooly Horse,
Stand back, Little Mack, now, stand back, Wooly Horse,
Stand back, Little Mack, now, stand back, Wooly Horse,
Kase Honest Abe's a-comin', de swiftest on de course.
    Tudle, taddle, etc.

                       (*Lincoln and Johnson Songster*)

Come, Gather Round
By Charles Githens, Esq.
Air—Dearest May

"Dearest May," one of the early minstrel type songs, appeared in *The Ethiopian Glee Book; a Collection of Popular Negro Melodies, Arranged for Quartet Clubs* (Boston 1850), in *Christy's Negro Songster* (New York 1855) and in *Minstrel Songs, Old and New, a Collection of World-wide, Famous Minstrel and Plantation Songs* (New York 1882). Authorship has been attributed to A.F. Winnemore and words by Francis

Lynch and music by L.V.H. Crosby. It was a popular song in its own right and as tune for other pieces.

> Come, gather round me, freemen, some truths I will relate,
> Of honest Abe Lincoln, the People's candidate;
> A man that's fit to guide the helm of our good ship of State—
> With pure and noble Johnson, a good and worthy mate.
>> Hurrah, hurrah, for honest Abe, hurrah!
>> Hark how the shout
>> Of the free rings out,
>> And swells from shore to shore.
>
> Sprung from the race of yeoman, their country's boast and pride,
> His stalwart form has braved the storms that lash the mountain's side;
> His manly forehead dripping with the sweat of honest toil,
> And side by side he labor'd with the tillers of the soil.
>> Hurrah, hurrah, for honest Abe, hurrah! (etc.)
>
> At eve, from toil returning, nought could his ardor damp;
> To pour oer Learning's mysteries, he trims the midnight lamp;
> The syren voice of Pleasure could not his youth enthrall,
> No fetters find the daring mind, no obstacles appall.
>> Hurrah, hurrah, for honest Abe, hurrah! (etc.)
>
> Thus noble has he struggled, and bravely bore the strife,
> And proudly has he conquer'd in the battle-field of life.
> From every hill and valley the trumpet-voice of Fame
> Rings out in loudest, clearest notes, our leader's spotless name.
>> Hurrah, hurrah, for honest Abe, hurrah! (etc.)
>
> Come, freemen, join the chorus, raise high the swelling notes;
> Like freemen give your suffrages, for Lincoln cast your votes.
> Let your rally cry be Union! in the coming fight,
> And victory'll be ours, and 'pon the side of right.
>> *(Lincoln and Johnson Songster)*

Old Abe's Preliminary Visit to the White House
Air—Villikins and Dinah

"Villikins and Dinah" or "Sweet Betsy from Pike" (1853) was possibly written by John A. Stone and set to traditional music. Easily parodied, the tune was used before the Civil War by Stephen Collins Foster in the 1856 Presidential campaign as "The Great Baby Show, or, The Abolition Show." The following song was written by Gen. Clarke, editor of the *Burlington* (Vt.) *Times*, and sung at a Lincoln and Hamlin ratification meeting at Burlington, at which the Hon. Geo. P. Marsh presided, by the "Bob-o-link" Glee Club.

One Abr'am there was who lived out in the West.
Esteemed by his neighbors the wisest and best,
And you'll see on a time if you'll follow my ditty,
How he took a straight walk up to Washington City.
    Ri ru, etc. (sic)

His home was in Springfield, out in Illinois,
Where he's long been the pride of the men and "the boys."
But he left his White House with no sign of regret,
For he knew that the people had another to let.

So Abr'am he trudged on to Washington straight,
And reached the White House through the avenue gate;
Old Buck and his cronies (some chaps from the South)
Sat round the East room, rather down in the mouth.

Old Abe seized the knocker and gave such a thump,
Buck thought the State ship had run into a slump;
He trembled all over and turned deadly pale,
"That noise," said he, "must be made with a rail."

"Run Lewis, run Jerry, and open the door"—
And the "functionary" nearly fell down to the floor—
"There's only one man that knocks that way, I'm bless'd,
And that is that tarnal old Abe of the West."

The Cabinet, frightened, sat still in their seats,
While Abr'am impatient, the rapping repeats,
"I hope it ain't Abe," said old Buck, pale and gray—
"If it is, boys, there'll be the devil to pay."

At last, though, reluctant, Buck opened the door,
And found a chap waiting six feet three or four.
"I have come, my fine fellows," said Abe to the ring,
"To give you fair notice to vacate next spring."

The people have watched you and made up their mind
That your management's running this country behind;
You're badly in debt, and your plan is a bold one,—
To make a new debt to pay off the old one.

"You and Douglas have so split your party in twain
That Spaulding's best glue can't unite it again;
And both parts are useless, the country don't need 'em—
For one goes for Slavery and the other 'gainst Freedom.

"So the people conclude that but one thing to do,
Is to right the state ship and hire a new crew,
And engage a new Captain as soon as they can,
And it is my duty to tell you that I am the man."

"Come in," says old Buck," and sit down Mr. Lincoln—
The remarks you have made are something to think on;
I don't care a cuss for the country, that's flat!
But if you best Douglas you can take my old hat!"

"Steve Douglas," said Abe, "he belongs in my state,
And I did beat him well in the year '58;
If I catch him again in the canvass he'll find
What it means when folks talk about 'running behind'."

"So you needn't fear Doug, let him scheme and conspire,—
He's as deep in the mud as you're in the mire.
And this moral he'll learn when his game is all played:
That it is not by 'squatting' that 'sovereigns' are made."

"Mr. Lincoln," says Buck," your notions, I think,
Are extremely correct, and I ask you to drink;
We've the best of 'J.B.,' 'green seal,' and old sherry,
And I've no great objections just now to be merry."

Says Abr'am: "My friends, I've come here to say
That the Democrat 'dog' has just had his day;
The people have trusted you more than they oughter,
And all that I ask is a glass of cold water."

"Cold water," said Buck, "we've got it I think,
Though tis not, with our party, a favorite drink;

Our tipple we take on its own naked merits,
And we need something strong to keep up our sperits."

The Cabinet searched the White House with a will,
But did not find water "put down in the bill;"
Jerry Black made report that, without any doubt,
The whiskey was plenty, but the water was out.

So Abe took his leave and returned to the West,
Leaving Buck and his Cabinet somewhat depressed,
For they saw with a glance how 'twould end without fail:—
They were bound for Salt River, this time on a rail!
                              (*Lincoln and Hamlin Songster*)

Campaign Song to The Wide-Awakes of Philadelphia
By G. Collins
Tune—Yankee Doodle

Old Uncle Abe! long time ago
    They said this to deride us;
But now we'll march to victory,
    And this's the tune to guide us.
              Old Uncle Abe! ha! ha! ha!
              Old Uncle Abe the honest;
              How the frightened Locos run
              From Uncle Abe the honest.

To fight is not a pleasant game,
    But if we must we'll do it;
As Uncle Abe began the fun,
    His boys will see him through it.
              Old Uncle Abe! ha! ha! ha! (etc.)

Once upon the prairies broad,
    Came a "giant" leader;
But Uncle Abe with a cedar rail
    Soon made him a Seceder.
              Old Uncle Abe! ha! ha! ha! (etc.)

Old Kentuck sent forth a man,
    A "horse and alligator";

But when he saw old Honest Abe,
    He didn't like his cedar.
        Old Uncle Abe! ha! ha! ha! (etc.)

Old Uncle Abe—how it brings
    The good old days before us.
Two or three begin to sing,
    Millions join the chorus.
        Old Uncle Abe! ha! ha! ha! (etc.)

Old Uncle Abe! not alone
    The continent will hear it!
But all the world shall catch the tune
    And every tyrant fear it.
        Old Uncle Abe! ha! ha! ha! (etc.)
        (*Lincoln and Hamlin Songster*)

Destruction of the Vandal Host at Manassas
A Parody

This parody is of Lord Byron's famous poem "The Destruction of Sennacherib" in which "The Assyrian came down like the wolf on the fold."

Abe Lincoln came down like the wolf on the fold,
And his cohorts were thirsting for silver and gold;
Though the sheen of their swords was like stars on the sea,
Yet is saved not their life-stream which crimsoned the lea.

Like the hordes of the forest, when the war-whoop is heard,
These serfs came by stealth on the braves whom they feared;
Like the leaves of the forest, when autumn hath blown,
These cowards their backs to the brave ones hath shown.

For our cannon and ball, spreading wide o'er the blast,
Carried death to the foe—sparing few as they passed;
And the eye of the Vandals waxed deadly and chill,
And our soil is now drenched by their vile crimson rill.

And there stood old Scott, sad, dejected, and pale,
When he heard from the hireling an heart-rending tale;

Beside him, the dying, —their wounds gaping wide,
In an instant to be like the dead by their side.

All hushed into silence, the dying alone
Interrupt the death-calm by a heart-breaking moan;
And the blood of the slain cries aloud to the Lord,
For his vials of wrath on the prince of the horde.

One Hundred Years Hence
Tony Pastor

Tony Pastor (1837?-1908) was one of the most famous vaudeville personalities during the Civil War. He seems to have had little love for Lincoln but great respect for the office of President and fierce love for the Union. On April 20, after Lincoln's call for 75,000 volunteers, a great rally was held in the afternoon in New York City. Pastor observed the electric effect the singing of "The Star Spangled Banner" created. He went to a store, bought a copy, learned the words and that night sang it to his audience, asking them to join him in the chorus. An anonymous patron of the show called the results "tremendous." Pastor sang some 1000 different Civil War songs, sometimes to his own endangerment by Southern sympathizers and mobs. In 1862 he published many songs in his *Tony Pastor's Union Songster*. In some of his acts Pastor used a stereopticon to flash likenesses of McClellan and Grant and other familiar military figures on a screen while his songs detailed their activities and virtues.

In his song "One Hundred Years Hence," Pastor demonstrated the feelings attached by many to Lincoln and to "Little Mac" (George Brinton McClellan, USA, 1826-85). McClellan was, in fact, a brilliant organizer and administrator and was wrapped in the blanket of his own ego. He always seemed to overestimate the strength of his adversary and to choose withdrawing his troops for more planning rather than taking advantage of any opportunity he might have. "Little Mac" would not fight. Lincoln once said that "Sending reinforcements to McClellan is like shoveling flies across a barn." But McClellan, because of his personality, was popular with the Northern populace. He ran for President in 1864. Pastor, though the "Dean of the vaudeville theater," was unable to predict the future, as the following song indicates.

Abe Lincoln is going it with a strong hand,
But still he's our ruler, and by him we'll stand;

Let us hope in the end he may prove he has sense,
For he'll be forgotten a hundred years hence.

There's little McClellan, of our army the boast,
He never complained when removed from his post—
The brave deeds he done bring their own recompense,
He *won't* be forgotten a hundred years hence.

(*Songs of the Civil War* 180)

Songs of Abraham Lincoln

McClellan is a humbug
And Lincoln is a fool,
All of them is liars
Of the highest greeting school.

Another Confederate ditty sympathized with Lincoln after the Battle of Bull Run:

King Abraham is very sick,
Old Scott has got the measles,
Manassas we have won at last,
Pop goes the weasel!

We Are Coming, Father Abraham

In July 1862, Lincoln issued a call for 300,000 volunteers to enlist for three years. Songwriter James Sloan Gibbons, Quaker abolitionist and friend of William Lloyd Garrison, responded with this song, which was printed in the *Evening Post*, July 16, 1862, and subsequently popularized by the famous Hutchinson family and by Stephen Foster. President Lincoln, for whom the song was performed several times, thought the piece "contained an excellent sentiment, and was sung in a manner worthy of the sentiment." For one performance Tad Lincoln took his father to Grover's Theater to see "The Seven Sister." Somehow during the performance Tad disappeared from the Presidential box and appeared on the stage, outfitted in oversize army blouse and cap and waving an American flag and led the singing of the song. During the New York City draft riots of 1863, Gibbons' luxurious house was ransacked and burned. His daughters escaped through a window and Gibbons stood in the front and watched the burning.

The song invited answers and parodies. Number one below was printed in the Philadelphia *Evening Journal*. Number two, "How Are You, Greenbacks?" in two versions attacked Lincoln on many issues, especially inflation.

We Are Coming, Father Abraham

James Sloan Gibbons

We are coming, Father Abraham, three hundred thousand more,
From Mississippi's winding stream and from New England's shore;
We leave our ploughs and workshops, our wives and children dear,
With hearts too full for utterance, with but a single tear;
We dare not look behind us, but steadfastly before;
We are coming, Father Abraham, three hundred thousand more.

Chorus
We are coming, we are coming, our Union to restore;
We are coming, Father Abraham three hundred thousand more,
We are coming, Father Abraham three hundred thousand more.

You have called us, and we're coming, by Richmond's bloody tide
To lay us down, for Freedom's sake, our brothers' bones beside;
Or from foul treason's savage grasp to wrench the murderous blade,
And in the face of foreign foes its fragments to parade.
Six hundred thousand loyal men and true have gone before;
We are coming, Father Abraham, three hundred thousand more.
Chorus

(*Songs of the Civil War* 186)

We Are Coming, Abraham Lincoln

We are coming, Abraham Lincoln,
  From mountain, wood, and glen;
We are coming, Abraham Lincoln,
  With the ghosts of murdered men.
Yes! We're coming, Abraham Lincoln,
  With curses loud and deep,
That will haunt you in your waking,
  And disturb you in your sleep.

There's blood upon your garments,
    There's guilt upon your soul;
For the lust of ruthless soldiers
    You let loose without control:
Your dark and wicked doings
    A God of mercy sees;
And the wail of homeless children
    Is heard on every breeze.

There's sadness in our dwellings,
    And the cry of wild despair,
From broken hearts and ruined homes
    Breaks on the midnight air;
While sorrow spreads her funeral pall
    O'er this once happy land;
For brother meets, in deadly strife,
    A brother's battle brand.
With desolation, all around
    Our dead lie on the plains;
You're coming, Abraham Lincoln,
    With manacles and chains,
To subjugate the white man,
    and set the *negro* free:
By the blood of all these murdered men
    This curse can never be.

You may call your black battalions
    To aid your sinking cause,
And substitute your vulgar jokes
    For liberty and laws.
No! by the memory of our fathers,
    By those green unnumbered graves,
We'll perish on ten thousand fields
    Ere *we* become your slaves.
Hark! hear you not the battle crash,
    See not the lightning's gleam:
The earth drinks up a brother's blood,
    Oh God! it is no dream.

                    (*Copperhead Minstrel*)

We Are Coming, Abraham Lincoln

We are coming, Abraham Lincoln,
From mountains, wood, and glen,
We are coming, Abraham Lincoln,
With the ghosts of murdered men.
Yes, we're coming, Abraham Lincoln,
With curses loud and deep,
That will haunt you in your waking
And disturb you in your sleep.

There's blood upon your garments,
There's guilt upon your soul,
For the host of ruthless soldiers
You let loose without control.
Your dark and wicked doings
A God of mercy sees,
And the wail of homeless children
Is heard on every breeze.

You may call your black battalions
To aid your stinking cause,
And substitute your vulgar jokes
For Liberty and laws.

(Songs of the Civil War 93)

How Are You, Greenbacks?

We're coming, Father Abraham, three hundred thousand more,
Five hundred presses printing us from morn till night is o'er.

We're willing, Father Abraham, one hundred thousand more
Should help our Uncle Samuel to prosecute the war;
But then we want a chieftain true, one who can lead the van,
Geo. B. McClellan, you all know, he is the very man.

We're coming, Father Abram, nine hundred thousand strong,
With nine hundred thousand darkies, sure the traitors can't last long,
with Corporal Cuff and Sergeant Pomp to lead us in the melee,
And at their head, without a red, our Brigadier General Greeley.

We're coming, Father Abram, nine hundred thousand more,
With the greatest fighting hero that lives upon our shore;
He fought in all the battles won, and shed his blood most freely,
But he's fought them with the Tribune, and his name is General
Greeley.

(Songs of the Civil War 92)

How Are You, Greenbacks?

We're coming, Father Abraham, One hundred thousand more,
Five hundred presses print us from morn till night is o'er;
Like magic, you will see us start and scatter thro' the land,
To pay the soldiers, or lease the border Contraband;
    Chorus: With our Promise to pay: How are you
        [Secretary Chase?
        Promise to pay: Oh! dat's what's de
        matter]

We're coming, Father Abraham, One hundred thousand more,
And cash was ne'er so easily evok'd from rags before,
To line the fat Contractor's purpose, or purchase transport craft,
Whose rotten hulks shall sink before the winds begin to waft:
    Chorus: With our Promise to pay: How are you,
        [Gideon Welles, Esquire?
        Promise to pay: Oh! can't you fix the
        date?]

We're coming, Father Abraham, Nine hundred thousand more,
With the greatest fighting Hero, that lives upon our shore;
He fought in all the battles won, and shed his blood most freely,
But he's fought them with the TRIBUNE, and his name is Gen'l
Greeley.
    Chorus: With our Promise to pay: How are you,
        [Black Brigade?
        Promise to pay: Three cheers for Father Abe!]
        (Copperhead Minstrel)

Abraham's Daughter
Words and Music by Septimus Winner

Various songs were composed to stir the Union spirits after the
early army reversals. Septimus Winner was violinist, composer and

arranger, who wrote songs under the pseudonyms of Percy Cruger, Mark Mason, Paul Stanton and Alice Hawthorne, under whose name "Abraham's Daughter" was published. He was author of such popular songs as "Listen to the Mocking Bird" and "Whispering Hope." "Abraham's Daughter" was written especially for the "Fire Zou-zous," a dashing regiment of the Union army. The song became popular in various versions. In it the nation ("Columbia") was synonymous with Lincoln, its personification. I give two versions.

> Oh, kind folks, listen to my song
> It is no idle story;
> All about a volunteer
> Who's going to fight for glory.
> Don't you think that I am right?
> For I am nothing shorter.
>
> *Chorus*
> And I belong to the Fire Zou-zous
> And don't you think you oughter?
> We're going down to Washington
> To fight for Abraham's daughter.
>
> Oh, should you ask me who she am,
> Columbia is her name, sir;
> She is the child of Abraham,
> Or Uncle Sam the same, sir;
> Now if I fight, why ain't' I right,
> And don't you think I oughter?
>
> *Chorus*
> The volunteers are pouring in
> From ev'ry loyal quarter,
> I'm going down to Washington
> To fight for Abraham's daughter.
>
> But let us lay all jokes aside,
> It is a sorry question;
> The man who would these states divide,
> Should hang for his suggestion.
> One country and one flag, I say,
> Whome'er the way may slaughter.

Chorus
And I belong to the Fire Zou-zous,
And don't you think I oughter?
We're going down to Washington
To fight for Abraham's daughter.

Abraham's Daughter, II

Oh! The soldiers here both far and near,
They did get quite excited,
When from their brethren of the South,
To war they were invited.
But it was to be, it is to be,
It can't be nothing shorter.
Oh! and if they call upon this child,
I'ze bond to die a martyr.

Chorus
For I belong to the Fire Zou-Zous
And don't you think I oughter?
I'm goin' down to Washington
To fight for Abraham's Daughter.

I am tired of a city life,
And I will join the Zou-Zous;
I'm going to try and make a hit
Down among the Southern foo-foos;
But if perchance I should get hit,
I'll show them I'm a tartar;
We are bound to save our Union yet,
'Tis all that we are arter.
Chorus

There is one thing more that I would state,
Before I close my ditty,
'Tis all about the volunteers
That's left our good old city.
They have gone to fight for the Stars and Stripes—
Our Union, now or never!
We will give three cheers for the volunteers,
And Washington forever.
Chorus
(*Songs of the Civil War* 102-103)

Abraham's Daughter
As sung by Ben Cotton, at Maguire's Opera House,
and encored to the echo

Oh, de soldiers here, both far and near, dey did get quite excited,
When from deir bredren from de Souf to war dey was invited;
But it was to be, it is to be, it can't be nothing shorter,
An' if dey call upon dis child, I'se bound to die a martyr.

Chorus:
For I belong to de Fire Zoo-zoos, an' don't you tink I orter?
An' I'm gwine down to Washington, to fight for Abraham's daughter.

I'm tired of a city life, an' I'm gwine to jine de Zoo-zoos;
I'm gwine to try an' make a hit, down 'mong de Southern foo-foos;
But if perchance I should get hit, I'll show dem I'm a tartar;
We are bound to save dis Union yet, 'tis all dat we are arter.

Dere is one ting more dat I would state, before I close my ditty,
'Tis all about de volunteers dat's left our good old city;
Dey've gone to fight for de stars an' stripes, our Union now or neber,
So we'll gib three cheers for de Volunteers, and Washington for ever!
(*John Brown and the Union Right or Wrong Songster*)

Black Brigade
A Walk-Around Dance—Composed by Old Dan Emmett

Solo:
Oh, where you gwine, Epheram? gwine to jine de Union?
    Oh, where you gwine, Epheram? hi ro we go;
Oh, where you gwine, Epheram? gwine to jine de Union?
Ha, ha, ha, ha! we are right from Lincom's land,

Chorus:
Den harness up de mule—be careful how you whip,
    An' mind your eye:
    Sam Johnson am de *nigger general*,
We's de Black Brigade, why don't you let her rip!
    Jeems Riber!   Massa Greeley, oh!

Solo:
Oh, we come from Ole Kentucky, gwine to jine de Union,
Oh, we come from Old Kentucky, hi ro we go;

Oh, we come from Old Kentucky, gwine to jine de Union;
Ha, ha, ha, ha! we are right from Lincom's Land.

Solo:
Oh, we come from Ole Missouri, gwine to jine de Union,
Oh, we come from Ole Missouri, hi ro we go;
Oh, we come from Old Missouri, gwine to jine de Union;
Ha, ha, ha, ha! we are right from Lincom's land.

(John Brown and the Union Right or Wrong Songster)

Abraham Lincoln
January First, Eighteen Hundred and Sixty Three
By W.D. Gallagher

Stand like an anvil, when 't is beaten
    With the full vigor of the smith's right arm!
Stand like the noble oak-tree, when 't is eaten
    By the Saperda and his ravenous swarm!
For many smiths will strike the ringing blows
Ere the red drama now enacting close;
And human insects, gnawing at thy fame,
Conspire to bring thy honored head to shame.

Stand like the firmament, upholden
    By an invisible but Almighty hand!
He whomsoever JUSTICE doth embolden,
    Unshaken, unseduced, unawed shall stand.
Invisible support is mightier far,
With noble aims, than walls of granite are;
And simple consciousness of justice gives
Strength to a purpose while that purpose lives.

Stand like the rock that looks defiant
    Far o'er the surging seas that lash its form!
Composed, determined, watchful, self-reliant,
    Be master of thyself, and rule the storm!
And thous shalt soon behold the bow of peace
Span the broad heavens, and the wild tumult cease;
And see the billows, with the clouds that meet,
Subdued and calm, come crouching to thy feet.

Kentucky, December, 1862
(Lyrics of Loyalty)

Abram Am De Man for Me
Air—Sally is the Gal

O, I'm a darkey sojer man,
But hab no vote, d'ye see.
Yet I am free to speak my mind,
"Uncle Abe am de man for me."
O white folks, list to me.
I'm glad dat I am free.
I'll drink dis toast from de old canteen:
"Uncle Abe am de man for me."

When dey marched us down to Washington,
Dare Honest Abe I see.
He made a speech, and said, boys, go,
"Your cause is Liberty."
O White folks, list to me. (etc.)
Dat's what dem darkies want so bad,
Dat libs in slavery,
I tink dey'll get it very soon,
"Uncle Abe am de man for me."
O white folks, list to me. (etc.)

Jeff Davis down in Dixie am,
But he won't long dare be.
Some day or odder he will swing
'Pon dat sour apple tree.
O white folks, list to me. (etc.)
Abram am de man for me,
And's a candidate again.
De white folks say now in deir songs,
Dey're gwine to 'lect him in.
O white folks, list to me. (etc.)
                    (*Lincoln and Johnson Songster*)

The Boat-Race
Original Ethiopian Song
By H.W. Egan
Air—Jamboree

I'm goin' to tell you of a race—
You'll find it somethin' new—

'Tween de rebel scow and Union boat,
  Wid a bully Yankee crew.

Chorus
  Je-ru-sa-lem—
  Je-ru-sa-lem—
De Union am a bully boat,
  And bound to get it through!

De scow was launched at Charleston,
  De captain's name was Jeff.
One Beauregard de steward,
  And de mate was Floyd de thief.
Chorus
  Je-ru-sa-lem— (etc.)

De boat was built in 'Seventy-six,
  And launched at Bunker Hill.
De Builder's name was Washington,
  De world owns his skill.
Chorus
  Je-ru-sa-lem— (etc.)

De scow at first shot out ahead—
  Dey hois'ed de rebel rag;
But Abe Lincoln jumped aboard de boat,
  And raised de Union flag.
Chorus
  Je-ru-sa-lem— (etc.)

General Scott was de captain,
  Wid de nation at his back;
And de only man to take de wheel
  Was gallant "Little Mac."
Chorus
  Je-ru-sa-lem— (etc.)

Soon de rebel scow was left behind,
  And all deir courage fled;
Fro while little Mac was kept aboard
  De "Union" went ahead.

Chorus
Je-ru-sa-lem— (etc.)

But de politicians jumped aboard,
    And nearly swamped de boat;
Now, de only way to save it
    Is to set dem all afloat.
Chorus
Je-ru-sa-lem— (etc.)

Now, de scow is up Salt River,
    Steerin' fast for dat "last ditch"—
And soon 'twill go to pieces,
    With each rebel son of a ——traitor.
Chorus
Je-ru-sa-lem— (etc.)
                              (*Black Diamond Songster*)

Bully for Him
Air—Bully for All

Huzza for Father Abraham,
    Bully for him, bully for him.
He's chief cook for Uncle Sam.
    Bully for him, bully for him.
With him our Uncle's satisfied,
    Bully for him, bully for him,
And asks no better for a guide,
    Bully for him, bully for him.
Fiddle it, whistle it, sing our song,
    Bully for him, bully for him,
Join in the chorus and help it along,
    Bully for him, bully for him.

'Midst all our troubles he has stood,
    Bully for him, bully for him,
And worked but for his country's good,
    Bully for him, bully for him.
His honesty'll retain him there,
    Bully for him, bully for him,

For four years more, in that same chair.
Bully for him, bully for him.
Fiddle it, whistle it, sing our song, (etc.)

Throw up your hats, and let us shout,
Bully for him, bully for him,
And let our foes know we're about,
Bully for him, bully for him.
To praise old Abe is our delight,
Bully for him, bully for him,
For he is on the side of right.
Bully for him, bully for him.
Fiddle it, whistle it, sing our song. (etc.)

There's Loyal Andy Johnson, too,
Bully for him, bully for him,
A spunky boy is he and true,
Bully for him, bully for him.
For Old Secesh he proved too smart,
Bully for him, bully for him,
He wouldn't side in their old cart.
Bully for him, bully for him.
Fiddle it, whistle it, sing our song, (etc.)

Now for Uncle Abe and Andy J.,
Bully for him, bully for him,
Let's roll the ball and clear the way,
Bully for him, bully for him.
Old issues now we'll cast aside,
Bully for him, bully for him.
Our Union is the "Nag" we ride.
Bully for him, bully for him.
Fiddle it, whistle it, sing our song, (etc.)
(Lincoln and Johnson Songster)

The Flag of Our Union
By A. Patriot

(2nd stanza)

Though God in his wisdom designed
That Rebels armed with weapons of thunder

Should in their unholy treason combined
    Cause the gallant Anderson to surrender:
Yet, the Union of lakes—the Union of lands—
    The Union of States none can sever;
For Uncle Abe Lincoln, and millions of hands
    Will sustain the Flag of our Union forever.
        And ever!
    The Flag of our Union forever.

              (*"Union" Songster*)

An Editor, announcing that he had been drafted,
discoursed as follows:

"Why should we mourn conscripted friends,
    Or shake at draft's alarms?
'Tis but the voice that Abr'am sends
    To make us shoulder arms.

        (*Civil War in Song and Story*)

Little Rhode Island
Air—Nice little, tight little Island

Comment on the valor and loyalty of Rhode Island in raising two regiments.

(4th of 4 stanzas)
Let traitors look out, for there's never a doubt
    That Uncle Abe's army will trip 'em;
And as for the loud Carolinian crowd,
    Rhode Island alone, sir, can whip em!
      Loyal and true little Rhody!
      Bully for you, little Rhody!
Governor Sprague is a very good egg.
And worthy to lead little Rhody!

        (*The Camp Fire Songster*)

Fillibuster Sam
An original Ethiopian act
Always received with immense applause
Air—Soap-Fat Man

(5 stanzas and chorus)

1)   Now, white folks, list to me tonight,
        For I'se gwine away wid de morning's light;
        By Uncle Abe I'm a soger made,
        And I'm goin' to fight wid de Black Brigade!
              My name is Fillibuster Sam,
              To fight de rebels I'm de man;
              Of old Jeff D. I'm not afraid
              Since I have joined de Black Brigade!

(Chorus and March)
I'll shoulder my old blunderbuss,
And jump right into de middle of de muss;
I'll fight like de debil, as hard as I can,
'Kase I'm a Union soger-man!

2)   I'll start right off to Richmond town,
        And den to Charleston I'll go down;
        De rebel roosters, all afraid,
        Will skedaddle from de Black Brigade,
              And den old Uncle Abe, you see,
              Will make a brigadier of me,
              'Kase I'm a Union soger-man—
              My name is Fillibuster Sam!
                        (*The Black Diamond Songster*)

Abraham, Our Abraham
Air—Maryland, My Maryland

Parodying songs or using their tunes for different words was common in both the North and South during the Civil War. "Maryland, My Maryland" or "Tannenbaum, O Tannenbaum!" was a favorite Southern song. The words were written by James Ryder Randall, in 1861, when he was twenty-two years old. The tune was originally based on the drinking song "Mini est Propositum" by Walter de Mapes, a 12th century Oxford deacon, and the later German folksong "Tannenbaum, O Tannenbaum." There were, of course, many parodies. The following two, one of which is light and the other especially vitriolic, are examples. The third is direct and serious.

Answer to "My Maryland"

The rebel feet are on our shore,
    Maryland, my Maryland!
I smell 'em half a mile or more,
    Maryland, my Maryland!
Their shockless hordes are at my door,
Their drunken generals on my floor,
What now can sweeten Baltimore?
    Maryland, my Maryland!

Hark to our noses' dire appeal,
    Maryland, my Maryland!
Oh unwashed Rebs, to you we kneel!
    Maryland, my Maryland!
If you can't purchase soap, oh steal
That precious article—I feel
Like scratching from the head to heel,
    Maryland, my Maryland!

You're covered thick with mud and dust,
    Maryland, my Maryland!
As though you'd been upon a bust,
    Maryland, my Maryland!

Remember, it is scarcely just,
To have a filthy fellow thrust
Before us, till he's been scrubbed fust,
    Maryland, my Maryland!

I see no blush upon thy cheek,
    Maryland, my Maryland!
It's not been washed for many a week,
    Maryland, my Maryland!
To get thee clean—'tis truth I speak—
Would dirty every stream and creek,
From Potomac to Chesapeake,
    Maryland, my Maryland!
       (*Songs of the Civil War* 73)

Kentucky! O Kentucky!

John Morgan's foot is on thy shore,
    Kentucky! O Kentucky!
His hand is on thy stable door,
    Kentucky! O Kentucky!
You'll see your good gray mare no more,
He'll ride her till her back is sore,
And leave her at some stranger's door,
    Kentucky! O Kentucky!

For feeding John you're paying dear,
    Kentucky! O Kentucky!
His very name now makes you fear,
    Kentucky! O Kentucky!
In every valley, far and near,
He's gobbled every horse and steer;
You'll rue his raids for many a year,
    Kentucky! O Kentucky!

Yet you have many a traitorous fool,
    Kentucky! O Kentucky!
Who still will be the Rebel's tool,
    Kentucky! O Kentucky!
They'll learn to yield to Abra'm's rule, .
In none but Johnny's costly school,
At cost of every "animule,"
    Kentucky! O Kentucky!
               (*Songs of the Civil War* 73)

Abraham, Our Abraham
Air—Maryland, My Maryland

We'll choose again for President,
    Abraham, our Abraham;
'Pon that we Union men are bent,
    Abraham, our Abraham.
Our ship will ride safe in his hands,
For he the helm understands,
And public sentiment demands
    Abraham, our Abraham.

As chief, Columbia greets him now,
    Abraham, our Abraham;
For honor marks his pallid brow,
    Abraham, our Abraham.
Retain him too, friends, we will there,
In that same Presidential chair,
Which freemen bid him guard with care,
    Abraham, our Abraham.

                        (*Lincoln and Johnson Songster*)

De Serenade

Get de bones and get de banjo, get de soundin' tamborine!
When de 'casion calls for moosic you can count dis nigger in;
And I feels de glow inspirin', as de instruments I take,
For de 'casion is a serenade for Mass Linkin's sake!
    Oh, limber up de fingers,
        Let the serenade begin!
    When de 'casion calls for moosic
        You can count dis nigger in.

Oh, de sangomingo darkeys had a standard which dey bore;
'Twas a pretty little baby's head, all dripping in its gore!
And if we undahstand aright de President's Proclaim,
He tells de Dixie niggers de may go and do de same!
    Oh, limber up de fingers,
        Let de serenade begin!
    When de 'casion calls for moosic
        You can count dis nigger in!

Oh, de Sangomingo darkies, dare old Massas took and tied,
And den dey got de handsaw and sawed 'em till dey died!
And after dey had sawed 'em till dey sawed away dare lives,
You may bet dey had a good time a kissin' ob dare wives!
    And if we understand him,
        Massa Linkin makes proclaim,
    Dat de niggers down in Dixie
        Have a right to do de same!

Massa Beecher! Massa Cheever! you must set apart a day,
And get your Congo-rations for the handsaws for to pay;

De little baby's curly head ourselves can easy get,
And spike it to de standard while its dripping warm and wet!
    On de old plantation homestead,
        Waits de woe widout a name,
    If darkeys undahstand aright
        The President's proclaim!

Oh, wake up, Massa Linkin! for the night is not far spent,
And hear de fee Americans ob African descent,
Wid de bones and wid de banjo, and de soundin' tamborine,
We have come to serenade you ere de sawin' we begin;
    We have come to serenade you,
        Ere we raise, with life blood red,
    De Sangomingo standard
        Of de little baby's head!
                (*Copperhead Minstrel*)

To President Lincoln

Proudest of all earth's thrones
    Is he who rules by a free people's choice;
Who, midst fierce party strife and battle groans,
Hears, ever rising in harmonious tones,
    A grateful people's voice.

Steadfast in thee we trust,
    Tried as no man was ever tried before;
God made thee merciful—God keep thee just;
Be true—and triumph over all thou must.
    God bless thee evermore!
        (*Civil War in Song and Story*)

White Soldier's Song
Air—John Brown

"John Brown's Body," one of the fierce songs of the Civil War, has a complex history. The words are anonymous though attributed to Charles S. Hall, or Henry Howard Brownell, or Thomas Brigham Bishop. The tune is based on "Glory, Glory, Hallelujah." The song was, of course, inspired by the hanging of John Brown (1800-1859) on

December 2, 1859 for his raid on Harper's Ferry (1859). The song was sung by the Boston Light Infantry at Fort Marion in 1861. The heavy marching tune was perfect for the tune of the new song "Battle Hymn of the Republic," by Julia Ward Howe (1862). The line in the John Brown song "Hang John Brown to a sour apple tree" served also in parodies to give the same fate to Abraham Lincoln and Jefferson Davis.

> Tell Abe Lincoln that he'd better end the war,
> Tell Abe Lincoln what we all came out here for,
> Tell Abe Lincoln 'twas the Union to restore,
> As we go marching on.—Chorus.
>
> Tell Abe Lincoln to let the nigger be,
> Tell Abe Lincoln that we don't want him free,
> Tell Abe Lincoln that to this he did agree,
> As we, (etc.)—Chorus.
>
> Tell Abe Lincoln the Constitution is our guide,
> Tell Abe Lincoln by the laws he must abide,
> Tell Abe Lincoln to let his proclamation slide,
> As we, (etc.)—Chorus.
>
> Tell Abe Lincoln and his wooly-headed crew,
> Tell Abe Lincoln his suspension writ won't do,
> Tell Old Abe we are going to put him through,
> As we, (etc.)—Chorus.
>
> Tell Abe Lincoln of Antietam's bloody dell,
> Tell Abe Lincoln where a thousand heroes fell,
> Tell Abe Lincoln and his gang to go to h—,
> And we'll go marching HOME.—Chorus.
> *(Copperhead Minstrel)*

It Reminds Him of a Story

In 1864, when General George B. McClellan was running for President, his supporters pulled all stops in their efforts to ridicule and denigrate Lincoln, as the following song demonstrates.

> We're in the Rebellion now, the greatest one in history!
> And why it isn't settled, remains to us a mystery:

Five hundred thousand slain and the battlefield's all gory,
But Abe Lincoln takes it cool, it reminds him of a story.
Abe Lincoln is always joking, and widows are all weeping,
Oh husbands lost in battle, and under Southern soil now sleeping.

McClellan is our choice, the favorite of the nation,
One whom we choose to lead us to our former glorious station;
Our enemies they curse him; for they know he's hunky-dory,
It's about time to tell Abe Lincoln: this reminds me of a story.
                              (*Songs of the Civil War* 90)

                         Booth Killed Lincoln

     The assassination of Lincoln was by all standards the greatest
tragedy that could have devastated the newly saved Union. The horror of
it broke many hearts. The following ballad about it is typical of folk ballads in giving the whole core of the event. This folk ballad was recorded
by ballad collector Bascom Lamar Lunsford of South Turkey Creek,
North Carolina, who said that the song was widespread in his family and
elsewhere:

     "The title of this ballad is 'Booth,' or 'Booth Killed Lincoln.' It's an
old fiddle tune, and there are a few variants of the song. I heard my
father hum and sing a few of the stanzas when I was just a boy about six
or ten years old."

                    Wilkes Booth came to Washington,
                    An actor great was he,
                    He played at Ford's theater,
                    And Lincoln went to see.

                    It was early in April,
                    Not many weeks ago,
                    The people of this fair city
                    All gathered at the show.

                    The war it is all over,
                    The people happy now,
                    And Abraham Lincoln
                    Arose to make his bow;

The people cheer him wildly,
Arising to their feet,
And Lincoln waving of his hand,
He calmly takes his seat.

And while he sees the play go on,
His thoughts are running deep,
His darling wife, close by his side,
Has fallen fast asleep.

From the box there hangs a flag,
It is not the Stars and Bars,
The flag that holds within its folds
Bright gleaming Stripes and Stars.

J. Wilkes Booth he moves down the aisle,
He had measured once before,
He passes Lincoln's bodyguard
A-nodding at the door.

He holds a dagger in his right hand,
A pistol in his left,
He shoots poor Lincoln in the temple,
And sends his soul to rest.

The wife awakes from slumber,
And screams in her rage,
Booth jumps over the railing
And lands him on the stage.

He'll rue the day, he'll rue the hour,
As God him life shall give,
When Booth stood in the center of the stage,
Crying, "Tyrants shall not live!"

The people all excited then,
Cried everyone, "A hand!"
Cried all the people near,
"For God's sake, save that man!"

Then Booth ran back with boot and spur
Across the backstage floor,
He mounts that trusty claybank mare,
All saddled at the door.

J. Wilkes Booth, in his last play,
All dressed in broadcloth deep,
He gallops down the alleyway,
I hear those horses feet.

Poor Lincoln then was heard to say,
And all has gone to rest,
"Of all the actors in this town,
I loved Wilkes Booth the best."
                    (*Songs of the Civil War* 111-112)

We'll Fight for Uncle Abe
Words by C.E. Pratt
Music by Frederick Buckley

The South, especially in the early years, was not solidly for secession. There were always pockets of resistance by the poor whites who
insisted that the idea of rebellion would be a rich man's war and a poor
man's fight. In the following song, Grant was at Vicksburg 29 April-July
1863. Richmond, after a long siege, fell April 3, 1865. There were
numerous C.S.A. generals named Johnson. George Brinton McClellan
(1826-1885) was a brilliant theoretician and strategist but would not
fight. He was relieved of command of the Union army after Antietam,
when he would not pursue Lee.

Way down in Old Varginni,
I suppose you all do know,
They have tried to bust the Union,
But they find it is no go;
The Yankee boys are starting out
The Union for to save,
And we're going down to Washington
To fight for Uncle Abe. *Chorus:*
Rip, Rap, Flip, Flap,
Strap your knapsack on your back,
For we're goin' down to Washington
To fight for Uncle Abe.

There is General Grant at Vicksburg,
Just see what he has done,
He has taken sixty cannon
And made the Rebels run,

And next he will take Richmond,
I'll bet you half a dollar,
And if he catches General Johnson,
Oh won't he make him holler.(*Chorus*)

The season now is coming
When the roads begin to dry;
Soon the Army of the Potomac
Will make the Rebels fly,
For General McClellan, he's the man,
The Union for to save;
Oh! Hail Columbia's right side up,
And so's your Uncle Abe. (*Chorus*)

You may talk of Southern chivalry
And cotton being king,
But I guess before the war is done
You'll think another thing;
They say that recognition
Will the Rebel country save,
But Johnny Bull and Mister France
Are 'fraid of Uncle Abe. (*Chorus*)
            (*Songs of the Civil War*)

Yankee Doodle for Lincoln

Lincoln both individually and symbolically represented the North in the Union and in the Confederacy. It was only natural therefore that he be brought into all kinds of songs as frequently as possible. Perhaps it was most natural that one of the pro-Union songs declare that even Yankee Doodle—famous symbol and song since the Revolution—was pushing for Lincoln. In that song, Hannibal Hamlin (1809-1891), Senator from Maine before joining Lincoln on the Presidential ticket, was a moderate former Democrat who was pro-emancipation and unsuccessfully pushed Lincoln toward freeing the slaves long before the Emancipation Proclamation, January 1, 1863. It was only natural also that there be "Confederate Yankee Doodle" answers, as the following examples demonstrate.

Old Abe's elected so they say
Along with Darkey Hamlin,

The Yankees think they'll gain the day
By nigger votes and gamblin'.
(Ozark Folksongs 11, 317)

Confederate Yankee Doodle
Air—Yankee Doodle

Yankee Doodle had a mind
To whip the Southern "traitors,"
Because they didn't choose to live
On codfish and potatoes.
    Yankee Doodle, doodle-doo,
    Yankee Doodle dandy,
    And so to keep his courage up
    He took a drink of brandy.

Yankee Doodle said he found
By all the census figures,
That he could starve the Rebels out
If he could steal their niggers.
    Yankee Doodle, doodle-doo,
    Yankee Doodle dandy,
    And then he took another drink
    Of gunpowder and brandy.

Yankee Doodle made a speech;
'Twas very full of feeling:
I fear, says he, I cannot fight,
But I am good at stealing.
    Yankee Doodle, doodle-doo,
    Yankee Doodle dandy,
    Hurrah for Lincoln, he's the boy
    To take a drop of brandy.

Yankee Doodle drew his sword,
And practiced all the passes;
Come, boys, we'll take another drink
When we get to Manassas.
    Yankee Doodle, doodle-doo,
    Yankee Doodle dandy,

They never reached Manassas plain,
And never got the brandy.

Yankee Doodle soon found out
That Bull Run was no trifle;
For if the North knew how to steal,
The South knew how to rifle.
> Yankee Doodle, doodle-doo,
> Yankee Doodle dandy,
> 'Tis very clear I took too much
> Of that infernal brandy.

Yankee Doodle wheeled about,
And scampered off at full run,
And such a race was never seen
As that he made at Bull Run.
> Yankee Doodle, doodle-doo,
> Yankee Doodle dandy,
> I haven't time to stop just now
> To take a drop of brandy.

Yankee Doodle, oh! For shame,
You're always intermeddling;
Let guns alone, they're dangerous things;
You'd better stick to peddling.
> Yankee Doodle, doodle-doo,
> Yankee Doodle dandy,
> When next I go to Bully Run
> I'll throw away the brandy.

Yankee Doodle, you had ought
To be a little smarter;
Instead of catching woolly heads,
I vow you've caught a tartar.
> Yankee Doodle, doodle-doo,
> Yankee Doodle dandy,
> Go to hum, you've had enough,
> Of Rebels and of brandy.
> > (*Songs of the Civil War* 203)

Yankee Doodle for Lincoln

Yankee Doodle does as well
  As anybody can, sir;
And like the ladies, he's for Abe,
  And Union to a man, sir.

Yankee Doodle never fails,
  When he resolves to try, sir;
To elect a man who can't split rails
  That's just "all my eye, sir."

Yankee Doodle's come to town and
  On mature reflection
He's gonna do the Slavites brown
  At the next election.

Yankee Doodle cuts a swell,
  Although he will not bet, sir,
Yet he goes in for Abraham and
  Hamlin of old Maine, sir.

And he invites you one and all,
  No matter what your station
To vote for Freedom and Free Soil
  (And that will save the nation!)
    (*Americans and Their Songs*)

Jeff in Petticoats

Men's disguising themselves by dressing in women's clothing
seemed especially comical to people during the Civil War period, especially when the disguised person was such a stiff, severe, dignified and
hated person as the President of the defeated Confederacy. In trying to
escape, Davis was apprehended in Georgia just seventy miles from the
Florida state line on May 10. He was in company with his wife when
Federal soldiers stopped him. One opened Mrs. Davis' trunk and pulled
out a hooped skirt she had never worn. Davis rushed forward to try to
prevent the soldier's turning out the trunk. Obviously Davis did not have
it on, but within a week word spread that he had been arrested wearing

his wife's skirt. The minstrel shows could not resist laughing at what would have been to them a comical figure, just as Lincoln had been accused of disguising himself in Baltimore when he was traveling to Washington for his Inauguration. "Jeff in Petticoats" has been identified as "Words by Henry Tucker, Music by George Cooper," and "Words by George Cooper, Music by Henry Tucker."

> Jeff Davis was a hero bold,
> You've heard of him, I know,
> He tried to make himself a King
> Where southern breezes blow;
> But "Uncle Sam," he laid the youth
> Across his mighty knee,
> And spanked him well,
> And that's the end
> Of brave old Jeffy D.
> *Chorus*:
> Oh! Jeffy D! You "flow'r of chivalree,"
> Oh royal Jeffy D!
> You'r empire's but a tin-clad skirt,
> Of charming Jeffy D.
>
> This Davis, he was always full
> Of bluster and of brag,
> He swore, on all our Northern walls,
> He's plant his Rebel rag;
> But when to battle he did go,
> He said, "I'm not so green,
> To dodge the bullets, I will wear
> My tin-clad crinoline." (Chorus)
>
> Now when he saw the game was up,
> He started for the woods,
> His bandbox hung upon his arm
> Quite full of fancy goods;
> Said Jeff, "They'll never take me now,
> I'm sure I'll not be seen.
> They'd never think to look for me
> Beneath my crinoline." (Chorus)
>
> Jeff took with him, the people say,
> A mine of golden coin,

Which he, from banks and other places,
Managed to purloin;
But while he ran, like every thief,
He had to drop the spoons,
And maybe that's the reason why
He dropped his pantaloons. (Chorus)

Our Union boys were on his track
For many nights and days,
His palpitating heart it beat,
Enough to burst his stays;
Oh! what a dash he must have cut
With form so tall and lean;
Just fancy now the "What is it?"
Dressed up on crinoline! (Chorus)

The ditch that Jeff was hunting for,
He found was very near;
He tried to "shift" his base again,
His neck felt rather queer;
Just on the out-"skirts" of a wood
His dainty shape was seen,
His boots stuck out, and now they'll hang
Old Jeff in crinoline. (Chorus)
(Songs of the Civil War 343)

President Lincoln's Inaugural Address
(in Advance of all Competitors.)
by a "Southern Rights" Man

I come at the people's mad-jority call,
To open the Nation's quarternary ball,
And invite black and white to fall into ranks
To dance a State jig on Republican planks.

I'll fiddle like Nero when Rome was on fire,
And play any tune that the people desire.
So let us be merry—whatever the clatter be—
Whilst playing: "O dear! O me! what can the matter be?"

I've made a great speech for the people's diversion,
And talked about billet-doux love, and coercion;

Of the spot I was born, of the place I was reared,
And the girl that I kissed on account of my beard.

I'll settle the tariff—there's no one can doubt it—
But, as yet, I know nothing or little about it;
And as for those Southerners' bluster and clatter,
I know very well that there's nothing the matter.

You've oft heard repeated those wonderful tales
Of my beating a giant in splitting up rails;
And ere I left home—you know the fact is true—
That I beat a small Giant at politics, too.

Should it now be the will of the North and the Fates,
I can do it up Brown by the splitting of States;
and then when the State-splitting business fails,
I'll resume my old trade as a splitter of rails.

Baltimore, April 23, 1861.   —*Baltimore Republican*

SONGS AGAINST LINCOLN

Lincoln was, of course, also the butt of many songs throughout the Copperheads of the Union and the Secessionists of the Confederacy. The following examples, though undoubtedly not exhaustive, catalogue the directions and means such songs followed.

Lincoln's Troops
Air—Dixie

"Dixie" or "Dixie's Land" (1860), words and music written by Daniel Decatur Emmett (1815-1904), was a "walk-around" for the closing number of Dan Bryant's minstrels, when the entire company paraded on stage. Undoubtedly it was the most famous and most-often sung piece during the Civil War, especially in the South. Its self-assuring magic with troops, especially Southern warriors, can be illustrated by an anecdote:

"I WISH I WAS IN DIXIE!"

PLAINTIVE AIR—Sung nightly in Washington by that Celebrated Delineator, ABRAHAM LINCOLN.

I wish I was in Dixie;
In Dixie's land
I'll take my stand,
And live and die in Dixie.
Away, away,
Away down South in Dixie—

A Negro's Account of the Wild Cat Retreat

A gentleman whose slave accompanied a young confederate officer on the Wild Cat expedition, asked the darky on his return to Nashville, how long the army was on the march from its encampment to the battle-field. "About four days," was the reply. "Well, how long were they in marching back?" "About two days, massa." "Why, how is that, Joe? Could the men travel any faster back, when they were broken down with four days' march and a severe fight, than they travelled forward after a good rest in camp?" "Oh! I'll tell you what made the difference, massa," said old Joe; "it was the music. They marched toward Wild Cat to the tune of Dixie. When they marched back, the tune was; "Fire in the mountains—run, boys, run!" (*Rebellion Record* 50)

The South's appropriation of "Dixie" for its own purposes thoroughly annoyed Emmett who was a War Democrat born in Ohio and loyal to the Union. Emmett, continuing in show business after the War, sang his song in his eightieth year when making successful tours with the Al G. Fields Minstrels and would "bring down the house," though many in the audience would admit that the quality of Emmett's voice was not what it once was. Emmett had sold his copyright to "Dixie" to his publisher for $500 and died poor on his farm in Ohio. "Dixie" served somewhat as the overture and finale of the Civil War. Davis had it played at his inauguration in Montgomery, Alabama, February 1861, and Lincoln, upon hearing of Lee's surrender at Appomattox, had the band at the White House play the song, which had always somewhat contained the essence of the South to him and had been one of his favorites. "I thought 'Dixie' one of the best tunes I ever heard," he said in ordering that it be played. The Daughters of the Confederacy collected twenty-two Southern versions of the song, which was probably only a fraction of the number in vogue during the War. The following three versions demonstrate the drift and treatment of many of those variants.

Southern Land
Air—Dixie's Land

I.

We dwell where skies are bright above us,
Cheered by smiles from all who love us.
    Sing away, sing away in our dear Southern land!
For to this home of our affection
Here we give our strong protection.
    Sing away, sing away, &c.

Chorus
For in freedoms' cause we rally,
　　　For aye, for aye.
In this dear land we take our stand;
　　　Till death we will defend her!
Then rise, boys, rise;
　　　We never will surrender!
With heart and hand
　　　We ever will defend her.

II
Our soil from tyrant hordes defending,
Freely life and fortune spending.
　　　Sing away, sing away, &c.
We'll never yield the rights we cherish;
Stand we firm, or nobly perish!
　　　Sing away, sing away, &c.

Chorus
For in freedom's cause we rally, &c.

III
Our chief is one whose praise and glory
Men shall read in future story.
　　　Sing away, sing away, &c.
He who defends the right shall merit
Brightest honor to inherit!
　　　Sing away, sing away, &c.

Chorus
For in freedom's cause we rally, &c.

IV
Then let us not give place to sadness;
All our songs should be of gladness.
　　　Sing away, sing away, &c.
No wrong or strife the truth can alter;
In duty's path we'll never falter.
　　　Sing away, sing away, &c.

Chorus
For in freedom's cause we rally, &c.

V

"No breach of faith" our honor staining;
Still our rectitude maintaining.
　　　Sing away, sing away, &c.
Our plighted words remain unbroken;
Deeds may best men's hearts betoken.
　　　Sing away, sing away, &c.

Chorus
For in freedom's cause we rally, &c.

Dixie

Southrons, hear your country call you!
Up! lest worse than death befall you!
To arms! to arms! to arms! in Dixie!
Lo! all the beacon-fires are lighted;
Let all hearts be now united!
To arms! to arms! to arms! in Dixie!
Advance the flag of Dixie!
　　　Hurrah! hurrah!

Chorus—For Dixie's land we'll take our stand,
To live or die for Dixie!
　　　To arms! to arms!
And conquer peace for Dixie!
　　　To arms! to arms!
And conquer peace for Dixie.

Hear the Northern thunders mutter!
Northern flags in South winds flutter!
Send them back your fierce defiance,
Stamp upon the accurs'd alliance!

Fear no danger! shun no labor!
Lift up rifle, pike and sabre!
Shoulder pressing close to shoulder,
Let the odds make each heart bolder!

How the South's great heart rejoices
At your cannons' ringing voices;

For faith betrayed and pledges broken,
Wrong inflicted, insults spoken.

Swear upon your country's altar
Never to submit or falter,
Till the spoilers are defeated,
Till the Lord's work is completed.

Halt not till our federation
Secures among earth's powers its station!
Then at peace, and crowned with glory,
Hear your children tell the story.

If loved ones weep in sadness,
Victory soon shall bring them gladness,
Exultant pride soon banish sorrow,
Smiles chase tears away to-morrow.

The Song of the Exile
Air—Dixie

Oh! here I am in the land of cotton,
The flag once honor'd is now forgotten;
    Fight away, fight away, fight away for Dixie's land.
But here I stand for Dixie dear,
To fight for freedom, without fear;
    Fight away, fight away, fight away for Dixie's land.

Chorus—For Dixie's land I'll take my stand, to live or die for
Dixie's land;
    Fight away, fight away, fight away for Dixie's land.

Abe Lincoln tore through Baltimore,
In a baggage-care with fastened door;
    Fight away, fight away, fight away for Dixie's land.
And left his wife, alas! alack!
To perish on the railroad track!
    Fight away, fight away, fight away for Dixie's land.
                    Chorus

We have no ships, we have no navies,
But mighty faith in the great Jeff Davis;
    Fight away, fight away, fight away for Dixie's land.
Brave old Missouri shall be ours,
Despite Abe Lincoln's Northern powers;
    Fight away, fight away, fight away for Dixie's land.
                  Chorus

Abe's proclamation, in a twinkle,
Stirred up the blood of Rip Van Winkle;
    Fight away, fight away, fight away for Dixie's land.
Jeff Davis' answer was short and curt:
"Fort Sumter's taken, and nobody's hurt!"
    Fight away, fight away, fight away for Dixie's land.
                  Chorus

We hear the words of this same ditty,
To the right and left of the Mississippi;
    Fight away, fight away, fight away for Dixie's land.
In the land of flowers, hot and sandy,
From Delaware Bay to Rio Grande;
    Fight away, fight away, fight away for Dixie's land.
                  Chorus

The ladies cheer with heart and hand
The men who fight for Dixie land;
    Fight away, fight away, fight away for Dixie's land.
The "Stars and Bars" are waving o'er us,
And independence is before us;
    Fight away, fight away, fight away for Dixie's land.
                  Chorus

I Wish I Was in Dixie

I wish I was in Dixie;
    In Dixie's land
    I'll take my stand,
And live and die in Dixie.
    Away, away,
Away down South in Dixie—

The Song of the Exile

Oh! here I am in the land of cotton,
The flag once honored is now forgotten;
   Fight away, fight away, fight away for Dixie's land.
But here I stand for Dixie dear,
To fight for freedom, without fear;
   Fight away, fight away, fight away for Dixie's land.

Chorus
For Dixie's land I'll take my stand,
To live or die for Dixie's land.
Fight away, fight away, fight away for Dixie's land.

Oh! have you heard the latest news,
Of Lincoln and his kangaroos;
   Fight away, etc.
His minions they would now oppress us,
With war and bloodshed they'd distress us!
   Fight away, etc.

Abe Lincoln tore through Baltimore,
In a baggage-car with fastened door;
   Fight away, etc.
And left his wife alas! alack!
To perish on the railroad track!
   Fight away, etc.

Abe Lincoln is the President,
He'll wish his days in Springfield spent;
   Fight away, etc.
We'll show him that Old Scott's a fool,
We'll never submit to Yankee rule!
   Fight away, etc.

At first our States were only seven,
But now we number stars eleven;
   Fight away, etc.
Brave old Missouri shall be ours,
Despite old Lincoln's Northern powers!
   Fight away, etc.

We have no ships, we have no navies,
But mighty faith in the great Jeff Davis;
    Fight away, etc.
Due honor too we will award,
To gallant Bragg and Beauregard!
    Fight away, etc.

Abe's proclamation in a twinkle,
Stirred up the blood of Rip Van Winkle;
    Fight away, etc.
Jeff Davis' answer was short and curt
"Fort Sumter's taken, and 'nobody's hurt'!"
    Fight away, etc.

We hear the words of this same ditty,
To the right and left of the Mississippi;
    Fight away, etc.
In the land of flowers hot and sandy,
From Delaware Bay to the Rio Grande!
    Fight away, etc.

The ladies cheer with heart and hand,
The men who fight for Dixie's land;
    Fight away, etc.
The "Stars and Bars" are waving o'er us,
And Independence is before us!
    Fight away, etc.
                   (Rebellion Record 51)

Lincoln's Troops
Air—Dixie

Lincoln's troops, infatuated fools,
    Taught in Abolition schools,
Are coming South to pull their triggers,
Kill our boys and free our niggers.
    But how cowardly they will feel
    When first approaching Southern steel
    With one hurrah! we'll sally forth
    And kill those rascals of the North.

Lincoln, in a fit of frenzy,
Will be seized with influenza.
His care's so great he can't be civil,
He'll follow John Brown to the devil.
   (*War Songs and Poems of the Southern Confederacy*)

Root Hog or Die

"Root Hog or Die" was a popular song on the minstrel stage in the 1850s. It was published in *The Dime Song Book* (Boston, 1859) with parodies in minstrel lingo. It appeared in *The Arkansas Traveller's Songster* (New York, c. 1864) and in *Poetry of the Civil War* (New York, 1866). The homily is a universal statement that in America one must make his own way or perish; in other words every hog has to provide his own food. Because the tune was catchy and easy to learn, it was used often for both Northern and Southern songs, often with snatches from other songs attached.

In this first version, "Sumpter" refers to Fort Sumter, chief Federal fort in Charleston Harbor, which fell April 14, 1861, to Confederate troops commanded by Gen. Pierre Gustave Toutant Beauregard, C.S.A. (1818-1893).

In the second version, "Colonel Seigle" is Gen. Franz Sigel (1824-1902) who was born in Germany but in 1848 emigrated to the U.S. and commanded troops in many Civil War battles. The Dutch are, of course, Germans. Ben McCulloch (1811-1862), C.S.A. was in command of Confederate troops at Wilson's Creek and at Pea Ridge, where he was killed March 7, 1862 by sharpshooters. "The Lion" is Nathaniel Lyon (1818-1861), USA, who, in the inconclusive battle at Wilson's creek, in which the Confederates claimed victory, was killed.

In the third version, "Root, Abe, or Die," the reference to defeat at Carthage is to the fact that on July 5, 1861, at Carthage, Missouri, Gen. Sigel had been outnumbered by Confederate troops and retreated without putting up much fight.

In the fourth version, "Root Hog or Die (Southern Version)," Beauregard is Pierre Gustave Beauregard (1818-1893), C.S.A. The battle of Trenton, Tennessee, occurred December 20, 1862.

Old Abe Lincoln keeps kicking up a fuss,
I think he'd better stop it, he'll only make it worse,
We'll have our independence, I'll tell you the reason why,
Jeff Davis he will make them sing Root Hog or Die.

When Lincoln went to reinforce Sumpter for the fight
He told his men to pass through the harbor in the night,
He said to them be careful, I'll tell you the reason why,
The Southern boys are mighty bad on Root Hog or Die.

Then Beauregard he called a halt according to the style,
The Lincolnists they faced about and looked mighty wild,
They couldn't give the password, I'll tell you the reason why,
Beauregard's countersign was Root Hog or Die.

They anchored out a battery upon the waters free,
It was the queerest looking thing that ever you did see,
It was the fall of Sumpter, I'll tell you the reason why,
It was the Southern alphabet of Root Hog or Die.

They telegraphed to Abraham they took her like a flirt,
They underscored another line, there was nobody hurt,
We are bound to have the capital, I'll tell you the reason why,
We want to teach old Abe to sing Root Hog or Die.
                    (*Ozark Folksongs* II, 164-165)

We are a band of brothers
Natives of our soil
Fighting for the property
We gained by honest toil.
And all along the ranks
They all did cry,
Tomorrow boys, we'll make the Dutch
Root hog or die.

Hurrah, boys, hurrah,
We rangers know our rights,
And if they trample on our toes
We'll make them see sights.
The Lion cease to roar
And old Segals' on the shy,

Big Abe, little Abe,
Root hog or die.

If Abe isn't satisfied
And wants to fight again
All he has to do is
Just muster up his men.
To whip old Ben McCulloch
He can always get to try,
But he'll find the southern boys
Won't root hog or die.

(*Ozark Folksongs* II, 319)

Root, Abe, or Die

The Dutch came to Missouri, as well you all do know,
To subjugate the rebel boys but couldn't make it go.
They can't whip the rebel boys, and I'll tell you the reason why:
The Southern boys made them run—Root hog or die.

Colonel Seigle came to Carthage to whip the rebel crew,
To feed us to the buzzards, and hang Claib Jackson too.
But they couldn't make the riffle; and I'll tell you the reason why:
The Southern boys made them get—Root hog or die.

Then Lyon came to Springfield to take another stand,
He said he's whip us this time and drive us from our land.
He found us down on Wilson's Creek, to whale us he did try;
But the Southern boys made them get—Root hog or die.

'Twas on the tenth of August we heard the Lyon roar.
The grape-shot and minnie balls around like hail did pour.
But our shotguns did the work for them, and I'll tell you the reason
why:
The Southern boys made them get. Root hog or die!

'Twas there Lyon bit the dust and Seigle ran away,
Just as he did at Carthage upon a former day.
They left their wounded on the field, and I'll tell you the reason
why:
The Southern boys were after them, root hog or die.

(*Ozark Folksongs* II, 361)

Root Hog or Die (Southern Version)

Old Abe Lincoln keeps kicking up a fuss,
I think he'd better stop it, he'll only make it worse,
We'll have our Independence—I'll tell you the reason why,
Jeff Davis he will make them sing "Root Hog or Die!"

When Lincoln went to reinforce Sumter for the fight
He told his men to pass through the harbor in the night,
He said to them be careful, I'll tell you the reason why,
The Southern boys are mighty bad on "Root Hog or Die!"

Then Beauregard he called a halt according to the style,
The Lincolnites they faced about and looked mighty wild,
They couldn't give the password, I'll tell you the reason why,
Beauregard's countersign was "Root Hog or Die!"

They anchored out a battery upon the waters free,
It was the queerest looking thing that ever you did see—
It was the fall of Sumter, I'll tell you the reason why,
It was the Southern alphabet of "Root Hog or Die!"

They telegraphed to Abraham they took her like a flirt;
They underscored another line—"There was nobody hurt."
We are bound to have the Capital, I'll tell you the reason why,
We want to teach Old Abe to sing "Root Hot or Die!"

When Abra'm read the dispatch, the tear came in his eye,
He walled his eyes to Bobby, and Bob began to cry.
They prayed for Jeff to spare them, I'll tell you the reason why,
They didn't want to *mark time* to "Root Hog or Die!"

The "Kentucky Braves" at Trenton are eager for the fight—
They want to help the Southern boys to set old Abra'm right;
They had to leave their native State, I'll tell you the reason why,
Old Kentucky wouldn't sing, "Root Hog or Die!"

(*Songs of the Civil War* 243)

Old Abe and Old Nick
Air—Lord Lovel

'Twas one winter night Abe Lincoln, he lay,
    Resting his weary head,
Strange stories to tell, the devil appeared,
    And unto Abe Lincoln he said-said-said,
    And unto Abe Lincoln he said.

If you'll sell me your soul I'll make you king,
    And destroy your countaree.
"It's a go," said Old Abe, almost out of breath,
    A man of my word I will be-be-be,
    A man of my word I will be.

Then he sent for Seward and Simon the thief,
    And Wells and Bates and Blair,
To these trusty old traitors, Abe Lincoln he said
    In my new nigger kingdom you'll share-share-share,
    In my new nigger kingdom you'll share.

The devil he came, and asked for his claim,
    Old Abe knew not what to do;
Said the devil, make haste, I've no time to waste,
    For Old Nick is waiting for you-you-you,
    For Old Nick is waiting for you.
                                        (*Copperhead Minstrel*)

Honest Old Abe

Honest old Abe, when the war first began,
Denied abolition was part of his plan;
Honest old Abe has since made a decree,
The war must go on till the slaves are all free.
As both can't be honest, will some one tell how,
If honest Abe then, he is dishonest Abe now.
                                        (*Copperhead Minstrel*)

True to His Name

In ancient days, Jehovah said,
    In voice both sweet and calm,
Be Abraham's name forever changed
    To that of Abraham!

'T was then decreed his progeny
    Should occupy high stations,
For Abraham, in Hebrew, means
    "Father of many nations!"

In our own land an Abraham,
    With speeches wise nor witty,
Went down to our Jerusalem,
    The famous Federal city.

True to his name, this Abraham,
    So changed are his relations,
Instead of one great nation, be
    "Father of many nations."

New Orleans True Delta.
    (*Rebel Rhymes and Rhapsodies*)

The Girl I Left Behind Me

The following fragment is the variant of "The Girl I Left Behind Me," a famous song in American history. The words were written by Samuel Lover, an Irish novelist, the melody we now have was "taken down by A. O'Neil, harper, A.D. 1800." The song is most widely known as a fife tune and was especially popular with both Federal and Confederate fifers. The spirit and direction of the original can be gathered from the concluding stanza of one early version:

Some future day shall crown us
    The masters of the main.
Our fleets shall speak in thunder
    To England, France and Spain;
And the nations o'er the ocean's spread
    Shall tremble and obey

The sons, the sons, the sons, the sons
Of brave America.

An anti-Lincoln version contained the following verse:

If ever I get through this war,
And Lincoln's chains don't bind me,
I'll make my way to Tennessee—
To the girl I left behind me.
                    (*Confederate Veteran*, Aug. 1895, 205)

Pop Goes the Weasel

"Pop Goes the Weasel" was one of the most famous tunes of the
Civil War period. It was written in 1853 possibly by Charles Twiggs,
based on a traditional English dance. In London in 1853, the custom was
for hatters to pawn ("pop") their hats ("weasels") on Saturday night.
"Old Scott" mentioned was General Winfield Scott (1786-1866), first
commander of the Union forces. Manassas refers to the first battle, July
1861, along Bull Run, VA., as it was called by Southerners or First Manassas, as called by Federals.

The second version is a longer and differently oriented folk version.

King Abraham is very sick,
Old Scott has got the measles,
Manassas we have now at last—
    Pop goes the weasel!

All around the cobbler's house
The monkey chased the people,
And after them in double haste
    Pop goes the weasel!

When the night walks in as black as a sheep,
And the hen on her eggs was fast asleep,
When into her nest with a serpent's creep
    Pop goes the weasel!

Of all the dance that ever was planned
To galvanize the heel and the hand,

There's none that moves so gay and grand
As pop goes the weasel!
(*War Songs and Poems of the Southern Confederacy* 387)

Old Abe is sick, old Abe is sick,
Old Abe is sick in bed.
He's a lying dog, a dying dog,
With meanness in his head.

He wants our cotton, he wants our cotton,
He wants our cotton, too.
He shall have it, he will have it—
Some tar and feathers, too.

Down with old Abe, down with old Abe,
And all his Yankee crew.
Up! up! with Jeff, hurrah for Jeff,
A Southern man so true.
(*Frank C. Brown Collection of Folklore*)

Old Honest Abe

An anonymous satire on Lincoln was printed in *Songs of the South* (Richmond 1863), which became a song of some distribution. As a song it varied in lines and words from the original. I give a somewhat "corrected" folk version according to the original text. "Scott" (Gen. Winfield Scott) and "Wool" (John Willis Wool, 1789-1869, fourth ranking general in Union Army).

Old honest Abe, you are a babe,
In military glory
An arrant fool—a party tool—
A traitor, and a tory.
You are a boss, a mighty hoss,
A-standing in the stable,
A racer too, a kangaroo—
So whup us if you're able
So whup up if you're able.

Dick Tater now is in a row
A-pulling of the trigger
Them that is on the South with the foaming mouth
Decoying of the nigger
　　　Decoying of the nigger

If Scott and Wool should at us pull
Across the country level,
We'll meet them there and fight them fair,
And trash them like the devil

For Wool and Scott will never squat,
But one thing you'll discover,
"That wool will fly," and Scott will die,
Before he whips his mother.
But you will fail and tuck your tail
You everlasting villain,
　　　You everlasting villain.

Oh Mr. Link, what do you think
About the Southern cattle
That horns you so wherever you go
And whups you every battle,
　　　And whups you every battle.
　　　　　　　(*Ballads and Songs* 356-357)

Irwin Silber, *Songs of the Civil War*, Columbia, Missouri, 1960.

Jeffdavise rides a white horse
Lincoln rides a mule.
Jeffdavise is a gentleman
And Lincoln is a fule.

Fight for the Nigger
Air—Wait for the Wagon

"Wait for the Wagon" (1851) was a famous song of the period. The words may have been composed by R. Bishop Buckley, who organized Buckley's Minstrels in 1843, with music by George P. Knauff. The catchy tune was widely used during the Civil War for songs advocating both Northern and Southern sentiments. The following "The Southern Wagon" and "Fight for the Nigger" both give Southern sentiments.

The Southern Wagon

Come, all ye sons of freedom, and join our Southern band;
We're going to fight the enemy, and drive them from our land.
Justice is our motto, Providence our guide,
So jump in the wagon, and we'll all take a ride.

> *Chorus*
> Oh! wait for the wagon,
> The dissolution;
> The South is our wagon,
> And we'll all take a ride.

Secession is our watchword, our rights we all demand,
And to defend our firesides we pledge our hearts and hand.
Jeff Davis is our President, with Stephens by his side;
Brave Beauregard, our general, will join us in the ride.

Our wagon is plenty big enough, the running-gear is good;
It's stuffed around with cotton, and made of Southern wood,
Carolina is our driver, with Georgia by her side,
Virginia will hold her flag up, and we'll all take a ride.

There are Tennessee and Texas also in the ring;
They wouldn't have a government where cotton wasn't king.
Alabama and Florida have long ago replied;
Mississippi and Louisiana are anxious for the ride.

Missouri, North Carolina, and Arkansas are slow;
They must hurry, or we'll leave them, and then what will they do?
There's Old Kentucky and Maryland won't make up their mind;
So I reckon, after all, we'll take them up behind.

The Tennessee boys are in the field, eager for the fray;
They can whip the Yankee boys three to one, they say;
And when they get in conflict, with Davis by their side,
They'll pitch into the Yankee boys, and then you'll see them slide.

Our cause is just and holy, our men are brave and true;
We'll whip the Lincoln cut-throats, is all we have to do.
God bless our noble army; in him we all confide;
So jump into the wagon, and we'll all take a ride.

(Rebellion Record 101)

Fight for the Nigger
Air—Wait for the Wagon

I calculate of darkies we soon shall have our fill,
With Abe's Proclamation and the Nigger Army bill;
Who could not be a soldier for the Union to fight?
Now, Abe's made the nigger the equal of the white.

   Fight for the nigger,
   The sweet-scented nigger,
   The woolly-headed nigger,
   And the Abolition crew.

Each soldier must be loyal and his officers obey,
Tho' he lives on mouldy biscuit and fights without his pay;
If his wife at home is starving, he must not be discontent,
Tho' he waits six months for green-backs worth forty-five per cent.
   Fight for the nigger, (etc.)

Moreover, if you're drafted, do not refuse to go,
You are equal to a nigger and can make as good a show;
And when you are in battle to the Union be true,
But don't forget the darkey is as good a man as you!
   Fight for the nigger, (etc.)

If ordered into battle go in without delay,
Tho' slaughtered just like cattle, it's your duty to obey;
For when old Jeff is captured, p'haps paid up you may be;
If you ain't, don't mind the money, don't you set the nigger free?
   Fight for the nigger, (etc.)

Three cheers for honest Abe, he will be a great man yet,
Tho' he's loaded us with taxes, and burdened us with debt;
He often tells us little jokes while pocketing our pelf,
And his last has made the nigger the equal of himself.
   Fight for the nigger, (etc.)

Guard well the *Constitution*, the Government and laws,
To every act of Congress don't forget to give applause;
And when you meet the rebels, be sure and drive them back,
Tho' you do *enslave* the white man, you must *liberate* the black.
    Fight for the nigger, (etc.)
                              (*Copperhead Minstrel*)

When This Cruel Draft is Over

This Copperhead song was a variant of "When This Cruel War is Over," a widely published and sung Union song by Charles C. Sawyer. The anti-war version differs only in necessary variants from the original, which had four stanzas. I quote the first and the chorus:

> Dearest love, do you remember,
> When we last did meet,
> How you told me that you loved me,
> Kneeling at my feet?
> In your suit of blue,
> When you vowed to me and country
> Ever to be true.
>
> *Chorus:*
> Weeping sad and lovely,
> Hopes and tears are vain.
> When this cruel war is over,
> Praying that we meet again.

When This Cruel Draft is Over

Dearest love, I fear they'll draft you,
    They'll put you on the list,
And they'll turn the wheel to grind you
    Into a Lincoln grist.
        Chorus: Weeping sad and lonely,
                All my tears are vain;
            When this cruel draft is over,
                Wilt thou come again.

O how fondly I adored you,
        When you first were mine,
All the time still growing dearer,
        All my soul is thine.
                Chorus: Weeping sad and lonely, (etc.)

But Old Abe I know will draft you,
        And drag you far from me;
O, I cannot live without you,
        My heart so cold will be.
                Chorus: Weeping sad and lonely, (etc.)
                        (*Copperhead Minstrel*)

                We'll Be Free in Maryland
                By Robert E. Holtz
                Air—"Gideon's Band"

The boys down South in Dixie's land,
The boys down South in Dixie's land,
The boys down South in Dixie's land,
Will come and rescue Maryland.
Chorus: If you will Join the Dixie band,
        Here's my heart and here's my hand,
        If you will join the Dixie band;
        We're fighting for a home.

The Northern foes have trod us down,
The Northern foes have trod us down,
The Northern foes have trod us down,
But we will rise with true renown.

The tyrants they must leave our door,
The tyrants they must leave our door,
The tyrants they must leave our door,
Then we'll be free in Baltimore.

There hirelings they'll never stand,
There hirelings they'll never stand,
There hirelings they'll never stand,
Whenever they see the Southern band.

Old Abe has got into a trap,
Old Abe has got into a trap,
Old Abe has got into a trap,
And he can't get out with his Scotch cap.

Nobody's hurt is easy spun
Nobody's hurt is easy spun
Nobody's hurt is easy spun
But the Yankees caught it at Bull Run.

We'll rally to Jeff Davis true,
Beauregard and Johnston, too,
Magruder, Price, and General Bragg,
And give three cheers for the Southern flag.

We'll drink this toast to one and all,
Keep cocked and primed for the Southern call;
The day will come, we'll make the stand,
Then we'll be free in Maryland.

Old Abe's Foot Down

The legion is armed for the battle,
    The charger is hot for the fray,
The thunders of musketry rattle,
    Yon eagles shall feast on the prey;
The corslets like diamonds are gleaming,
    The standard of blood is unfurled;
Yes, put your foot down, Mr. Lincoln,
    And trample them out of the world.

The hosts of the land are in motion,
    On, on with a ravenous pack,
Like waves on a pitiless ocean,
    When the heavens above them are black:—
They fire the mountain and prairie,
    The banner of death is unfurled;
Yes, put your foot down, Mr. Lincoln,
    And trample them out of the world.

The stars in their course are silent,
    The willows in agony weep,
The wind o'er the wave murmurs sadly
    Where the ashes of Washington sleep;
But crack your low jokes Massa Lincoln,
    Only white men to ruin are hurled,
So put your foot down, Massa Lincoln,
    And trample them out of the world.
                  (Copperhead Minstrel)

Song of the Abolitionists

O ring the bells a joyful peal,
    And rend with shouts the main,
We've learned that "freedom" means *to steal,*
    And fire the fruitful plain.

A burning wheatfield is our pride,
    A pillaged home our joy,
And then a stolen nag to ride,
    Is bliss without alloy.

Old Abe, a merry man is he,
    And we are merry all;
To swim in blood is to *be free—*
    Roll on the fiery ball!
                  (Copperhead Minstrel)

Conservative Chorus

Abraham, spare the South,
    Touch not a single slave;
Nor e'ern by word of mouth
    Disturb the thing, we crave.
'Twas our forefathers' hand
    That slavery begot;
There, Abraham, let it stand;
    Thine acts shall harm it not.
            (Civil War in Song and Story)

There's Nothing Going Wrong
Dedicated to "Old Age"

There's a general alarm,
The South's begun to arm,
And every hill and glen
Pours fourth its warrior men;
Yet, "There's nothing going wrong,"
Is the burden of my song.

Six States already out,
Beckon others on the route;
And the cry is "Still they come!"
From the Southern sunny home;
Yet, "There's nothing going wrong,"
Is the burden of my song.

There's a wail in the land,
From a want-stricken band;
And "Food! Food!" is the cry;
"Give us work or we die!"
Yet, "There's nothing going wrong,"
Is the burden of my song.

The sturdy farmer doth complain
Of low prices for his grain;
And the miller, with his flour,
Murmurs the dullness of the hour.
Yet, "There's nothing going wrong,"
Is the burden of my song.

The burly butcher in the mart,
He, too, also takes his part;
And the merchant in his store
Hears no creaking of his door.
But, "There's nothing going wrong,"
Is the burden of my song.

Stagnation is everywhere;
On the water, in the air,
In the shop, in the forge,
On the mount, in the gorge;

With the anvil, with the loom,
In the store and counting-room;
In the city, in the town,
With Mr. Smith, with Mr. Brown!
And "yet there's nothing wrong,"
Is the burden of my song.
> New Orleans, March 4, 1861. A.M.W.
> (*Songs and Ballads of the Southern People*)

King Scare

The monarch that reigns in the *warlike* North
   Ain't Lincoln all I ween,
But old King Scare, with his thin, fast legs,
   And his long sword in between;
The world has not for many a day
   Seen merrier king or lord;
But some declare, in a playful way,
   Scare should not wear a sword.
      Yes, I have heard, upon my word,
        And seen in prose and rhyme,
That if old Scare no sword would wear,
      He'd make much better time.

I cannot tell why he put it on,
   Nor tell where he got the heart,
But guess he intended it all for fun,
   And not for a tragedy part;
But well make up with his togs and wear,
   With his boots and sword and gun,
Not one of us knew it was old King Scare,
Till we saw the monarch run.
      It did us good, to see him scud
        And put the miles behind him;
      His friends now say, "put your sword away."
        But old Scare doesn't mind 'em.

He is ruler of twenty terrible States,
With ships and soldiers and tin;
But the state that all of these out-rates
Is the terrible state he is in;

With just nowhere for his ships to move,
With his tin more terribly rare,
With his soldiers on every field to prove
True subjects of old King Scare.
  The English "Times" and "Punch" in rhymes
    Both say the *Republic's nil,*
  That after the war, just as before
    Scare will be despot still.

Scare rides a horse in his "own countrie,"
And a high horse rides King Scare,
And a mighty host in his trail there be
Who nor gun nor falchion wear;
Now, these be the freedom-shriekers bold
Who keep off the war-'gine's track,
Who shut off the white race dungeon doors,
And send "braves" to steal the black.
  For Abolition is but a mission
    Of white-skinned niggers, to pray,
  And steal, and make the blacks they take
    As free and as mean as they.

This monarch Scare is imperious quite,
And he loves to swear and chafe
At the "rebel" foe that, in every fight,
He can always run from—safe;
And all his gazettes in great round words
His "brave volunteers" bepraise,
Whom Scare drives up against "rebel" swords,
And the swords drive otherways.
  Thus into battle, driven like cattle,
    Come his "brave volunteers;"
  Then from the fight, with all their might,
    Each gallantly—disappears.

Hurrah for the land of old Scare, then;
Hurrah for the Yankee land!
What a proud old war were this if their men
Could only be made to stand;
How the guns would roar, and the steel would ring,
And the soul up to heaven would flare,

If all the Yankees had now for king
Old Courage, and not old Scare.
But never they that lie and pray
And the wives of the Vandals are heard in their wail
With high imprecations Abe Lincoln to hail;
And the Saracen's might, yet untouched by our sword,
Shall share the same fate, for our trust's in the Lord.

J.J.H.

(Rebel Rhymes and Rhapsodies)

The Printers of Virginia to "Old Abe"
By Harry C. Treakle

Though we're exempt, we're not the *metal*
    To keep in when duty calls;
But onward we will *press*, to settle
    This knotty *case*, with leaden *balls*;
For our dear old mother State, the *fount*
    From which we each our life did *take*,
Is *locked up* by a Vandal horde,
    For the honor of the craft's at stake.

For *lean-faced* Lincoln's after us—
    His *slim shanks* moving like a scout;
But so long before his *job* is done,
    He'll find that all his *quads* are *out*.
For with Lee our *headline*—worthy *guide*—
    We, *galley*-slaves will never be,
But still press onward by his side.
    For that *fat take*, sweet liberty!

Soon Abe will find what he's about
    Will cost him such a pile of rocks,
Before his cherished *work* is *out*,
    He'll have no *sorts* in any *box*!
For his bank is now so very low,
    He scarce can *chase* up *quoins* to pay
The hired scum, the foreign foe,
    Who comes to steal our rights away.

And his *chums* now see, by his *foul matter*,
    To set *clean proof* he ne'er was *cast*,
And fears are felt that the gaunt old *ratter*
    Will go *broadside* to hell at last,
Where his friend, the *devil*, will welcome him,
    With *accents* sweet—to his bosom fly,
Revise his *foul proof-sheets* once more,
    And *knock* his naked *form* in *pi*.

And so to rush the base old *monk* along,
    And bring the quiet soon about,
We'll swell our *lines* to *columns* strong,

Southern Sentiment
By Rev. A.M. Box

The North may think that the South will yield,
    And seek for a place in the Union again;
But never will Southrons abandon the field
    And place themselves under *tyrannical reign*.

Sooner by far would we yield to the grave,
    Than form an alliance with so hated a foe;
To joint the "old Union" would be to enslave
    Ourselves, our children, in want and in woe!

What! sons of the South! submit to be ruled
    By the minions of Abraham Lincoln, the fool?
Our fair ones insulted—our wealth all controlled
    By Yankees, free negroes, and every such tool!

Heaven forbid it! and arm us with might,
    To drive back our foes, and grind them to dust!
In every conflict may we put them to flight,
    Aided by thee, thou God of the just!

Our bosoms we'll bare to the glorious strife,
    And our oath is recorded on high,
To prevail in the cause is dearer than life,
    Or crushed in its ruins to die!

The battle is not to the strong we know,
    But to the just, the true, and the brave—
With faith in our God, right onward we'll go,
    Our country our loved ones, to save.
        (Songs and Ballads of the Southern People)

A Southern Scene

Oh! mammy have you heard the news?
    Thus spoke a southern child,
As in the nurse's aged face
    She upward glanced and smiled.

What news, you mean, my little one?
    It must be mighty fine,
To make my darling's face to red,
    Her sunny blue eyes shine.

Why, Abraham Lincoln, don't you know,
    The Yankee president,
Whose ugly picture once we saw,
    When up to town we went—

Well, he is going to free you all,
    And make you rich and grand,
And you'll be dressed in silk and gold,
    Like the proudest in the land.

A gilded coach shall carry you,
    Where e'er you wish to ride;
And mammy, all your work shall be
    Forever laid aside.

The eager speaker paused for breath,
    And then the old nurse said
While closer to her swarthy cheek
    She pressed the golden head:—

My little missus stop and rest,
    You're talking mighty fast;
Jes look up dere, and tell me what
    You see in yonder glass?

You sees o'd mammy's wrinkly face,
    As black as any coal;
And underneath her handkerchief
    Whole heaps of knotty wool.

My darlin's face is red and white,
    Her skin is soft and fine,
And on her pretty little head
    De yallar ringlets shine.

My chile, who made dis difference
    'Twixt mammy and 'twixt you?
You reads de Lord's blessed book,
    And you kin tell me true.

De dear Lord said it must be so,
    And honey, I for one,
Wid thankful heart will always say,
    His holy will be done.

I tanks mas Linkum all de same,
    But when I wants for free,
I'll ask de Lord ob glory,
    Not poor buckra man like he,

And as for gilded carriages,
    Dey's notin' 'tall to see;
My massa's coach what carries him,
    Is good enough for me.

And, honey, when your mammy wants
    To change her homespun dress,
She'll pray like dear old missus,
    To be clothed with righteousness.

My works' been done dis many a day,
    And now I takes my ease,
Awaitin' for de master's call
    Jest when de master please.

And when at last de time's done come,
    And poor old mammy dies,

Your own dear mother's soft white hand
   Shall close dese tired old eyes.

De dear Lord Jesus soon will call
   Old mammy home to him,
And he can wash my guilty soul
   From ebery spot of sin.

And at his feet I shall lie down,
   Who died and rose for me;
And den, and not till den, my chile,
   Your mammy will be free.

Cabinet Pictures

There was an attorney named Lincoln,
The last for a statesman you'd think on;
   All danger was smoke,
   If he had but his joke,
And could browse, and tell stories, and wink on.

There was an old pilot named Seward,
Who never believed that it blew hard;
   So he woke up too late,
   When the ship of the state
Was drifting on sand banks to leeward.

There was a purse-bearer named Chase,
Who made paper and gold run a race,
   And invented the green-back
   That was ne'er to be seen back
At the customs—a very hard case.

There was an old fogie named Welles,
Quite worthy of cap and of bells,
   For he thought that a pirate,
   Who steamed at a great rate,
Would wait to be riddled with shells.

There was an attorney named Bates,
Chief advisor at law for the State;

But as never a word
Of his pleading is heard,
Who can possibly tell how he rates?

There was an old post-man named Blair,
Disposed to do something quite fair,
    But fanatical fury
    Made Blair of Missouri,
In the pranks of the cabinet share.

There was an old war-ass named Stanton,
Almost an American Danton,
    Though he thinks he's designed
    To astonish mankind
Round the world from Chicago to Canton.

There was an old poet named Bryant,
On Parnassus by no means a giant,
    Yet he scowls like a ghost
    As he doles from a *Post*
His humanities grim and defiant.

There was a queer parson named Beecher,
Not of Christ, but of bloodshed, a teacher;
    It was always a trifle
    Whether—Bible or rifle,
Wrought the aim of this blasphemous preacher.

Song of the "Loyal" Leaguers

We're going to fight for darkies now,
    Glory hallelujah!
At Lincoln's negro altars bow,
    Glory hallelujah!

Come, jolly white men, come along,
    Glory hallelujah!
Fall in, and sing this merry song,
    Glory hallelujah!

O, when we get the negroes free,
    Glory hallelujah!

As good as negroes we shall be,
　　Glory hallelujah!
(Copperhead Minstrel)

Lincoln's Thanksgiving

O God of Battles! once again
　　With banner, trump, and drum,
And garments in Thy wine-press dyed,
　　To give Thee thanks, we come!

No goats or bullocks garlanded,
　　Unto Thine altars go—
With brothers' blood, by brothers shed,
　　Our glad libations flow.

From pest-house and from dungeon foul,
　　Where, maimed and torn, they die;
From gory trench and charnel-house,
　　Where, heap on heap, they lie:

In every groan that yields a soul,
　　Each shriek a heart that rends—
With every breath of tainted air—
　　Our homage, Lord, ascends.

We thank Thee for the saber's gash,
　　The cannon's havoc wild;
We bless Thee for the widow's tears,
　　The want that starves her child.

We give Thee praise that Thou hast lit
　　The torch and fanned the flame;
That lust and rapine hunt their prey,
　　Kind Father! in Thy name.
(Songs of the Civil War 340)

During Civil War days, people in both South and North were deeply interested in the origins and meanings of words. Obviously interpretation could be manipulated to one's own purpose, as the following example demonstrates.

The Rev. Dr. Moore, of Richmond, Va., delivered a lecture in that city on the origin and meaning of words, in which many curious facts were developed, among which were that the word *Davis* means, "God with us," and that *Lincoln*, when subjected to etymological analysis, means, "On the verge of a precipice."

Chapter 5

Slave-Lore

Slaves had to resort to the secret language of metaphor and symbol—so far-fetched at times that they were meaningless to whites—to
speak their messages about hated slavery. But slave owners and other
whites recognized that there was more meaning in the language than the
uneducated ear could understand, and they were wary and apprehensive.
Carl Sandburg (*Abraham Lincoln: The War Years*, III, 61) said that to
blacks Lincoln was "the Liberator, the Chain-Breaker, the Giver of
Freedom." (See cartoon of Lincoln in Richmond.) To ignorant slaves,
Lincoln signified far more than mere human being, at times reaching the
status of God. Eugene Genovese (*Roll, Jordan, Roll* 273) reports that
one Yankee soldier once asked in a school for freedman "Who is Jesus
Christ?" heard "Him's Massa Linkum," and "Massa Linkum! our 'dored
Redeemer an' Saviour an' Frien'!" Another soldier reported (Coffin,
Four Years of Fighting, 203) that an old 69 year old slave called Yankee
soldiers "Jesus's aids, and I call you head man de Messiah." One Negro
was reported by the American Freedman's Inquiry Commission as saying, "Mass Linkum be ebrywhere. He walk de earth like de Lord." Upon
hearing of the Emancipation Proclamation, many blacks cheered,
laughed, sang and cried. "God bress Massa Linkum! De Laws save
Fader Abraham! De day of jubilee am come, shuah." But Lincoln's reputation was not always positive. One ex-slave from Natchez, filled with
the "high manners" of Southerners characterized Lincoln: "Mr. Lincum
was a good man, but dey tells me he was poor an' never cut much figger
in his clothes. Dat's why he never did un'erstan' how us felt 'bout us
white folks. It takes de quality to un'erstan' such things. (Genovese,
Roll, Jordan, Roll, 115) Genovese also reported how a slave resorted to
folk analogy to describe her tempered optimism about the Union's hope
for success (*Roll, Jordan, Roll* 438):

God won't let Massa Linkum beat de South till he do right ting. Massa
Linkum he great man, and I'se poor nigger; but dis nigger can tell Massa
Linkum how to save de money and de young men. He do it by setting de niggers free. S'pose dar was awfu' big snake downdar, on de floor. He bite you.
Folks all skeered, cause you die. You send for doctor to cut de bit; but snake he
rolled up dar, and while doctor dwine it, he bit you again. De doctor cut out dat
bit; but while he dwine it, de snake he spring up and bite you agin, and so he
keep dwine, till you kill him. Dat's what Massa Linkum orta know.

In Savannah a congregation of slaves attending a public baptism one Sunday was arrested, imprisoned and punished with thirty-nine lashes for singing the song below. Another version was popular in Florida. A little slave boy explained to the collector of the lines, "Dey tink de Lord mean fo' to say de Yankees calls us."

Slave Song (South Carolina version)

My mother! how long! Mothers! how long! mothers! how long!
　　Will sinners suffer here?
Chorus—It won't be long! It won't be long! It won't be long!
　　That sinners'll suffer here!

We'll walk de golden streets! we'll walk de golden streets! we'll walk de golden streets
　　Where pleasures never die!
Chorus

My brother! do sing! my brother! do sing! my brother! do sing! my brother! do sing!
　　De praises ob de Lord!
Chorus

　　　　　　　　　　　　(Allen, Ware, Garrison 95)

Negro Soldiers' Civil War Chant

Old Abe (God bless 'is ole soul!)
Got a plenty good victuals, an' a plenty good cloes,
Got powder an' shot, an' lead,
To bust in Adam's liddle Confed'
In dese hard times.

Oh, once dere was union, and den dere was peace;
De slave, in de cornfield, bare up to his knees.
But de Rebels' in gray, an' Secesh's in de way,
An' de slave'll be free
In dese hard times.

　　　　　　　　　　　　(Talley 98-99)

We'll *soon* be free! we'll *soon* be free! we'll *soon* be free!
De Lord will call us home!
Chorus. My brother! do sing! my brother! do sing! my brother! do sing!
De praises ob de Lord!

Another version was more militant and threatening.

We'll fight for liberty,
We'll fight for liberty,
We'll fight for liberty,
When de Lord will call us home.
And it won't be long,
And it won't be long,
And it won't be long,
When de Lord will call us home.
(*Confederate Veteran*, Aug. 1895, 352)

Pray On

This "spiritual" obviously carried more uplift in the spirit than the words. It was sung on the rice plantations of the Port Royal Island when news of impending freedom reached the slaves.

Pray on—pray on;
Pray on, den light us over;
Pray on—pray on,
De Union break of day.
My sister, you come to see baptize
In de Union break of day,
In de Union break of day.
(*Confederate Veteran*, Aug. 1895, 352)

Where Lincoln Wrote His Name

I

I think Abe Lincoln was next to the Lord. He done all he could for the slaves; he set 'em free. People in the South knowed they'd lose their slaves when he was elected president. 'Fore the election he traveled all over the South, and he come to our house and slept in Old Mistress' bed. Didn't nobody know who he was. It was a custom to take strangers in and put them up for one night or longer, so he come to our house and he watched close. He seen how the niggers come in on Saturday and drawed four pounds of meat and a peck of meal for a week's rations. He also saw 'em whipped and sold. When he got back up North he writ Old Master a letter and told him he was going to have to free his slaves, that everybody was going to have to, that the North was going to see to it. He also told him that he had visited at his house and if he doubted it to go in the room he slept in and look on the bedstead at the head and he'd see where he'd writ his name. Sure enough, there was his name: A. Lincoln.

II

Abraham Lincoln gits too much praise. I say, shucks, give God the praise. Lincoln come through Gallitan, Tennessee, and stopped at Hotel Tavern with his wife. They was dressed just like tramps, and nobody knowed it was him and his wife till he got to the White House and writ back and told 'em to look 'twixt the leaves in the table where he had set and they sure enough found out it was him.

When Lincoln Came Down to Free Us

I

Oooh, child, you ought to been there when Mr. Linktum come down to free us. Policeman ain't in it. You ought to seen them big black bucks. Their suits was so fine trimmed with them eagle buttons and they was gold too. And their shoes shined so they hurt your eyes. I tell you I can't remember my age but it's been a long time ago.

I wouldn't take $100 for living in slavery days, and I 'member when they all parted out. Mr. Linktum come down. Yes'm, Mr. Abe Linktum and his partner, Horace Greeley, comed down. Lieutenants and Sarges all comed. And some big yellow buck niggers all dressed up fine. I served Mr. Linktum myself with my own hands. Yes 'm, I did. I fotched cold water from the spring on a waiter, and I stood straight and held it out just like this in front of me. Yes'm and his partner, Mr. Horace Greeley, too. And them big yellow buck niggers went in the kitchen where my mammy was cooking and told her: "Git outa here, nigger. You don't have to wait on these white folks no more." Yes'm, they did. And they done said; "You ain't' got no more master and no more missus. You don't have to work here no more." But my mother said: "I's putting Old Master's victuals on to cook. Wait till I gets 'em on." And they told her again that she didn't have no more master and no more missus. I told my mammy to kick him down the step, but she said she was afeared he would shoot her. All I hates about them Sarges and Lieutenants is they never did shave. Them days all wore whiskers...

II

I knowed the time when Abram Linkum come to the plantation. He come through there on the train and stopped over night oncet. He was known by Dr. Jameson, and he came to Perry to see about the food for the soldiers.

We all had part in entertaining him. Some shined his shoes, some cooked for him, and I waited on the table, I can't forget that. We had chicken hash and batter cakes and dried venison that day. You be sure we knowed he was our friend and we catched what he had to say. Now, he said this (I never forget that so long as I live): "If you free the people, I'll bring you back into the Union. [To Dr. Jameson.] If you don't free your slaves, I'll whip you back into the Union. Before I'd allow my wife and children to be sold as slaves, I'll wade in blood and water up to my neck."

Now he said all that. If my mother and father were living, they'd tell you the same thing. That's what Linkum said.

He came through after freedom and went to the Sheds' first. I couldn't 'magine what was going on, but they came running to tell me, and what a time we had.

Linkum went to the smokehouse and opened the door and said, "Help yourselves; take what you need; cook yourselves a good meal!" and we sure had a celebration.

III

When Fillmore, Buchanan, and Lincoln ran for President, one of my old bosses said, "Hurrah for Buchanan," and I said, "Hurrah for Lincoln." One of my mistresses said, "Why do you say, 'Hurrah for Lincoln'?" And I said, "Because he's going to set me free."

During that campaign, Lincoln came to North Carolina and ate breakfast with my master. In those days the kitchen was off from the house. They had for breakfast ham with cream gravy made out of sweet milk, and they had biscuits, poached eggs on toast, coffee and tea, and grits. They had waffles and honey and maple syrup. That was what they had for breakfast.

He told my old boss that our sons are conceiving children by slaves and buying and selling our own blood, and it will have to be stopped. And that is what I know about that.

IV

I was looking right in Lincoln's mouth when he said, "The colored man is turned loose without anything. I am going to give a dollar a day to every Negro born before Emancipation until his death—a pension of a dollar a day." That's the reason they killed him. But they sure didn't get it. It's going to be an awful thing up yonder when they hold a judgment over the way that things was done down here.

When the war was declared over, Abraham Lincoln came South and went to the capitol [in Atlanta], and there was so many people to meet him he went up to the tower instead of in the State House. He said, "I did everything I could to keep out of the war. Many of you agreed to turn the Negroes loose, but Jeff Davis said that he would wade in blood up to his neck before he would do it."

He asked for all of the Confederate money to be brought up there. And when it was brought, he called for the oldest colored man around. He said, "Now, is you the oldest?" The man said, "Yes, sir." Then he threw him one of those little boxes of matches and told him to set fire to it and burn it up.

Then he said, "I am going to disfranchise every one of you [the white folks], and it will be ten years before you can even vote or get back into the Union."

Maybe Mr. Lincoln Ain't So Bad

In them days they was peddlers gwine round the country selling things. They toted big packs on they backs filled with everything from needles and thimbles to bedspreads and frying pans. One day a peddler stopped at Miss Fanny's house. He was the ugliest man I ever seed. He was tall and bony with black whiskers and black bushy hair and curious eyes that set 'way back in his head. They was dark and look like a dog's eyes after you done hit him. He set down on the porch and opened his pack, and it was so hot and he looked so tired that Miss Fanny give him a cool drink of milk that had done been setting in the springhouse. All the time Miss Fanny was looking at the things in the pack and buying, the man kept up a running talk. He ask her how many niggers they had; how many men they had fighting on the 'Federate side, and what was she gwine do if the niggers was set free. Then he ask her if she knowed Mr. Abraham Lincoln.

'Bout that time Miss Virginia come to the door and heard what he said. She blaze up like a lightwood fire and told that peddler that they didn't want to know nothing 'bout Mr. Lincoln, that they knowed too much already, and that his name wasn't 'lowed called in her house. Then she say he wasn't nothing but a black devil messing in other folks' business, and that she'd shoot him on sight if she had half a chance.

The man laughed. "Maybe Mr. Lincoln ain't so bad," he told her. Then he packed his pack and went off down the road, and Miss Virginia watched him till he went out of sight round the bend.

Two or three weeks later Miss Fanny got a letter. The letter was from that peddler. He told her that he was Abraham Lincoln heself; that he was peddling over the country as a spy; and he thanked her for the rest on her shady porch and the cool glass of milk she give him.

When that letter come, Miss Virginia got so hopping mad that she took all the stuff Miss Fanny done bought from Mr. Lincoln and made us niggers burn it on the ash pile. Then she made Pappy rake up the ashes and throw them in the creek.

(Lay My Burden Down 16-19)

Chapter 6

Lincoln in the Illustrated Newspapers

Frank Leslie's Illustrated Newspaper, from which most of the following cartoons were taken, had a spectacular if brief career in American journalism. Frank Leslie (1821-1880) was born Henry Carter in Ipswich, England. After successful work on the *Illustrated London News*, the first graphic newspaper, Carter immigrated to New York in 1848. He worked as engraving supervisor for a year on P.T. Barnum's short-lived *Illustrated News*. Developing a new technique of engraving sketches that reduced the time needed to transfer sketch to print from 3-4 weeks to a maximum ten days, Leslie, who had changed name from Carter, launched in January 1854 his first publication *Frank Leslie's Ladies' Gazette of Paris, London, and New York Fashions*. In December 1855 he initiated *Frank Leslie's Illustrated Newspaper*.

The American public could not get enough illustrated news. Within four years, *Harper's Weekly* and the *New York Illustrated News* joined in the effort to supply the needed illustrated news. At its heyday Leslie's had a circulation 10,000 higher than *Harper's*. He worked with a staff of 130 engravers and printers. At the beginning of the Civil War, his staff consisted of the best sketch artists of the time, including such individuals as the British brothers William and Lafred Laud, Eugene Benson, Arthur Lumley, C.S. Hall, Edwin Forbes, Henri Lovie and many others, many of whom, called "specials," did countless sketches of life in both the North and South, then after the beginning of the War, scenes of battle, life in the army, generals and other people and events. *Leslie's* was most successful during the early war years. But Leslie could not get his political stance quite right, his attitude toward paying his artists was off-center, at times his dedication to journalism wavered and *Harper's* could afford to hire his artists away. By war's end Leslie's preeminence had waned. In its brief life, however, it had recorded the actions and the pulse of a nation. The following sketches demonstrate how it illustrated those pulses in editorial sketches.

On his railroad trip to Washington for the Inauguration, in Philadelphia Lincoln was told of a plot uncovered by Allen Pinkerton, head of a private detective agency, to murder him in Baltimore. Lincoln scoffed at the idea and insisted on speaking at Philadelphia and Harrisburg. Thereafter, however, convinced of the truth of the rumor to assassinate him, Lincoln and his friend, burly Ward Lamon, a rough and tumble fighter armed with two pistols, two derringers and two large knives, left Harrisburg in a special train. In Baltimore at half past three a.m., the sleeping car was pulled through silent streets to Camden Station, which serviced Washington. On the streets Lincoln heard a drunk singing "Dixie." Lincoln arrived in Washington at 6 a.m. with the detail of four army officers assigned to accompany him. As soon as news of Lincoln's extraordinary arrival in Washington became known, he was ridiculed and lampooned mercilessly. Joseph Howard, a reporter for the World and Lincoln's eternal nemesis was responsible for inventing the story of Lincoln's disguise in "a scotch cap and long military cloak."

THE FLIGHT OF ABRAHAM.

(*As Reported by a Modern Daily Paper.*)

(1.) THE ALARM.

"On Thursday night, after he had retired, Mr. Lincoln was aroused, and informed that a stranger desired to see him on a matter of life and death. * * A conversation elicited the fact that an organized body of men had determined that Mr. Lincoln should never leave the City of Baltimore alive. * * Statesmen laid the plan, Bankers indorsed it, and Adventurers were to carry it into effect"

(2.) THE COUNCIL.

"Mr. Lincoln did not want to yield, and his friends cried with indignation. insisted, and he left,"

Frank Leslie's Illustrated Newspaper.

(4.) THE OLD COMPLAINT.

"Mr. LINCOLN, accompanied by Mr. SEWARD, paid his respects to President spending a few minutes in general conversation."

(3.) THE SPECIAL TRAIN.

"He wore a Scotch plaid Cap and a very long Military Cloak, so that he was entirely unrecognizable."

Frank Leslie's Illustrated Newspaper.

Lincoln was Inaugurated March 4, 1861. As the following two cartoons demonstrated, even before his Inauguration, Lincoln was bombarded with suggestions as to how to run his office. The first pictures him as a peacemaker who, through proper inducements, can bring the two sides together again. The second suggests that Lincoln was finding the prospects of force uncomfortable.

A job for the new cabinet maker. *Frank Leslie's Illustrated Newspaper*, February 2, 1861.

Old Abe—"Oh, it's all well enough to say, that I must support the dignity of my high office by Force—but it's darned uncomfortable sitting—I can tell yer." *Frank Leslie's Illustrated Newspaper*, March 2, 1861.

Lincoln's reputation as a jokester and humorist was widespread in Illinois, preceded him to Washington and was often despised by those more solemn people who did not understand that it was therapy for the President. Lincoln once told Congressman James M. Ashley (R. Ohio), who protested Lincoln's apparent levity during times of national disaster, "If I couldn't tell these stories, I would die." Some people, however, appreciated Lincoln's ways, as the following paragraph from *Vanity Fair* (August 30, 1882) demonstrates:

A Joke Explained

Need we say that the President is a wag? The mirth-moving tales of which his head is full, and the dogged persistency with which he retails them, regardless of the flying buttons and purpling faces of the laughing philosophers by whom he is surrounded, are among the few jolly and refreshing things which serve to give a jocular and comic turn to the present bloody and terrible war. Sometimes there is a hidden meaning in his humor, which is *caviare* to the General—as for instance, when he said to General Sykes, referring to the Fifth New-York Zouaves, that there was "no such thing as beating them even round a stump." The *Herald* reporter quotes this remarkable expression, but furnishes no key to its occult signification. Permit us, whose province it is to sift the grain of wit from the "chaff" of the day, to pluck the heart out of the mystery. The boys of the Fighting Fifth, is seems are fond of solacing such leisure moments as they can snatch from their military labors, with a turn at "Old Sledge," a game in which they are believed to be unrivalled. Stumps are often the only tables to be found in the sylvan bivouac, and around these primitive pieces of furniture they may occasionally be seen squatting in groups of four each, betting their piles on all fours. The President, having been informed of their proficiency in this absorbing pastime, no doubt intended to pay a compliment to their skill in remarking that there "was no such thing as beating them *even*, round a stump." It was neatly said, and we are not surprised that the Fighting Fifth should show their appreciation of the joke by cheering the perpetrator.

OUR PRESIDENTIAL MERRYMAN. "The Presidential party was engaged in a lively exchange of wit and humor. The President Elect was the merriest among the merry, and kept those around him in a continual roar." —*Daily Paper. Frank Leslie's Illustrated Newspaper*, March 2, 1861.

Upon being inaugurated as President, Lincoln was showered with suggestions for changing government to handle the question of slavery and Secession. The Chicago Convention had drafted several moderate planks designed to appeal to differing groups. On slavery the platform avoided any strong condemnation and acknowledged the right of each state to dictate its own policy. The most serious suggestion Lincoln was handed was a thirteenth amendment to the Constitution which Congress had passed just before adjournment the preceding December forever guaranteeing slavery in the states free from Federal interference. Lincoln promised to support this amendment, saying, "I have no objection to its being made express, and irrevocable." But Lincoln was always educable and wanted to do what was right. In this cartoon, the artist has attributed to Columbia Lincoln's own words of caution and determination: "First be sure you're right, then go ahead!"

CONSULTING THE ORACLE.
President Lincoln. "And, what next?"
Columbia. "First be sure you're right, then go ahead!"
Frank Leslie's Illustrated Newspaper, April 13, 1861.

Lincoln always looked upon the Civil War as a rebellion and was dedicated to restoring the Union at whatever the cost. But slavery was the cornerstone of the Confederacy. Lincoln was forced to countermand the orders of military commanders and of Congress liberating the slaves. Lincoln put saving the Union as his one and only purpose in the War. The cartoonist obviously agreed with the President.

Lincoln—"I'm sorry to have to drop you, Sambo, but this concern won't carry us both!" *Frank Leslie's Illustrated Newspaper*, October 12, 1861.

John Charles Fremont (1813-1890) became a national hero when, in the 1840s, he trailblazed across the Rocky Mountains and led the campaign to take California from Mexico. Appointed Major General by Lincoln at the beginning of the Civil War, Fremont proved inept and an embarrassment. Acting on his own authorization on August 3, 1861, he proclaimed that Missouri's slaves were forever free. He informed the President of his actions a week later. Lincoln ordered Fremont to reverse his proclamation since it ran contrary to the Confiscation Act of 1861, which freed only those slaves used by Confederates in their war effort. Fremont was suspected of higher political aspirations and he did make a feeble effort to run on a third party for the Presidency in 1864. Lincoln felt the effort premature.

Lincoln—"Well, Master Fremont, that's rather a long reach, ain't it? You might fetch it with your sword, perhaps, in the proper time, but it isn't ripe yet." *Frank Leslie's Illustrated Newspaper*, October 26, 1861.

In need of battle ships, Confederate Secretary of the Navy Stephen R. Mallory used the hull and engines of the USS *Merrimac*, abandoned by the U.S. Navy at Norfolk, VA, to construct his famous ironclad gun casement that seemed to float on the water with the body of the ship submerged below the waterline. Capt. Franklin Buchanan took his ship out March 8, 1862, on what was supposed to be a test of its machinery and handling. Instead he attacked, rammed and sank the U.S. *Cumberland* and the *Congress*, which burned. Buchanan brought his *Virginia* out the next day to face the U.S. *Monitor*. The two ships fought two hours. Neither was able to destroy the other. The threat of the *Merrimac* caused panic in the Cabinet and White House, and Lincoln, as the cartoonist suggests, recognized the dawn of a new day in naval warfare.

SINBAD LINCOLN AND THE OLD MAN OF THE SEA.

Frank Leslie's Illustrated Newspaper.

Horace Greeley (1811-1872), through his New York *Tribune*, continuously brought pressure on Lincoln with suggestions on how to win the War and save the Peace. Lincoln chafed under the harassment.

VANITY FAIR.

The Monotonous Minstrel.

President Lincoln, (to H. G.)—" Go away, you tiresome vagrant! It's always the same old croaking tune, 'Abolition, Abolition, Marching On!'"

Vanity Fair, August 30, 1862.

Benjamin Franklin Butler (1818-1893) was a tempestuous lawyer from New Hampshire, the first Major General of volunteers appointed by President Lincoln. He quelled the riots of Baltimore, May 13, 1861. He was known as "Spoons" Butler for allegedly stealing the silverware from the house he occupied in New Orleans after troops were sent there in May 1862 under his command. His most notorious order in New Orleans was that women there who did not treat Union soldiers with respect were to be treated like women of the streets, i.e., whores. Butler was relieved of his command in December 1862.

Uncle Abe. "Hello! Ben, is that you? Glad to see you!"
Butler. "Yes, Uncle Abe. Got through with that New Orleans Job. Cleaned them
out and scrubbed them up! *Any more scrubbing to give out?*" *Frank Leslie's
Illustrated Newspaper.*

Something of a mystic, Lincoln sometimes had dreams/visions of future events in his life. Here he is shown dreaming of how some of his former generals have lost their heads in battle and of how he is going to have to behead his Cabinet. The individuals approaching the chopping block and having passed it from left to right are Halleck, Welles, Stanton, Seward, Lincoln, Burnside, McClellan and McDowell.

Frank Leslie's Illustrated Newspaper, February 14, 1863.

The cartoonist is suggesting that Lincoln, after many disappointments over the "size" of his military commanders and their accomplishments, might turn to the acknowledged dwarfs of famous showman P.T. Barnum (1810-1891) and his little people, Gen. Tom Thumb, Commodore Nutt, Lavinia Warren and others.

THE COMING MEN! The Great Snowman—"Mr. President, since your naval and military heroes don't seem to get on, try mine!"

Mr. Lincoln—"Well, I'll do it to oblige you, Friend Phineas, but I think mine are the smallest. *Frank Leslie's Illustrated Newspaper,* February 28, 1863.

Richmond, Virginia, Confederate capital and military nerve center, was obviously a necessary union military objective. The battle to take Petersburg, 20 miles south of Richmond, and Richmond itself, lasted from June 15, 1864, to April 3, 1865. Contrary to the desires of Generals Lee and Grant, because of Federal ineptitude, the assault became a siege of trenches, tunnels and mudholes Grant insisted his generals break through. They did not succeed. This mud bath was the longest sustained campaign of the war.

THE BAD BIRD AND THE MUDSILL.

Frank Leslie's Illustrated Newspaper, February 21, 1863.

The Confederate cotton policy was flawed from the outset. Confederates assumed that their cotton was so vital to the British economy that they had to have the "white gold" at any price, even to intervention in the war. But though the British blustered and posed, they never seriously planned to intercede on the side of the confederacy. The British did not feel the dire shortage of Southern cotton until late 1862 and within a year they had discovered new sources in India, Egypt and Brazil.

MR. BULL (*Confiding Creature*). "Hi want my Cotton, bought at Fi' Pence a Pound."

MR. LINCOLN. "Don't know any thing about it, my dear Sir. Your friends, the Rebels, are burning all the Cotton they find, and I confiscate the rest. Good Morning John!" *Harper's Weekly.*

William Cornell Jewett, known as "Colorado Jewett," was a shadowy person who, in January 1863, got involved with Horace Greeley to have the French mediate an end to the war. Under Greeley's direction, Jewett visited the French minister, Henry Mercier, and suggested mediation. Greeley and Jewell's efforts were written up in the Tribune. Greeley and Jewett were later involved in the so-called Niagara Falls meeting with representatives of the Confederacy.

"Enough to kill him." *The Colorado grand Peace Prescription. Frank Leslie's Illustrated Newspaper*, March 28, 1863.

Horace Greeley (1811-1872) was the fiery editor of the New York *Tribune*, which he founded in 1841. He demanded immediate freedom for slaves. He was ever ready to give advice to Lincoln. After the Battle of Shiloh (April 6-7, 1861), which was a bloody victory for General Grant, Greeley said "Grant should be hung." Lincoln, however, who liked Grant's determination to beat the Confederate Army, did not want to sweep the General onto the growing pile of cashiered Union army commanders.

RIGHT AT LAST. Old Abe—"*Greeley be hanged! I want no more new brooms. I begin to think that the worst thing about my old ones was in not being handled right.*" Frank Leslie's Illustrated Newspaper, June 13, 1863.

Clement Laird Vallandigham
(1820-1871), a fiery states righter, a
democrat and native of Dayton, Ohio,
addressed a large audience in Colum-
bus, Ohio, and contrary to an order by
Major General Ambrose E. Burnside
against attacking the President, made
derogatory remarks about President
Lincoln. Convicted by a military court,
Vallandigham was sentenced to two
years in a military prison. Lincoln com-
muted the sentence to banishment in the
Confederacy. In the South, Vallandigham objected to Davis' handling
of the war and was ejected. He slipped
through the blockade to Nassau and
lived in Canada until June 1864 when,
ignored by Lincoln, he returned to the
U.S. and made the keynote speech at
the June 1864 Democratic Convention.
He was subsequently defeated for Governor of Ohio. He may have been the
model for Edward Everett Hale's work
"The Man Without a Country" (1863).
The cartoonist here shows no sympathy
for Vallandigham.

A Rare Old Game of "Shuttlecock."
Jeff—*"No good sending him here. I'll have to send him back."*
Abe—*"He's none of mine, anyhow." Frank Leslie's Illustrated Newspaper,*
June 20, 1863.

By the summer of 1863, Jefferson
Davis began encouraging the abuse of
captured Union soldiers and Blacks in
the Confederacy. In retaliation, on July
31, Lincoln prepared "General Order
No. 252": "That for every soldier of the
United States killed in violation of the
laws of war, a rebel soldier shall be exe-
cuted; and for every one enslaved by
the enemy or sold into slavery, a rebel
soldier shall be placed at hard labor on
the public works."

THE PRESIDENT'S ORDER NO. 252. Mr. Lincoln. "Look here, Jeff. Davis! if you lay a finger on that boy, to hurt him, I'll likc this *Ugly Cub of yours* within an inch of his life!" *Harper's Weekly*, August 15, 1863.

New York generally supported the
Union in the Civil War despite the dis-
couragement of numerous military fail-
ures. In 1863, when Congress adopted
conscription New York mobs, at least
partly manned by working men who
feared emancipated blacks would take
their jobs, ransacked the draft office,
looted, lynched Negroes and burned
some abolitionists' residences. The cartoonist pictures a cajoling President
trying to get compliance with the draft
order.

THE NAUGHTY BOY GOTHAM, WHO WOULD NOT TAKE THE DRAFT.
Mammy Lincoln—"*There now, you bad boy, acting that way, when your little sister Penn takes hers like a lady!*" *Frank Leslie's Illustrated Newspaper*, August 29, 1863.

Though Lincoln was a most controversial President during his first term in office, his nomination for a second term at the Republican national convention held in Baltimore guaranteed to most people prosecution of the war and ultimate triumph over Jefferson Davis. The cartoonist looks upon the nomination as Davis' deathblow.

THE HARDEST SHELL YET.
Jeff Davis's breakfast spoilt by a shot from Baltimore. Frank Leslie's Illustrated Newspaper, July 2, 1864.

Throughout the war, at various times, negotiations for peace were undertaken. In May 1864, Congressman Dawson asked the North to "tender the olive branch of peace" and a peace effort was initiated in July when a group, including the shadowy figure George N. Sanders of Kentucky, then resident of Canada, tried to work through Horace Greeley and get Lincoln to come to terms. Several meetings were held at Niagara Falls, Canada, between Union and Confederate representatives but nothing came of them. Abolitionists felt that Lincoln might be indecisive on the issue of slavery. The cartoonist, however, saw Lincoln as accepting no peace without emancipation.

G.N. Sanders—"Won't you accept an Olive branch from me? the emblem of Peace, you know."
Mr. Lincoln—"What! an Olive branch with Blackberries growing upon it? Never!"
Frank Leslie's Illustrated Newspaper, October 8, 1864.

With the failure of the "Radical Democracy" party to mount serious opposition and with Grant's military successes, Lincoln was nominated for and elected to a second term. With this election, defeat of the South was assured. By the time of the Civil War, tall people had been called "Long" from at least Elizabethan times when "Long Meg" was a heroine who disguised herself as a man and fought with her man in the wars. In Lincoln's day, one of the more famous "long" men was Sweet Betsy's lover, "Long Ike," in the song "Sweet Betsy from Pike," words possibly by John A. Stone, music a folk tune, first published in 1853 though possibly older. The song was parodied during the 1856 Presidential campaign as "The Great Baby Show" or "The Abolition Show," by Stephen Collins Foster.

Frank Leslie's Illustrated Newspaper, December 3, 1864.

Francis P. Blair, Union politician,
believed that the North and South could
be reunited under the purpose of driving
the French out of Mexico. Lincoln
hoped such a move might soften Radical Republican attitudes toward the
South during Reconstruction. Jefferson
Davis felt it might stiffen Southern attitudes and prolong the War another year.
The Hampton Road Peace Conference
was held February 3, 1865, with the
Southern group led by Alexander
Stephens, Vice-President of the Confederacy but critic of Davis. Nothing came
of the Conference. Actually, Lincoln
was not as hopeful as the cartoonist pictured him.

THE PEACE COMMISSION.
Flying to ABRAHAM's Bosom. *Harper's Weekly*, February 18, 1865.

Lincoln's Emancipation Proclamation of September 22, 1862, declared that on January 1, 1863, all slaves in rebellious sections of the United States were free. But it left many Negroes still enslaved. His proposal of the Thirteenth Amendment to the U.S. Constitution, having passed the Senate, came up for ratification in the House on January 31, 1865. An astute politician, Lincoln had maneuvered behind the scenes to guarantee its passage. The clerk whispered the tally to Speaker Confax: Ayes 119, Nays 56, not voting 8. Colfax asked to be called and voted aye. Thus, finally, Lincoln's dream as a young man in Illinois to stamp out slavery had come to pass. At a slave auction in New Orleans he had once declared: "If I ever get a chance to hit that thing, I'll hit it hard." Through many broken promises and dreams, he had persisted and prevailed. Lincoln called the Thirteenth Amendment "A king's cure for all evils. It winds the whole thing up."

UNCLE ABE'S VALENTINE SENT BY COLUMBIA.
An envelope full of broken chains. *Frank Leslie's Illustrated Newspaper*, February 25, 1865.

City Point, VA, seven miles east of Petersburg on the south bank of the James River, was General Grant's headquarters for the last ten months of the war. On March 29, 1865, Lincoln, Mrs. Lincoln and son Tad visited Grant in his campaign against Lee. Lincoln remained at City Point while Grant maneuvered around Lee, telegraphing reports on his movements back to Lincoln. Lincoln, "having no great deal to do" sent Grant's dispatches on to the Secretary of War and they were released to the press. On April 2, at 4:30 p.m., Grant wired the President: "The whole captures since the army started out will not amount to less than 12,000 men, and probably fifty pieces of artillery.... All seems well with us, and everything is quiet just now." Petersburg, site of a prolonged bungled siege, fell on April 2 and Richmond on April 3. Six days later Lee surrendered at Appomattox. Little wonder that *Harper's* was pleased with the news that Lincoln had forwarded.

FROM OUR SPECIAL WAR CORRESPONDENT.
"City Point, Va., *April—*, 8:30 A.M. "All seems well with us."—A. Lincoln.
Harper's Weekly, April 15, 1865.

On April 4, 1865, after Richmond
had fallen the day before, Lincoln
decided to go to the conquered capitol
of the Confederacy since it had stood as
a symbol of Secessionism. His party
arrived by boat and, with no escort, he
walked nearly two miles to the heart of
the city, having horse guards only for
the last distance to the Confederate
Executive Mansion. Lincoln shook
hands with several blacks. One older
Negro said: "Go 'way, dat ain' no
Fadder Abraham. Why, dat man look
lak a 'ornery ol' famah [farmer], he
do." After lunch, Lincoln with a cavalry
escort rode over the city. On one street a
Negro woman held up her sick child
and said: "See yeah, honey, look at de
Savior, and you'll git well. Touch de
hem of his gahment, honey, and your
pain will be gone."

President Lincoln riding through Richmond, April 4, and the enthusiastic cheers of the inhabitants.—From a sketch by our special artist, J. Broker. *Frank Leslie's Illustrated Newspaper*, April 22, 1865.

The assassination as seen by the artist for *Frank Leslie's Illustrated Newspaper* (April 29, 1865). The picture was accompanied by this poem by Edmund C. Stedman taken from the New York Tribune (which denied mercy):

"Forgive them, for they know not what
    they do!"
        He said, and so went shriven to
            his fate—
Unknowing went, that generous heart
    and true,
        Even while he spoke the slayer
            lay in wait,
        And when the morning opened
            Heaven's gate
There passed the whitest soul a nation
    knew.
        Henceforth all thoughts of
            pardon are too late;
They, in whose cause that arm its
    weapon drew,
        Have murdered MERCY. Now
            alone shall stand
BLIND JUSTICE, with the sword
    unsheathed she wore.
        Hark, from the eastern to the
            western stand,
The swelling thunder of the
    people's roar:
        What words they murmur—
            FETTER NOT HER HAND!
SO LET IT SMITE, SUCH DEEDS
SHALL BE NO MORE!

Booth.　　Mr. Lincoln.　　Mrs. Lincoln.　　Miss Harris.　　Major Rathbun. Assassination of President Lincoln in his private box at Ford's Theatre, Washington, April 14. *Frank Leslie's Illustrated Newspaper*, April 29, 1865.

Frank Leslie's Illustrated Newspaper needed money to survive. From its beginning, therefore, it accepted advertising of all kinds, running together under large and small headlines and large and small type announcements of all kinds of commercial businesses. The following pages illustrate how, in *Leslie's*, one read almost in one breath commemorations of Lincoln's assassination and the cure for pimples, musical tributes to Lincoln and a new song called "Scandal on the Brain." America was a new, boisterous, developing new gilded world where all things jostled one another for visibility and importance. The author of the song "Mourn Not, O ye People," Mrs. E.A. Parkhurst, was a popular song writer of the period. She also wrote "Dying Drummer," "This Hand Never Struck Me, Mother," "Sanitary Fair Polka, "Little Joe, the Contraband" and "The New Emancipation Song."

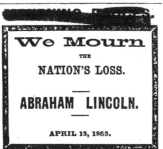

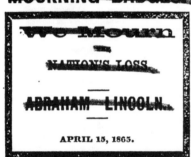
May 20, 1865.

May 20, 1865.

May 27, 1865.

Bibliography

Abraham Africanus I. New York: J.F. Feeks, 1861.

Adderup, Andrew. *Lincolniana; or the Humors of Uncle Abe.* New York: J.F. Feeks, 1864.

Belden, H.M. *Ballads and Songs Collected by the Missouri Folk-Lore Society.* Columbia, Mo.: Univ. of Missouri Studies, 1940.

Book of Anecdotes, Joker's Knapsack, Including Witticisms of the Late President Lincoln and Humors, Incidents and Absurdities of the War. Philadelphia: John E. Potter & Co., 1866.

Book of the Prophet Stephen, Son of Douglas. Wherein Marvellous Things Are Foretold of the Reign of Abraham. New York: Feeks & Bancker, 1863.

Book of the Prophet Stephen, Son of Douglas. Book Second. New York: J.F. Feeks, 1864.

Botkin, B.A. *Lay My Burden Down.* Chicago: Univ. of Chicago Press, 1945.

Brown, Frank C. *Frank C. Brown Collection of North Carolina Folklore.* Durham, N.C.: Duke Univ. Press, 1950.

Confederate Veterans Magazine. Nashville, 1893.

Luther, Frank. *Americans and Their Songs.* New York: Harpers, 1942.

Moore, Frank. *Civil War in Song and Story.* New York: Collier, 1889.

——. *Lyrics of Loyalty.* New York: Putnam, 1864.

——. *Rebel Rhymes and Rhapsodies.* New York: Putnam, 1864.

——. *Rebellion Record.* New York: Putnam, 1861-68.

——. *Songs and Ballads of the Southern People.* New York: D. Appleton, 1886.

Randolph, Vance. *Ozark Folksongs.* Columbia, Mo.: Univ. of Missouri Press, 1946-50.

Sandburg, Carl. *American Songbag.* New York: Harpers, 1927.

Silber, Irwin. *Songs of the Civil War.* New York: Columbia Univ. Press, 1960.

Wharton, Henry Marvin. *War Songs and Poems of the Southern Confederacy.* Philadelphia, 1904.

Songsters

Brower, Frank. *The Black Diamond Songster*. New York, 1864.
The Camp Fire Songster. New York, 1862.
The Copperhead Minstrel. n.p., n.d.
Hutchinson, John Wallace. *The Bobolink Minstrel; or, Republican Songster for 1860*. New York, 1860.
The John Brown "Union Right or Wrong" Songster. New York [?], 1863.
The Lincoln and Hamlin Songster; or, The Continental Melodist, comprising a choice collection of original and selected songs, in honor of the people's candidates Lincoln and Hamlin, and illustrative of the enthusiasm everywhere entertained for "Honest Old Abe" of Illinois, and the noble Hamlin of Maine. Philadelphia, 1860.
The Lincoln and Johnson Union Campaign Songster. Philadelphia, 1864.
The "Little Mac" Songster.... New York, c. 1862.
The "Union" Songster...National and Patriotic Melodies. San Francisco, 1861.
Upson, Theodore F. *With Sherman to the Sea. The Civil War Letters, Diaries and Reminiscences of Theodore F. Upson*. Indiana Univ. Press, 1958.